# FIRE FROM
# HEAVEN

Thanks for praying!

Mark I. Bubeck

Ps 85: 4-7

# FIRE FROM HEAVEN

*God's Provision for Personal Spiritual Victory*

## MARK I. BUBECK

*The Bible Teacher's Teacher*

COOK COMMUNICATIONS MINISTRIES
Colorado Springs, Colorado • Paris, Ontario
KINGSWAY COMMUNICATIONS LTD
Eastbourne, England

Victor® is an imprint of
Cook Communications Ministries, Colorado Springs, CO 80918
Cook Communications, Paris, Ontario
Kingsway Communications, Eastbourne, England

FIRE FROM HEAVEN
© 2007 by Mark I. Bubeck

Portions of this book are taken from the previously titled *The Rise of Fallen Angels* (Moody Publishers © 1995, ISBN 0802471897), which was a minor revision of *The Satanic Revival* (Here's Life/Thomas Nelson © 1991, ISBN 0898403146). More than 50 percent new material.

Any Web addresses (URLs) recommended throughout this book are solely offered as a resource to the reader. The citation of these Web sites does not in any way imply an endorsement on the part of the author or the publisher, nor does the author or publisher vouch for their content for the life of this book.

First Printing, 2007
Printed in the United States of America

1 2 3 4 5 6 7 8 9 10

Unless otherwise noted, Scripture quotations are taken from the *Holy Bible, New International Version®. NIV®.* Copyright © 1973, 1978, 1984 by International Bible Society. Used by permission of Zondervan. All rights reserved. Scripture quotations marked NASB are from the *New American Standard Bible*, © Copyright 1960, 1995 by The Lockman Foundation. Used by permission. Scripture quotations marked KJV are taken from the King James Version of the Bible. (Public Domain.) Italics in Scripture quotations have been added by the author for emphasis.

ISBN 978-0-7814-4375-3

LCCN 2007925285

*To the encouragement of all believers
whom God has called and empowered to
be prayerfully responsive to His loving
burden for our broken world (John 3:16)*

# CONTENTS

Available online at www.cookministries.org/firefromheaven:

*Appendix A: Buying from Jesus Christ*

*Appendix B: The Five Commandments That Convict Us All*

*Appendix C: Romania and Spiritual Renewal*

*Appendix D: Quick Reference Guide to Revival Praying*

*Appendix E: Some Helpful Tools*

# PRAYER PATTERNS FOR REVIVAL*

* These seven prayers are available in booklet form, and may be ordered for quantity distribution by calling 877-467-4222 or by writing:

    ICBC International
    18741 N. Union St.
    Westfield, IN 46074

# FOREWORD

Two thousand years ago religious legalism was the order of the day. As the Pharisees stifled worship of God through their laws, the Roman rulers suffocated the Jewish people with their politics. The oppression could not have been much worse for the chosen people of God. It was the perfect time for God to intervene. As the apostle Paul observed, "For while we were still helpless, at the right time Christ died for the ungodly" (Rom. 5:6 NASB).

I believe it is the "right time" for God's people today. Western culture is rapidly sinking into a cesspool of sexual madness. Truth telling has been abandoned for face saving. Trust in our leaders, both political and moral, is at an all-time low. The pornography industry is ever increasing. Through abortions, innocent unborns still are being slaughtered for the sake of personal convenience.

As Mark Bubeck points out in this book, more and more people are becoming involved or interested in paganism and occult activity; interest in the spirit world, including fallen angels, is high. Many of our churches seem ineffective in this spiritual war, as they struggle with apathy, materialism, scandal, and division. If Christians seem helpless to do anything about it, it's because we have leaned on our own understanding and relied on our own strength and resources. Only when we come to the end of our resources are we able to discover God's.

The signs of a coming revival are vivid. It will not (because it cannot) be centered in any one individual or program. Our part is to stop leaning on our own understanding and start acknowledging God in every way, declaring our dependence upon Him. We accomplish this only through prayer, and there is no better pastoral model to follow than Dr. Mark Bubeck.

My dear friend Mark has kept his daily appointment with God for many years. In the early seventies he discerned that revival was coming and that we had to come to terms with the spiritual battle we are in. He was a leader before his time. His book *The Adversary* was groundbreaking for most evangelicals.

Now in his latest book, Mark looks at the potential for spiritual renewal in a pagan-era church, showing why it is urgent and how Christians can bring renewal to themselves and contribute to revival in their land.

Significantly, Mark has a key focus on the power of prayer in cultural revival. He includes his seven "Prayer Patterns for Revival." Those prayers, available in booklet form and used in our conferences, have benefited my ministry tremendously, as has this book.

Don't just read *Fire from Heaven* to expand your knowledge or understanding. Pray through this book and become an instrument in God's hand for the coming revival.

It is the right time.

Neil T. Anderson
Author, Founder of Freedom in Christ Ministries

# PREFACE

God called me to have a vision for revival very early in my adult life. My Lord's assignment for me to see the need for His merciful, loving hands to revive His people has endured throughout my lifetime. From my early years of ministry to the present, God has kept that fire burning in my heart.

I first submitted a manuscript containing the major thrust of this book to a publisher in 1988. That publisher chose to give it a vogue title for the time: *The Satanic Revival*. Another publisher comparably changed the title in 1995 to *The Rise of Fallen Angels* with the subtitle, *Victory Over the Adversary through Spiritual Renewal*. Although both books kept the need for spiritual awakening before the readers, the choice of titles may have suggested an undue focus upon opposition from the realm of darkness, and some of the contents of those versions were perhaps force-fitted in their spiritual warfare emphasis in order to justify the titles. However, all of the focus for revival awakening needs to remain upon our Lord!

*Fire from Heaven* helps capture what this author longs to communicate. It's a title that conveys what God's people really need, and the contents have been revised to match the heart of this message. Fire that brings spiritual renewal is always heaven's fire; it is all of God and all of grace!

God's wind and His fire from heaven visited those early disciples gathered in the upper room in prayer as they waited upon God: "Suddenly a sound like the blowing of a violent wind came from heaven and filled the whole house where they were sitting. They saw what seemed to be tongues of fire that separated and came to rest on each of them" (Acts 2:2–3). Heaven's fire transformed human lives and energized them. They in turn impacted their world for God. Their critics complained, "These that have turned the world upside down are come" (Acts 17:6 ᴋᴊᴠ). Opposition was very much present, but God's wind and fire blew it away. The power of the gospel and the Holy Spirit's fullness overflowed to the whole world in which they lived. Our trembling, wounded world of human beings needs to see that again.

I once heard a respected pastor make this statement: "When properly understood, prayer is not getting man's will done in heaven; it is getting God's will done on earth." God's Word supports such insight on prayer. It is the purpose of this book to help God's people pray in faith and harmony with what God desires to do. As we await our Lord's return in these days of climactic history, may it please God to refresh, renew, and transform His people. The challenges before us are daunting. Only fire from heaven can light the way and break through the darkness. Encouraging believers to participate in such a move of God's grace sums up the message of this book.

May God be pleased to so bless and motivate each reader.

# ACKNOWLEDGMENTS

My deepest appreciation goes to my fellow members of the Ambassador's Class of Palmcroft Baptist Church in Phoenix, Arizona. Known for their prayer support for the needs of others, they have held a covering of prayer over my efforts to complete the writing of this renewed call to pray for revival. Those prayers have provided a shield of protection and a surrounding of enabling grace.

The publishers, editors, and staff at Cook Communications Ministries have from the inception of this project provided the covering of encouragement and help that every writer needs. Special thanks in particular to my editor, Craig Bubeck, for his acquisition, oversight, and development of this revision; to Jack Campbell for ensuring the copyedit quality and for his sharp proofing eye; and to Susan Vannaman for her artful design of the interior.

Most of all, without the loving devotion of my wife, Anita; my three daughters and their husbands; and my extended family support, this writing project could not have been completed. All glory to God for His provision of such enablers.

# Introduction

*At the time of sacrifice, the prophet Elijah stepped forward and prayed: "O LORD, God of Abraham, Isaac and Israel, let it be known today that you are God in Israel and that I am your servant and have done all these things at your command. Answer me, O LORD, answer me, so these people will know that you, O LORD, are God, and that you are turning their hearts back again."*

*Then the fire of the LORD fell and burned up the sacrifice, the wood, the stones and the soil, and also licked up the water in the trench.*

*1 Kings 18:36–38*

It has to be one of the most powerful images of God's intervention in all of the Old Testament—certainly for many of us the image has become burned into our imaginations from as far back as our flannel-graph Sunday school days. The great prophet, calling out boldly to his God, before all of the pagan priests and fickle Israelites—and God sends down fire from heaven, to consume the sacrifice and even to lick up all the water that should have been a resistance to any normal fire. Incredible!

Fire came down from heaven, and the people believed. There was going to be a revival in the land! And yet … in his natural, human giftedness, the prophet Elijah really was not a very brave man.

In the drama of these unfolding events, Jezebel's threatening words sent him running: "May the gods deal with me, be it ever so severely, if by this time tomorrow I do not make your life like that of one of them" (1 Kings 19:2). Even though Elijah had just come from facing down King Ahab and bringing God's judgment on the prophets of Baal, Jezebel's words panicked him: "Elijah was afraid and ran for his life" (v. 3).

It's important to understand that Elijah was not very different from us. James's words support that assessment: "Elijah was a man just like us. He prayed earnestly that it would not rain, and it did not rain on the land for three and a half years. Again he prayed, and the heavens gave rain, and the earth produced its crops" (James 5:17–18). In fact, to this day, God's people praying in harmony with God's will still see divine interventions akin to Elijah's experiences. God's grace and mercy are constants that flow from His unchanging attributes.

God had made Elijah a man of prayer. We don't really know much else about him other than that he was "the Tishbite, from Tishbe in Gilead" (1 Kings 17:1). His importance and place in history is as James states: "He prayed."

Doubtlessly, it was in one of Elijah's shut-away times of prayer that God had told him to find a time and place to confront King Ahab. That would not have been a pleasant thought to Elijah. Ahab was a wicked, ruthless king, known for using his brutal power to crush all opposition. Elijah's natural temerity would not seek out such confrontation, but God's assignments need not accommodate our personal comfort zone.

Nevertheless, dressed in his prophet's garb, Elijah waited for a time to confront the king. Perhaps it was when Ahab was in his royal chariot riding to his next stop in his round of kingly duties. A retinue of mounted horsemen and armed guards accompanied him. Suddenly, Elijah stepped into the king's path, stopping the whole procession. (His action brings to mind the famous image of that Chinese youth who faced down a military tank in the Tiananmen Square uprising.) All grew quiet.

The fire burning in the eyes of God's prophet was formidable. The ruthless, powerful king felt compelled to listen as the thunder of Elijah's voice rang out: "As the LORD, the God of Israel, lives, whom I serve, there will be neither dew nor rain in the next few years except at my word" (v. 1). The words burned into Ahab's mind with branding-iron permanence. He heard the fire of God's judgment ringing in every word. He would not forget this encounter with Elijah.

As suddenly as he had come, Elijah disappeared from public view. Chapter 17 of 1 Kings recounts God sending him to the Kerith Ravine east of the Jordan River, where God hid him. He drank from the flowing brook and ate the bread and meat God assigned the ravens to bring him each morning and evening. He was alone—tucked away and hidden from Ahab's frantic attempts to find him (18:10–11). The brook eventually dried up from the drought of Elijah's pronouncement, and God sent him on to Zarephath of Sidon.

God had arranged a stay for him in a prophet's room provided by a widow and her young son. God kept him active in prayer and in his prophet's role while he waited for the absence of rain to accomplish God's full purpose. Miraculously, at Elijah's pronouncement the destitute widow's cooking oil kept flowing and her flour jar never lacked that precious commodity necessary to maintain life. There was always enough to feed Elijah, the widow's young son, and the widow herself. God even used Elijah to raise the widow's son from death to life during his sojourn in the room she'd prepared for God's prophet. All the while, Elijah patiently waited for the famine and drought to accomplish God's sovereign purpose.

In the third year of the drought, God's word again came to Elijah. God's orders were clear: "Go and present yourself to Ahab, and I will send rain on the land" (18:1). Certainly those words were intimidating to Elijah. He knew that as time had gone on and the drought had produced its full disaster, Ahab's fury had become explosively volatile. Everyone around Ahab felt the murderous rage of the king. They were afraid even to mention Elijah's name lest they die in Ahab's fury (vv. 9–14).

As a first contact with the king, God sent Elijah to meet Obadiah. He was in charge of King Ahab's palace and was a God-fearing believer who loved and respected Elijah. God in His sovereignty had placed Obadiah in that strategic position. We learn that Obadiah had hidden and fed one hundred of God's prophets from Queen Jezebel's murderous plans to kill them. She had used her high position to promote the wicked worship of Baal throughout Israel. Obadiah was a wise and courageous man. He could arrange a proper confrontation between Elijah and the infuriated Ahab.

The day of the tense meeting took place. Ahab went to meet Elijah. As they stood facing each other, Ahab spoke threatening, contentious words: "Is that you, you troubler of Israel?" (v. 17). He and his kingdom had just experienced three and one half years without the falling of any rain at the word of Elijah. His rage was there but restrained by his respect for God's prophet. He knew he was dealing with the God of Israel and not just a man. God has ways of gaining the respectful attention of even the most profane.

"'I have not made trouble for Israel,' Elijah replied. 'But you and your father's family have. You have abandoned the LORD's commands and have followed the Baals. Now summon the people from all over Israel to meet me on Mount Carmel. And bring the four hundred and fifty prophets of Baal and the four hundred prophets of Asherah, who eat a Jezebel's table'" (vv. 18–19). Those words got Ahab's attention to the point that he followed Elijah's instructions. He ordered those false prophets and invited Israel's leaders and the common people to meet with Elijah on Mount Carmel. The disastrous consequences of three and one half years without a drop of rain falling had gotten all of their attention. This was a desperate hour. The entire nation was impacted. It was a life-or-death issue. If Elijah had any answer, they wanted to hear what he had to say.

The drama of the moment was electric. Fierce tensions were flowing. A religious and political power struggle of great magnitude was taking place. The power of God's Holy Spirit was upon Elijah as he spoke: "How long will you waver between two opinions? If the LORD is God, follow him; but if Baal is God, follow him" (v. 21).

Everyone remained silent. No one dared to speak. God's searching power was impacting them through Elijah's words. Most of the people still held a passive loyalty to the Lord, the historic God of Israel, but they also continued their corrupt involvement with the worship of Baal. Religious immoralities associated with Asherah practices were also part of the mix. Although God later assures Elijah that He had reserved for Himself seven thousand people in Israel, even they remained silent. They had not bowed down to Baal or "kissed him" to express love and devotion to Baal, but the political climate and the sin of the times had intimidated them into speechless silence. Elijah faced this challenge alone.

Elijah did have their attention, however. They were hanging on his every word. In that strategic moment, Elijah presented a logical, powerful challenge: "Then Elijah said to them, 'I am the only one of the LORD's prophets left, but Baal has four hundred and fifty prophets. Get two bulls for us. Let them choose one for themselves, and let them cut it into pieces and put it on the wood but not set fire to it. I will prepare the other bull and put it on the wood but not set fire to it. Then you call on the name of your god, and I will call on the name of the LORD. The god who answers by fire—he is God'" (vv. 22–24). That challenge brought an instant response from the people. To see fire fall on the prepared sacrifice would be compelling evidence: "What you say is good," the people cried out with enthusiasm. They saw an opportunity for their confusion and doubts to be blown away. Clarification was about to emerge. Is Jehovah the almighty God of Israel or is Baal the true god? Is Elijah a prophet of the true and living God or will Baal's prophets be able to prove their legitimacy?

Wickedness always carries its own baggage of deception, guilt, and uncertainty. As the context unfolds, it seems that the prophets of Baal were confident about the challenge. Like those Egyptian wise men, sorcerers, and magicians who had advised the Pharaoh in Moses' day, Baal's prophets also had no doubt seen numerous displays of supernatural power attributed to Baal.

Counterfeit miracles produced by the realm of darkness can appear very real to limited human perceptions. What appears as miracles to the nondiscerning eye are in reality an important part of Satan's deceptive work. Elijah's challenge did not discourage them. It seems evident that they expected supernatural power from Baal to burn up their sacrifice. What they did not know was that they were now dealing with the true and living God of Israel. He's in charge. He retains full control over all of His creation. In this situation, only what the God of Israel permits will happen. He will honor Elijah's proposed test: "The god who answers by fire—he is God."

From morning until noon, Baal's prophets cried out to their god to send his fire upon their sacrifice. It was a pathetic scene of deceived people seeking an answer that would never come: "'O Baal, answer us!' they shouted. But there was no response; no one answered. And they danced around the altar they had made" (v. 26).

As Elijah watched this scene of blasphemous worship of a false god, his righteous anger moved him. At noon he began to taunt the prophets of Baal:

"'Shout louder!' he said. 'Surely he is a god! Perhaps he is deep in thought, or busy, or traveling. Maybe he is sleeping and must be awakened'" (v. 27). The fervor of Baal's prophets accelerated. They yelled louder, cut themselves, and let their blood flow in their frantic efforts to defend and prove the reality of their god. "But there was no response, no one answered, no one paid attention" (v. 29). What a dismal conclusion for false prophets and false gods. Their experience of following the god of a false religious zeal was not unlike that which Jesus spoke about: "Then he will say to those on his left, 'Depart from me, you who are cursed, into the eternal fire prepared for the devil and his angels'" (Matt. 25:41). The fire of God's judgment eventually will come with terrible finality upon the rebellious and deceived.

At the time of the evening sacrifice, Elijah took center stage in the unfolding drama. "Come here to me," Elijah invited all of the people. In their curiosity, even Baal's prophets doubtlessly joined the throng pressing together to watch Elijah prepare for the sacrifice. Ahab must have had a choice seat for watching. Methodically, Elijah chose twelve stones upon which to rebuild the altar of the LORD, which was in ruins. Some have supposed that Baal's prophets may have destroyed the altar in their vain efforts to please the spirit realm of darkness. That may be a possibility, but a more likely scenario is that no one in Israel had been worshipping at the LORD's altar with an evening sacrifice for a long time. The altar was in disrepair from lack of use. Passive indifference had done its work. Pagan Baal worship had taken over the religious life of the majority of people.

As Elijah took the twelve stones, he reminded the people what they represented: "One for each of the tribes descended from Jacob, to whom the word of the LORD had come, saying, 'Your name shall be Israel'" (1 Kings 18:31). Elijah was preaching while he worked. He was helping the people remember their heritage; the roots of their faith and their responsibility to the God of Israel had been made clear throughout Israel's history.

After repairing the altar, he cut the bull into pieces and laid it carefully on the wood. He also dug a trench around the altar large enough to hold several gallons of water. When the sacrifice was prepared, he ordered them to bring four large jars of water and pour the water over the sacrifice, the wood, and the stones. When done, he ordered them to do it again. Then, even a third time they doused the sacrifice scene with fire-quenching water: "The water ran down around the altar and even filled the trench" (v. 34).

The text speaks for itself concerning what happened next: Elijah prayed (vv. 36–37). You can almost see the people pulling away from being too close to the sacrifice, sensing what was about to happen.

Suddenly, fire from heaven came in blazing power, consuming not only the sacrifice on the altar but also the wood, the stones, the soil, and all the water filling the trench.

The people promptly saw everything clearly. They fell prostrate before Elijah and the God he serves as they cried out: "The Lord—he is God! The Lord—he is God!" (v. 39).

God had two major purposes to accomplish in bringing His "fire from heaven" upon the prepared sacrifice. The first purpose was to turn the hearts of the people He loved back again to Himself. He desired them to serve and worship only the true and living God of Israel. The beginning of that work was instantaneous. No one remains standing in the presence of God when He draws near. Although it is not stated clearly, even Baal's prophets probably fell prostrate. The fear of approaching judgment was before them. God's presence—His holiness and His justice—overwhelm people. God's people fall on their faces in a state of broken repentance and worship before the awesome wonder of their Lord.

God's second purpose for His "fire from heaven" was to let it serve as a message of God's impending judgment upon wicked, rebelling, unbelieving people.

"Then Elijah commanded them, 'Seize the prophets of Baal. Don't let anyone get away!' They seized them, and Elijah had them brought down to the Kishon Valley and slaughtered there" (v. 40). That was not Elijah's decision. The command was from God. When it's judgment time, God brings it swiftly. When it's God's time for wrath, there is no place to hide; there is no escape. The fire from heaven will also do God's work of establishing His justice and truth.

As the scene of judgment came to its conclusion, Elijah told Ahab to go eat and drink because he heard the sound of "heavy rain" coming. The king went off to eat and drink, but Elijah climbed to the top of Mount Carmel. There he "bent down to the ground and put his face between his knees" and prayed (v. 42).

What he had just been through made him want to worship his Lord. He needed to be alone with God. Sending his servant away to look toward the sea for the signs of rain, he prayed. His servant came back and reported that there was no sign of rain yet. He did that seven times. Each time, Elijah sent him back to keep looking while he kept praying. The seventh time the servant reported that a cloud the size of a man's hand was on the horizon over the sea. Elijah knew it was time to go. He sent his servant to tell Ahab to get in his chariot and head for his Jezreel palace. He needed to do it quickly before the full impact of the rain would stop him.

God had planned a unique way to implant Ahab's encounter with Elijah deeply into the king's memory. As Ahab rode through the rain in his chariot, Elijah was never out of his sight. God kept him visible up ahead of Ahab, running through the rain and lightning, all the way from Mount Carmel to Jezreel.

After reaching his palace, the king related to Jezebel all that had happened. She was furious. The execution of all of Baal's prophets motivated her to threaten Elijah's life, since she regarded herself as the protector of Baal worship. His prophets were her treasured religious guides.

What followed shows us how very much Elijah was just like us. Fear gripped him, and he began running from Jezebel's murderous plot to kill him. With God's help and the providing of holy angel escorts, he ran all the way to Mount Horeb, the mountain of God, where he found shelter in a cave.

It was there that once again the word of the Lord came clearly to Elijah: "What are you doing here, Elijah?" (19:9). God's servant poured out a litany of excuses, but God told him to go out to the mouth of the cave and wait there in the presence of the Lord, because the "LORD is about to pass by." As Elijah waited, a sudden, powerful wind of hurricane and tornado proportions began to tear the mountain apart and shatter the rocks. Elijah and we are assured that "the LORD was not in the wind" (v. 11). After the wind an earthquake began to rumble and shake the whole mountain. Again we are told "the LORD was not in the earthquake. After the earthquake came a fire, but the LORD was not in the fire" (vv. 11–12). God was showing Elijah that He had many means of displaying His almighty power and authority, but He did not need those things to speak to His people.

It was at that moment that a powerful event took place: "After the fire came a gentle whisper. When Elijah heard it, he pulled his cloak over his face and went out and stood in the mouth of the cave" (vv. 12–13).

The context communicates to us that God was definitely in the "gentle whisper." The gentle voice of the LORD spoke again to Elijah: "What are you doing here, Elijah?" Once again, the context reveals that the Lord still had important work for His prophet to do, and Elijah needed to get on with the Lord's work.

The message in this "gentle whisper" is important. God doesn't need powerful winds, the terror of earthquakes, or even blasting blaze from heaven to bring His message to His people. Sometimes it's His gentle, flickering flame: His whisper—the quiet, convicting voice that only we can personally sense, but that touches us most deeply.

The gentle whisper is the way the Lord brought me to Christ. It was the means He used to call me into ministry. Multitudes of times He has used that same gentle whisper to bring me back to Him when I have strayed to my own way. He did that for Elijah. The gentle whisper started Elijah back on the path of great usefulness that stayed with him until one of the most eventful days of history.

God had appointed Elisha to succeed him, and 2 Kings 2 records this marvelous scene: "As they were walking along and talking together, suddenly a chariot of fire and horses of fire appeared and separated the two of them, and Elijah went up to heaven in a whirlwind. Elisha saw this and cried out, 'My father! My father! The chariots and horsemen of Israel!' And Elisha saw him no more" (vv. 11–12).

It's fitting that fire from heaven had a part in Elijah's departure for heaven.

Fire from heaven—it's a sign of God at work in the lives of His people; it's a sign of God's work of purifying, judgment, renewal, and new life. The powers of evil want desperately to quench it in God's people—to soak and saturate what should be our sacrificial service to God with the stifling waters of fear, depression, or sin. But no amount of dousing can quench God's Spirit. When God's people call upon the name of their Lord in faith—faith that is authentically intimate with God through Christ Jesus—His fire will come.

It might begin with a whispering, flickering flame of God's quiet voice; or it might come in a spectacular conflagration. But when God ignites the spirits of His people, the gates of hell cannot prevail.

*Chapter 1*

# IGNITING GOD'S PEOPLE TO JOIN THE BATTLE

*Then Elijah said to all the people, "Come here to me."*
*They came to him, and he repaired the altar of the*
*LORD, which was in ruins. Elijah took twelve stones,*
*one for each of the tribes descended from Jacob, to*
*whom the word of the LORD had come, saying, "Your*
*name shall be Israel." With the stones he built an altar*
*in the name of the LORD, and he dug a trench around*
*it large enough to hold two seahs of seed. He arranged*
*the wood, cut the bull into pieces and laid it on the*
*wood. Then he said to them, "Fill four large jars with*
*water and pour it on the offering and on the wood."*
*"Do it again," he said, and they did it again.*
*"Do it a third time," he ordered, and they did it the*
*third time. The water ran down around the altar and*
*even filled the trench.*

*1 Kings 18:30–35*

I wonder what the world might look like if Elijah were with us today. Would Christ's church be characterized as "on fire" or soaking wet? Would our altar be in disrepair ... crumbled and scattered about?

The truth is, we are facing a sopping spiritual malaise among professing believers today that will not be easy to penetrate—not any easier, anyway, than what Elijah faced in his increasingly pagan nation.

Can anyone reasonably deny that our situation is much like what Jesus Christ spoke to when He addressed the church at Laodicea?

I know your deeds, that you are neither cold nor hot. I wish you were either one or the other! So, because you are lukewarm—neither hot nor cold—I am about to spit you out of my mouth. You say, "I am rich; I have acquired wealth and do not need a thing." But you do not realize that you are wretched, pitiful, poor, blind and naked. (Rev. 3:15–17)

I am sure that Jesus' words must have been shocking when read by that assembly of professing believers making up the church at Laodicea. Jesus Christ wanted them to be shocked. He was not pleased with their spiritual condition. But He was offering them revival—the opportunity to return to Him—and He wanted them to see their need through His eyes.

It is also noteworthy that although His offer was to the corporate body of the church, Jesus kept it in a personal, individual focus: "Here I am! I stand at the door and knock. If anyone hears my voice and opens the door, I will come in and eat with him, and he with me" (v. 20). Revivals are always intensely personal. The changes take place within each believer's innermost person. The corporate effect flows out from each person's personal encounter with God.

## REVIVAL MEANS YOUR PERSONAL TRANSFORMATION ... FROM WITHIN

It has been said so many times that to repeat it almost seems clichéd: The spiritual condition of the church at Laodicea was remarkably similar to today's evangelical congregations.

Getting past the apparent cliché, though, it can also seem rather harsh. I hope that does not seem too judgmental. I don't mean it that way. I write in the same spirit that many followers of Christ look at Christ's body today: with tears of grief and a longing hunger for change. I include my family, my church, most of my Christian friends, and myself within the parameters of our Lord's words.

Jesus Christ knew Laodicea to be a very needy church. And He knows that about us. We too are very needy. If we are to experience His healing, we need to listen. This is our Lord Jesus Christ speaking: "These are the words of the Amen, the faithful and true witness, the ruler of God's creation" (Rev. 3:14).

He is competent to speak—that's the sense of that strange syntax: "These are the words of the Amen." Jesus Christ has the final word. He is the "so be it" One. He speaks with authority. Likewise, He is "the faithful and true witness." Jesus Christ is faithful because God is faithful, and Jesus Christ is God. He is the "true witness." He not only speaks the truth, but also He declared Himself to be the truth (John 14:6).

Jesus is also "the ruler of God's creation." The apostle Paul enlarged upon that infinitely expansive claim with these words: "For by him all things were created: things in heaven and on earth, visible and invisible, whether thrones or powers or rulers or authorities; all things were created by him and for him. He is before all things, and in him all things hold together" (Col. 1:16–17). How wonderfully reassuring to know that Jesus Christ speaks with unchallenged competence. Every created thing and every created being in the universe answers to Him. He is the One who holds it all together.

This is the voice that speaks the hard words, "I know your deeds, that you are neither cold nor hot" (Rev. 3:15). These are the words of the omniscient One, the all-knowing Creator. When He declares that He knows, He really knows. He reads it as it is. His knowledge surpasses our own awareness. He knows in the sense of absolute truth. None of us can hide from His analysis of our true condition. We must accept it. For a believer to be "lukewarm" is offensive to the Lord. That kind of spiritually insipid condition is so nauseous to Him that He resorts to graphically descriptive terms: "I am about to spit you out of my mouth."

Our highest level of repentance may need to begin right here: "Lord Jesus Christ, You have helped me see that my indolent, lukewarm spiritual apathy is grossly offensive to You. I acknowledge this sinful condition to have a serious hold on my life. I repent of it and ask You to relight the fires of joyful obedience to do Your will within the wholeness of my person. In Your precious name, I look to You to meet my need."

## Lord, Diagnose My True Condition

> You say, "I am rich; I have acquired wealth and do not need a
> thing." But you do not realize that you are wretched, pitiful, poor,
> blind and naked. (Rev. 3:17)

The process by which true believers degenerate into a lukewarm spiritual condition is extremely subtle. At Laodicea, Jesus showed that it began with their move away from spiritual values into a desire for material wealth. Their sense of contentment and well-being focused upon their bank accounts and investment portfolios. The apostle Paul warned his "son in the faith" concerning these dangerous perils of materialism: "People who want to get rich fall into temptation and a trap and into many foolish and harmful desires that plunge men into ruin and destruction. For the love of money is a root of all kinds of evil. Some people, eager for money, have wandered from the faith and pierced themselves with many griefs" (1 Tim. 6:9–10). This speaks to what is probably the most dangerous temptation being overlooked by most believers in our day.

My Lord dealt deeply with me on this very issue in recent days when I really didn't think this spiritual problem was an issue in my life. I love to give and have rejoiced to be a faithful steward of all that the Lord sends our way. But the Lord stripped off my blinders and let me see some things that I did not know; perhaps *admit* is a better word choice. When He showed me that certain practices in my life all really amounted to a subtle love-of-money issue, He gave me the grace to enter into some deep repentance and important changes.

The problem is as common to both those who are not rich and those who have wealth. The focus is upon the attitude and the mind-set, characteristically made evident by our life practices. Since we all live in a society given over to materialism, we need the Holy Spirit's wisdom to avoid and escape from this deadly peril with its pull toward making us lukewarm.

Christ helps us see how very serious this "love of money" is by His truthful diagnosis of the Laodicean believers: "But you do not realize that you are wretched, pitiful, poor, blind and naked" (Rev. 3:17). Those are very humbling words. He is not describing some homeless, hungry, sick, tattered beggar living on the street or under a bridge down by the city dump. He is describing the spiritual state of "a good Christian person" who has a nice home, an acceptable car to drive, money for retirement, and all the visible amenities that we deem important.

Yet spiritually he's "wretched"—his true spiritual joy has evaporated. And he is "pitiful"—he is so out of touch with reality that he is not even aware of his true spiritual state. He is also "poor"—true spiritual riches have disappeared from what he owns. He is "blind"—he just does not see why he needs revival—yes, other people perhaps, but he knows he's saved and he's on his way to heaven. And finally he is "naked" of that spiritual clothing, which is a likeness to Jesus Christ: "Clothe yourselves with compassion, kindness, humility, gentleness and patience" (Col. 3:12).

What a terrible way to appear—naked before our Lord Jesus Christ. If this diagnosis isn't changed by our response to Jesus' corrective words, it might suggest one reason why, at the judgment seat of Christ, God will be wiping away tears from some eyes (Rev. 7:17). Dare we dismiss this very serious, warning word from our Lord Jesus Christ?

His revival is desperately needed. He wants us to have what we need. As you are reading these words, pause and ask the Holy Spirit to enable you to see your own need for revival.

### Lord, Counsel Me about What I Need

I counsel you to buy from me gold refined in the fire, so you can become rich; and white clothes to wear, so you can cover your shameful nakedness; and salve to put on your eyes, so you can see. (Rev. 3:18)

The prophet Isaiah in speaking of the coming of the expected Messiah wrote, "For to us a child is born, to us a son is given, and the government will be on his shoulders. And he will be called Wonderful Counselor, Mighty God, Everlasting Father, Prince of Peace" (Isa. 9:6). In Revelation 3:18 that "Wonderful Counselor" offers His counsel to the church at Laodicea and to all of us who know that we fit the diagnosis our Lord gave concerning Laodicea's spiritual condition.

"I counsel you to buy from me." The Lord Jesus Christ lets us know that He has the answers we need for our serious state, and we may "buy" from Him what we need. His counsel is that lukewarm people need three things from Him: (1) They need gold refined in His fire that will remove their wretched, pitifully poor state of spiritual poverty and credit true riches to their account; (2) His counsel is that they can buy from Jesus Christ "white clothes to wear" that will be effective to provide the Lord's covering for their "shameful nakedness"; and (3) the Great Physician counsels them to "buy" His healing—to have "salve to put on [their] eyes" so that they would be able to see what He knows they need to see.

Christ does not specify the meaning of these three things that they need to buy from Him. Yet one can recognize that the "gold refined in the fire" has reference to His chastening discipline; this enables a person to see his sinful attitudes and practices that need repentance and to experience freedom from those defeats He addresses.

Indeed, Hebrews 12 reminds us of the spiritual riches that come from welcoming our Lord's loving discipline: "No discipline seems pleasant at the time, but painful. Later on, however, it produces a harvest of righteousness and peace for those who have been trained by it. Therefore, strengthen your feeble arms and weak knees. 'Make level paths for your feet,' so that the lame may not be disabled, but rather healed" (vv. 11–13).

Revelation 3:19 makes it clear that this is the meaningful purpose of our Lord wanting us to buy gold from Him: "Those whom I love I rebuke and discipline. So be earnest, and repent." It's amazing how quickly spiritual poverty can be turned into spiritual riches when true repentance comes. The riches are what take place in the heart that brings forth the blessings of revival.

The buying of "white clothes to wear, so you can cover your shameful nakedness" may refer to many things that counter our impotence to impact our world for our Lord Jesus Christ. In part, at least, it must include moral cleanness and purity of thoughts and practices. Our shameful nakedness in this matter is epidemic. Living in a morally bankrupt culture takes its toll even on God's people.

If not dealt with in our Lord's victory, the pornography problem on the Internet and in every facet of our society can have an explosively destructive and defiling influence upon our Lord's blood-washed saints. Our Lord Jesus Christ knows the full measure of the problem. Only He can bring freedom from that bondage and return His healing purity into the hearts and lives of His people. The Wonderful Counselor knows how much buying His white clothes is needed in these times when so much defilement is happening to His own.

The "salve to put on your eyes, so you can see" certainly must include the enlightenment and illumination of the Holy Spirit. He is the One who gives the Lord's people the capacity to see and understand God's truth: "The Spirit searches all things, even the deep things of God. For who among men knows the thoughts of a man except the man's spirit within him? In the same way no one knows the thoughts of God except the Spirit of God. We have not received the spirit of the world but the Spirit who is from God, that we may understand what God has freely given us" (1 Cor. 2:10–12). It was very important to Jesus that His disciples wait in Jerusalem until the Holy Spirit had been poured out upon them (Acts 1:8; Luke 24:49). The Holy Spirit provided the power they needed to carry out their Lord's commission and provide the illumination of God's Word so they could see spiritual truth and understand God's will and plans.

Jesus Christ offered the essence of revival to these believers who made up the church at Laodicea. Although, as He had just stated, they had fallen into in a very serious state of deception and spiritual decline, Jesus Christ offered them great hope for full restoration and some phenomenal spiritual rewards. There is prophetic significance here. This is one of several strong passages that provide hope for God to grant us a tremendous spiritual revival in the last days.

If Christ offered Laodicea such great promise for revival, He has the same offer for us. Laodicea was the last of the seven churches He addressed in Revelation 2 and 3, and as such, it would seem to have special significance for the end times. In the understanding of many, this church represents the predominate condition that will characterize evangelical churches in the end times.

We need to listen to our "Wonderful Counselor" and begin to "buy" from Him.

## Buying from the Lord

For those of us yearning for this promised revival, there is an important question: How does one "buy" what he needs from the Lord Jesus Christ? The Lord seemed to assume that the believers at Laodicea would discern how they were to follow through on His counsel. Perhaps that assumption was based on the fact that He knew the issue had been addressed by His Old Testament prophet in Isaiah 55.[†]

In my understanding, when we harmonize our Lord's counsel to Laodicea with the message of Isaiah 55, we will be brought to promised revival. God's people who obediently listen to our Lord's counsel in Revelation 3:18 and faithfully "buy" from Him will experience His revival. Such a conclusion fits what Jesus Christ conveys in His continuing words to the church at Laodicea. After urging them to "buy" from Him what is needed and to respond to His discipline with earnest repentance, He becomes very personal and conveys clearly how much He is both able and ready to meet their needs: "Here I am! I stand at the door and knock. If anyone hears my voice and opens the door, I will come in and eat with him, and he with me" (Rev. 3:20).

These words have often been applied to what happens to a person when he or she becomes a Christian believer. Although it may be appropriate to use this text to illustrate what happens in our personal lives when we are saved, proper appreciation of the context does not focus on salvation. Jesus is offering His healing for their lukewarm spiritual disaster. He wanted them to experience His renewal. He offers them the essence of revival.

Clearly, the personal aspects of revival remain much of the focus. As one offering help, Christ forcefully interjects Himself: "Here I am!" Jesus Christ knows He is the answer to what His people need. In the confusion that a lukewarm, materialistic spiritual condition produces, God's people may fall into the fallacy of thinking that our Lord is reluctant to bring them to

---

† Appendix A provides an outline for more in-depth study of this fascinating chapter.

revival. This text refutes such thoughts. In essence Jesus Christ is saying, "Here I am. I am ready to bring My healing to you!"

The intimacy of His offer keeps probing: "I stand at the door and knock." Don't miss the tenderness and the caring love of these words. The door represents the personal, intimate core of each person. It's what we commonly call our heart. Jesus comes up to that door and speaks: "Here I am!" Knowing the personal nearness of the Lord Jesus Christ is a tender moment in anyone's life, but He doesn't stop there; He knocks and keeps speaking your name: "Mary, Mark, John; I am here. Open your door and invite Me in." Our Lord's eagerness to heal and turn around their lukewarm condition climaxes with His promise: "I will come in and eat with him, and he with me."

On the personal level, those words of Jesus define revival. Personal revival is knowing the intimate presence and fellowship with Jesus Christ at the deepest levels of one's total person. It's knowing that He has made you clean. It's having assurance that your "wretched, pitiful, poor, blind and naked" condition has been washed in His blood and removed from your record. It's knowing that He has replaced your lethargic, indolent ways with a holy, passionate desire for obedience to do His will. It's experiencing a continuing intimate flow of joy and spiritual communion with Him every moment of your life.

What do the attitudes and conduct of a person's life look like when revived in the same manner that our Lord Jesus Christ offered to Laodicea? Nancy Leigh DeMoss has a passionate heart for revival. Her radio ministry, conference speaking, and extensive writings have contributed much toward calling God's people to revival. She has developed a study of the attitudes and conduct differences between Proud People and Broken People that is germane to help answer our question. She has graciously granted permission to include those contrasts in this book. They provide helpful insights concerning how Christlike attitudes and daily conduct would manifest in the life of a Christian believer who has been revived and changed by our Lord Jesus Christ.

They bring our understanding of revival into clearer focus—to the point of hearing the Lord's knocking, perhaps even upon our own personal doors.

| PROUD PEOPLE[†] | BROKEN PEOPLE |
|---|---|
| • Focus on the failures of others | • Overwhelmed with the sense of their own spiritual need |
| • Self-righteous; have a critical, fault-finding spirit; look at own life/faults through a telescope but others with a microscope | • Compassionate; forgiving; look for best in others |
| • Look down on others | • Esteem all others better than self |
| • Independent/self-sufficient spirit | • Dependent spirit/recognize need for others |
| • Maintain control; must be my way | • Surrender control |
| • Have to prove that they are right | • Willing to yield the right to be right! |
| • Claim rights | • Yield rights |
| • Demanding spirit | • Giving spirit |
| • Self-protective of time, rights, reputation | • Self-denying |
| • Desire to be served | • Motivated to serve others |
| • Desire to be a success | • Desire to be faithful to make others a success |
| • Desire for self-advancement | • Desire to promote others |
| • Driven to be recognized/appreciated | • Sense of unworthiness; thrilled to be used at all; eager for others to get credit |
| • Wounded when others are promoted and they are overlooked | • Rejoice when others are lifted up |
| • "The ministry is privileged to have me!" | • "I don't deserve to serve in this ministry!" |
| • Think of what they can do for God | • Know that they have nothing to offer God |
| • Feel confident in how much they know | • Humbled by how much they have to learn |
| • Self-conscious | • Not concerned with self at all |
| • Keep people at arm's length | • Risk getting close to others/willing to take the risks of loving intimately |

† Used by permission, © Revive Our Hearts, www.ReviveOurHearts.com.

| Proud People[†] (continued) | Broken People (continued) |
|---|---|
| • Quick to blame others | • Accept personal responsibility—can see where they were wrong |
| • Unapproachable | • "Easy to be entreated" |
| • Defensive when criticized | • Receive criticism with a humble, open heart |
| • Concerned with being "respectable" | • Concerned with being real |
| • Concerned about what others think | • All that matters is what God knows |
| • Work to maintain image/protect reputation | • Die to own reputation |
| • Find it difficult to share their spiritual needs with others | • Willing to be open/transparent with others |
| • Want to be sure nobody finds out about their sin | • Willing to be exposed (Once broken, you don't care who knows—nothing to lose!) |
| • Have a hard time saying, "I was wrong; will you please forgive me?" | • Are quick to admit failure and to seek forgiveness |
| • When confessing sin, deal in generalities | • Deal in specifics |
| • Concerned about the consequences of their sins | • Grieved over the cause/root of their sins |
| • Remorseful over their sin—got caught/found out | • Repentant over sin (forsake it) |
| • When there is a misunderstanding or conflict, wait for others to come and ask forgiveness | • Take the initiative to be reconciled; see if they can get to the cross first! |
| • Compare themselves with others and feel deserving of honor | • Compare themselves to the holiness of God and feel desperate need for mercy |
| • Blind to their true heart condition | • Walk in the light |
| • Don't think they have anything to repent of | • Continual heart attitude of repentance |
| • Don't think they need revival (Think everybody else does!) | • Continually sense their need for a fresh encounter with the filling of His Spirit! |

## Chapter 2

# GOD SENDS THE FIRE

*Oh, that you would rend the heavens and come down,*
*that the mountains would tremble before you! As when*
*fire sets twigs ablaze and causes water to boil, come*
*down to make your name known to your enemies and*
*cause the nations to quake before you. For when you did*
*awesome things that we did not expect, you came down,*
*and the mountains trembled before you. Since ancient*
*times no one has heard, no ear has perceived, no eye has*
*seen any God besides you, who acts on behalf of those*
*who wait for him.*

*Isaiah 64:1–4*

The prophet Isaiah had an understanding about the kind of revival that will be required to elicit God's power to bring change into the lives of His people in our day. In Isaiah 64, He spoke during those sinking moments just before Judah would be invaded, captured, and destroyed by Babylon. That heathen nation was God's chosen instrument of judgment upon His willfully disobedient people.

D. Martyn Lloyd-Jones, the late British pastor and renowned Bible teacher, wrote these words concerning Isaiah's message in verse 1:

So we have here his final great petition—"Oh, that you wouldest rend the heavens, that thou wouldest come down." I do not hesitate to assert that it is the ultimate prayer in connection with revival. It is right, of course, always to pray to God to bless us, to look upon us and to be gracious unto us, that should be our constant prayer. But this goes beyond that, and it is here that we see the difference between what the Church should always be praying for, and the special, peculiar, urgent prayer for a visitation of God's Spirit in revival.... This is a prayer for something unusual, something quite exceptional, and it is at the same time a reminder to us of what revival really is, there is no better way of putting it than this. It is indeed God's coming down. God, as it were, no longer merely granting us the blessings.... Everything that God does is marvelous and wonderful and transcends our highest imagination and yet we find these contrasts in the Scriptures between God doing what he normally does, and God doing the unusual, God coming down. (305–6)

## Unless God Does the Work

Lloyd-Jones helps us capture the dramatic essence of Isaiah's prayer. This prayer is asking God for a "Damascus road" kind of visitation from God. There are times when God's people become so hardened, so spiritually lethargic that they are incapable of responding and correcting their situation without a special, divine intervention. Isaiah is asking for the glory and power of almighty God to come down—to become manifest before His people in a powerful encounter. Isaiah knew the situation Judah was facing required that kind of direct intrusion of God's power to confront him and his nation.

I believe that the people of God are in a similar condition today. For revival to happen, God Himself will need to bring it to pass by the means only He knows to be necessary. Consider this illustration from a simple jail ministry.

### Setting Prisoners Free

A number of men in the Sunday school class my wife and I attend have been wonderfully used of God in jail ministry. In recent months a movement of revival has broken out in that ministry. Recent converts are manifesting transformed lives and are leading their fellow inmates to Christ. God has powerfully used my friend Jake Malenke in this unique touch of grace evident in the jails.

In response to my request, he has given me some of his thoughts related to what is happening. Some of Jake's insights are pertinent to the special manifestation of God's power to bring conviction upon the inmates.[†]

I have been involved in prison work for about fifteen years, and most recently the Lord enabled me to change my ministry to the county jail. God was also in process of changing my whole approach to ministry with these hardened criminals. Some of the men I became involved with in my visitation were considered most dangerous. When they were moved they were handled by four officers dressed in body armor. These inmates were chained at the feet and hands, were handcuffed, and fastened to a leather belt at their waist. Most of these people plea-bargain and eventually go to state prison to serve out their sentences. I knew they desperately needed to know my Lord Jesus Christ.

After reading evangelist Ray Comfort's book *Hell's Best Kept Secret*, God opened my eyes to see the importance of confronting these men with God's law. They needed to see their guilt in the eyes of our awesome, holy God. I had always had moderate success in seeing prisoners profess faith in Christ, but evidence of dramatically transformed lives was rare. After recognizing that old-time evangelists like John Wesley, Charles Finney, and others had stressed the importance of a sinner feeling his guilt before God, I changed my approach to reaching these men. I still used our evangelistic tract, but I added my own insert where I have written out five of the Ten Commandments.

The young man God used to start the revival was Bobby. His sister sent me a written request to visit him with the warning: "Bobby is a manipulator and a con-artist. He knows the Bible and has gone forward several times in his youth. He has gone to college for five years to become a lawyer, but tragically he became involved with drugs."

---

[†] In respect for their privacy, I have substituted fictitious names for the prisoners mentioned by name, and I've edited from his report the pertinent information for this book.

As I visited Bobby, I used the same approach I always had used, but with this added insert concerning God's law. After going through the booklet and the added focus on the five commandments with Bobby, it was obvious that God was dealing with him. The focus on God's law powerfully impacted him.[†]

When I asked him if he thought he would go to heaven or hell, Bobby hung his head. Through his tears he admitted that he would probably go to hell. After sharing God's plan of salvation, he responded wonderfully to the gospel. He accepted Christ as his Savior with obvious evidence that a miracle of change had taken place.

I started him in the 30-lesson Bible study follow-up that we use and urged him to go and share his faith with other inmates by using the same little booklet with the five commandments that we had just been through. He gave me the name of an inmate friend and promised to share the gospel with him during the week.

The revival started that day with Bobby. When I met with him the next week, Bobby had led his friend Tim to confess faith in Christ. Each week he had more names to give me of those he had witnessed to and needed a visit from me. I had to enlist more workers just to keep up with what God was doing through Bobby and those he had influenced to put their faith in Christ. Eight men and two women are now a part of our evangelism-discipleship team. Since that beginning, I have had the personal joy of seeing more that 130 men and women prisoners come to know Christ.

## The Power of God's Law

In Psalm 19, King David exalts the power of God's law to initiate revival with these striking words:

> The law of the LORD is perfect, reviving the soul. The statutes of the LORD are trustworthy, making wise the simple. The precepts of the

---

† See Appendix B, "The Five Commandments that Convict Us All."

LORD are right, giving joy to the heart. The commands of the LORD are radiant, giving light to the eyes. The fear of the LORD is pure, enduring forever. The ordinances of the LORD are sure and altogether righteous. They are more precious than gold, than much pure gold; they are sweeter than honey, than honey from the comb. By them is your servant warned; in keeping them there is great reward. (vv. 7–11)

David's words contain the heart core ingredients of what happens in revival awakening. Jake's experience with the law of God—how it so powerfully impacted the lives of the prisoners—was key to starting a "mini-revival" at the county jail; and it provides a contemporary illustration of the truth of Psalm 19.

It is not difficult to see why the Devil has his schemes to remove any focus upon the Ten Commandments from our public schools and the whole of our national public life. God still uses His law to startle and impact people. It convicts and shocks people into knowing their need of God. The Devil and his kingdom, including people under his control, fight that outcome with all the schemes they can muster. We are in a great battle between light and darkness. The battle is fierce. It will continue heating up as the time of the end draws nearer. Satan will fight revival with every tool under his influence and command.

We must know that many of the politically correct agendas advocated by certain pressure groups upon our politicians and judicial systems are most certainly supported by the kingdom of darkness. Much of such agendas are in direct defiance of God's laws and the principles set forth in God's Word that are designed to protect and bring blessings to humanity.

## REVIVAL REQUIRES GOD'S PEOPLE

What is revival? We have been reaching for a biblical answer. We are not yet there, but perhaps we are coming closer. We are seeking to understand those essentials, those ingredients necessary to bring us to the kind of biblical revival that we so desperately need. Two essential elements have so far kept coming into view.

As we have considered from the counsel of our Lord Jesus Christ to the church at Laodicea, a human responsiveness to our Lord's love is necessary. Believers can and must participate in the coming of revival. All biblical evidence supports this conclusion. God requires human participation in His sovereign plans. Even in such sovereign works of His grace as the birth of Jesus Christ, the Lord had His Simeon interceding for His coming. He let Simeon know that he would see his Messiah before he died, and he did (Luke 2:21–35).

God also had His prophetess Anna there. Although she was eighty-four years old, she never left the temple. She had a call to be fasting and praying for her Messiah to come. God let her know of His sovereign work in bringing His Messiah, and she gave forth her praise and her witness of His presence (Luke 2:36–38). Surely they are representatives of others who were passionate in prayer for the coming of the long awaited Messiah of Israel. The point is that God had His people who were participating, even in God's ultimate sovereign plan.

Likewise, before the coming of the Holy Spirit and the revival at Pentecost (Acts 2), God had His people prepared and ready to participate. For three years His disciples had walked, learned, and lived with Jesus Christ. They together with 108 other followers of Christ waited those ten days in the upper room in prayerful expectation of the event God planned for Pentecost. They were participants with God in the miraculous events related to that outpouring of the Holy Spirit.

We may not feel that our feeble intercessions and continuing prayers for revival are very significant, but these are false feelings. Our prayers are tremendously significant and our responsiveness to God's plans is part of His sovereign moving.

## REVIVAL BEGINS WITH GOD MOVING IN POWER

"Oh, that you would rend the heavens and come down," (Isa. 64:1). Isaiah understood that there are certain times in history when the need for God's supernatural intervention is a necessary ingredient to the fulfillment of God's plan. Getting the attention of rebellious, spiritually blind people is not a small task.

As I am writing, our nation has just observed another anniversary of the terrorist attacks upon the United States, perpetrated on September 11, 2001.

At the World Trade Center, 2,749 people were killed; at the Pentagon, another 184 people died; near Shanksville, Pennsylvania, at the crash sight of United Airlines Flight 93, an added 40 passengers and crew members died.

In appropriate ceremonies, the brothers and sisters of the nearly 3,000 people who died in those terror attacks read the names of their deceased loved ones. As was the actual event, the remembrance was a sobering moment for all. We faced the startling reminder that the terrorists launched a bold war against all freedom-loving people on that infamous day.

God in no way initiated the carnage, death, and terror of that awful attack, but He did permit it to happen. In God's sovereign ways, He used the attack to awaken His people to the urgency of our times. He desires an urgency of response from His people:

> When I shut up the heavens so that there is no rain, or command
> locusts to devour the land or send a plague among my people, if my
> people, who are called by my name, will humble themselves and
> pray and seek my face and turn from their wicked ways, then will
> I hear from heaven and will forgive their sin and will heal their
> land. (2 Chron. 7:13–14)

God is speaking powerfully through shocking world events, and only those who are truly His people can participate with Him in what God desires to do.

### God Is Speaking, but Who Is Listening?

Terrorist attacks in Spain, London, Asia, Palestine, and Israel, and the insurgency in Iraq with murderous suicide bombings, keep the suffering chaos of war constantly before the world. We are also being confronted with so-called "natural disasters" like the earthquake-caused Indian Ocean tsunami, the hurricanes that devastated Florida in 2004 and the 2005 hurricane Katrina that destroyed New Orleans and devastated the coastal areas of several southern states.

People by the multiplied thousands died, were rendered homeless, or experienced injury. They went through indescribable sufferings and total economic chaos in these disasters wrought by the elements. The media news accounts have even invoked some familiar Christian lingo in their published statements describing the carnage: "These disasters have reached biblical proportions!" or "New Orleans is an apocalyptic disaster zone!" Some people are hearing God speak, but is that making a difference?

Surely God is speaking to His entire world in these chaotic times. Many of us have no doubt that God's sovereign, attention-grabbing power is on display. He has authority to judge and require accountability from all people. This fact is on display in sometimes shocking dimensions.

Yet, for the most part, the world in its wisdom espouses answers that totally bypass God. The politically powerful environmentalist movement declares that increasing pollution has led to global warming that is wreaking havoc upon our oceans and weather patterns. Geologists study the shifting of continental plates to try to explain and even predict approaching earthquakes. Other scientists and astronomers consider the sun's recent explosive flares to have a detrimental influence upon telecommunications. Some suggest that these sunspots may have negative effects on weather patterns and other issues that could contribute to calamities of nature.

The world searches for answers and legitimately so. But any admission that earth's problems might be related to how our sins have offended the holiness of God remains a closed door. The fact that a holy, judicious God might hold humanity accountable for what the Bible defines as wickedness is not allowed to come up for consideration by the world of public opinion. The world will not readily recognize the involvement of almighty God in any world happenings.

Yet this is where God's people need to begin. God's people must know God's sovereign power at work. He is involved. Our Lord Jesus Christ foretold these happenings in prophetic utterances that are strikingly relevant today.

> Then he said to them: "Nation will rise against nation, and kingdom against kingdom. There will be great earthquakes, famines and pestilences in various places, and fearful events and great signs from heaven.... There will be signs in the sun, moon and stars. On the earth, nations will be in anguish and perplexity at the roaring and tossing of the sea. Men will faint from terror, apprehensive of what is coming on the world, for the heavenly bodies will be shaken." (Luke 21:10–11, 25–26)

## The People Who Wouldn't Listen to God

In my personal devotional time, I have been reading through the Old Testament book of Jeremiah again. My heart has been significantly moved to note the similarity between Judah's spiritual condition and that which characterizes so much of the professing Christian community in our own nation. As Jeremiah bravely gave out God's words of warning, the Lord's patient endurance with Judah's sins was near its limit. The beginning winds of God's judgment were becoming more and more visible:

> Judah mourns, her cities languish; they wail for the land, and a cry goes up from Jerusalem. The nobles send their servants for water; they go to the cisterns but find no water. They return with their jars unfilled; dismayed and despairing, they cover their heads. The ground is cracked because there is no rain in the land; the farmers are dismayed and cover their heads. Even the doe in the field deserts her newborn fawn because there is no grass. Wild donkeys stand on the barren heights and pant like jackals; their eyesight fails for lack of pasture. (Jer. 14:2–6)

God often speaks through the calamities of nature. God kept sending to Judah drought, famine, storms, and the nasty incursions of warlike invasions, all in support of the messages of His prophet. As the people of Judah hardened their hearts and refused to believe God's warnings, increasingly intense crises kept coming.

As Jeremiah spoke God's coming-judgment words to his nation, they did not listen. Threats, beatings, imprisonment, ridicule, and disgrace were heaped upon God's faithful prophet for speaking truth. The magnitude of that tragedy is measured by the fact that the respected religious leaders of Judah were the major perpetrators of Jeremiah's sufferings. They stubbornly refused their opportunity to hear what God was saying. They were locked into their limited frame of reference and left no room to hear what God was really saying.

As noted above, the nations of today's world are (like Judah) receiving numerous warnings concerning approaching perils of judgment from God's judicious hand—the proverbial "handwriting is on the wall!" Foreboding dark clouds of sovereign judgment from God are becoming increasingly evident; but at least at this moment, few seem to be responding.

Even among Bible-believing Christians, the response to these times of distress and severe natural disasters remains mostly insipid. Programs and new approaches to ministry still attract some attention, but calls for prayer and times set apart for travail and intercession for God's merciful intervention—prophetic voices on the order of Jeremiah, beseeching God—are rare at best.

What is needed to change stubborn hearts and closed minds into seeking, broken, responding hearts? It is evident in God's Word that something more than judicious acts on God's part is necessary. Neither Israel nor Judah responded to God's beginning of judgments upon them in ways that pleased God and changed the course of their demise. Their hearts were too hardened by sin. Judah had some short reprieves but returned quickly to their erring ways.

During the times of God's coming judgments described in the book of Revelation, statements like these are repeated several times:

> The rest of mankind that were not killed by these plagues still did not repent of the work of their hands; they did not stop worshiping demons, and idols of gold, silver, bronze, stone and wood—idols that cannot see or hear or walk. Nor did they repent of their murders, their magic arts, their sexual immorality or their thefts. (9:20–21; see also 6:15–17; 16:9, 11)

God's sovereign acts of His judicious judgments upon humanity do gain attention and offer the world a glimpse of His holiness, but more of God's grace and mercy seem necessary for a significant revival to impact humanity. I and others share a conviction that God intends to do just that.

## A MOVE BY GOD OF OVERWHELMING MAGNITUDE

On the day of Pentecost, God originated His powerful move of overwhelming magnitude. The disciples assembled in "one place" for prayer and a quiet waiting upon God for His promise of the coming of the Holy Spirit. These followers of Jesus Christ had little concept concerning what the arrival of the Holy Spirit might mean.

On the day of Pentecost, a powerful sound "like the blowing of a violent wind came from heaven" (Acts 2:2). The sound filled the entire house where they were sitting. Although the heavenly sound was concentrated within the house, the magnitude of the windlike noise startled and attracted many people in the city: "Now there were staying in Jerusalem God-fearing Jews from every nation under heaven. When they heard this sound, a crowd came together in bewilderment" (vv. 5–6).

A second physical manifestation appeared concurrently. The disciples "saw what seemed to be tongues of fire that separated and came to rest on each of them" (v. 3). As the violent wind sound and the "tongues of fire" washed over those waiting, praying disciples, "all of them were filled with the Holy Spirit and began to speak in other tongues as the Spirit enabled them" (v. 4). Suddenly, these disciples were filled with overflowing hearts that were declaring the wonders of God.

Then another miracle happened. Everyone was able to understand the disciples in their own tongues. Some sixteen different languages and dialects are listed as being represented in the crowd, but each person heard the disciples' words in his or her own native language. God's miracle got their attention. "What does this mean?" was the astonished question of these confused people observing the manifestations of the Holy Spirit's coming. Some skeptics dismissed the strange scene with the careless charge that these 120 disciples had too much wine to drink.

The apostle Peter was prompted by the Holy Spirit to deliver his first sermon after having been filled with the Holy Spirit. That must have been a profound and powerful moment for Peter and the rest of the disciples as well. He was the same Peter everyone knew, and yet he was totally different. Humility, authority, and commanding power flowed from his person and message. Everyone was energized by the Holy Spirit's presence as they listened with rapt attention.

After assuring his listeners that they were not drunk at that early morning hour, Peter chose this text from the prophet Joel:

In the last days, God says, I will pour out my Spirit on all people. Your sons and daughters will prophesy, your young men will see visions, your old men will dream dreams. Even on my servants, both men and women, I will pour out my Spirit in those days, and they will prophesy. I will show wonders in the heaven above and signs on the earth below, blood and fire and billows of smoke. The sun will be turned to darkness and the moon to blood before the coming of the great and glorious day of the Lord. And everyone who calls on the name of the Lord will be saved. (vv. 17–21)

Peter went on expounding his Christ-exalting sermon, and the results were phenomenal. Three thousand professed faith in Christ. They were all baptized and added to that first fairly megachurch body of believers. Phenomenal evidences of transformed lives; Holy Spirit–empowered witnessing; and miraculous, sovereign interventions of God overwhelmed the opposition.

Those early chapters of Acts unfold an explosive story of startling magnitude. Jesus Christ launched His church with the power of the Holy Spirit, mightily moving upon and through the witness of God's people. Threats, imprisonments, beatings, and even Stephen's martyrdom seemed only to energize the believers on to greater effectiveness. Then, in Acts 9:1–18, Jesus Christ miraculously confronted the most zealous persecutor of the church, Saul of Tarsus, on the road to Damascus. He was totally transformed by that encounter and became his Savior's most explosive and expansive witness.

### In the Last Days

As we consider revival in these closing days of history, the pouring out of the Holy Spirit at Pentecost has significant purpose for our encouragement. Peter uses the above quoted text from the Old Testament book of Joel to help explain the miraculous, phenomenal happenings being observed at Pentecost. The coming of the Holy Spirit was a move by almighty God that was of overwhelming importance. It would have been hard to miss the fact that God was at work.

In my judgment, as we pray and anticipate revival, this is what God's people and our world scene needs from God again. I believe we need another miraculous work of God's grace on the level of this magnitude. God's people and our world scene need to be confronted by that which God is obviously doing.

No, I am not suggesting that we need the Holy Spirit to be poured out again in the same way that He came at Pentecost. That has already taken place. Peter makes it clear that a major purpose of Joel's prophecy was to foretell just what the disciples were experiencing and the observers were seeing. But it needs to be asked, "Was that the only purpose?" Could it be that Joel's prophecy is meant also to encourage believers to look for an equally dramatic intervention by God at the close of the ages? Many of us believe it does.

Peter begins by quoting Joel's expansive statement, "In the last days, God says, I will pour out my Spirit on all people" (v. 17). The initial coming of the Holy Spirit certainly must be regarded as being a part of "the last days" of which Joel was prophesying. Those last days began nearly two thousand years ago with the launching of Christ's church. However, the larger context makes clear that those "last days" have continuing expression throughout the end times.

For example, Joel 3 opens with a prophetic reference to the coming judgment of the nations:

> In those days and at that time, when I restore the fortunes of Judah and Jerusalem, I will gather all nations and bring them down to the Valley of Jehoshaphat. There I will enter into judgment against them concerning my inheritance, my people Israel, for they scattered my people among the nations and divided up my land. (vv. 1–2)

This statement and others would seem to have particular intent to bring focus upon the very end times of history. Those are "the last days" in consummate dimension. For the encouragement of all who recognize the need for a mighty revival and are praying for God's plan to bring it about, Joel's text seems to hold promise for another mighty intervention of God's power in these closing days of history. God's people, the nations, and all people need to see God's infinite power displayed in compelling certainty.

Do we see in the prophetic passages of Scripture promise of such an event? Has God planned a coming world occurrence where a miraculous, divine encounter of a similar magnitude to Pentecost would be probable to occur? Will there be a time where God speaks to His world with such authority and power that all humanity will be forced to recognize that God is speaking?

I believe the answer to such questions is a resounding "Yes!"

## Chapter 3

# THE FIRE FROM HEAVEN DOES BURN

*When all the people saw this, they fell prostrate and cried, "The LORD—he is God! The LORD—he is God!" Then Elijah commanded them, "Seize the prophets of Baal. Don't let anyone get away!" They seized them, and Elijah had them brought down to the Kishon Valley and slaughtered there.*

*1 Kings 18:39–40*

While we can get very excited over the triumphant image of God sending fire from heaven to ignite the sacrifice (and the hearts) of his people toward revival, there is another meaning that we must associate with "fire from heaven"—one that is usually ironically less popular, though if we're honest, the more commonly understood.

Most of the time, when we speak of "fire from heaven," we are referring to God's judgment. For instance, fire from heaven immediately evokes for many of us the fate of Sodom and Gomorrah. And there are many other repeatedly frightening images of God's consuming wrath being sent down upon rebellious people: upon complaining Israelites under Moses' leadership (Num. 11:1–2); Elijah's calling down fire from heaven upon those poor captains and soldiers sent by an apostate King Ahaziah (2 Kings 1:9–14); and then there is even Jesus' disciples (James and John) and their indignant threat to do the same to the Samaritan village that would not welcome him (Luke 9:52–56).

Fire from heaven for blessing and revival, and fire from heaven for judgment—they would seem as about as opposite in purpose as possible. But in truth, God's judgment is often intrinsically linked to his work of revival. It was very much the case when God sent fire down from heaven to consume Elijah's soaked sacrifice.

We don't like to dwell on it much, but immediately after God's decidedly supernatural victory, revival among his people was ushered in next by a fierce cleansing—eight hundred and fifty prophets "slaughtered" in the valley of Kishon at Elijah's behest.

Fire from heaven is indeed an attention getter—but often our attentions are captured because of the powerful judgment that accompanies it. Those who had been deceived into believing that perhaps God is out of touch come to realize with bitter certainty that God is not mocked (Gal. 6:7). But the reality that attentions are captured is key to revival—God's divine intervention can shake his people out of their slumbering delusions and bring them before God's throne.

The prophet Ezekiel devotes chapters 38 and 39 of his book, two rather long sections in prophetic writ, to proclaim such a miracle of powerful divine intervention in coming world affairs. Ezekiel describes in remarkable detail a time when God will place His almighty power on miraculous display for the entire world to see. These two chapters describe swift, deadly judgments by God that supernaturally fall upon His enemies while they are attempting to invade Israel. God expresses His divine "No" in His judicious wrath, and the invasion stops. Under God's holy judgment, virtually all of the invaders are judged by death.

## ENTER GOG OF MAGOG

Although it would be a worthy study, it is not the purpose of this book to do an in-depth study of these two prophetic chapters. We will, however, attempt to look at some of the pertinent matters that contribute to our hope for revival. I recommend Ezekiel 38 and 39 for frequent reading. These two chapters relate God-honoring, Christ-exalting truth; and they have singular importance for these closing days of history.

Through His prophet, God tells of a coming time of invasion of Israel by a consortium of nations. Some of the nations participating in this coming invasion attempt are specifically identified with nations existing today, but others are more difficult to identify with certainty. A personage designated as "Gog, of the land of Magog" spearheads this coming military effort to "settle" the Israel and Middle East problems on the invaders' terms. God defines the invasions purpose as "an evil scheme" (38:10).

Treachery and betrayal make up a part of the invasion's scheme: "You will say, 'I will invade a land of unwalled villages; I will attack a peaceful and unsuspecting people'" (v. 11). This would seem to suggest that the present peacemaking initiatives for the Middle East by the diplomacy of Israel and other world powers could reach a measure of success. On the human level of perception these efforts appear to hold great promise for Israel to live in peace with the Palestinians and the rest of her Arab neighbors. However, generations of hate, greed, and desire to control the wealth of the Middle East prevails, and a betrayal of the peace initiatives will cause it to fail. The invasion begins.

"Gog" is convinced that his scheme to come with overwhelming numbers and tremendous military power will prevail. The invaders are described as "a great horde, a mighty army"; their numbers are "like a cloud that covers the land" (vv. 15–16). It's probable that a million or more invaders, energized by their generations of hatred, make up the troops. Humanly speaking, Gog is sure of success. On the international level of diplomatic efforts to prevent war and "keep the peace," only some words of weak warning are addressed to Gog and the nations making the massive invasion: "Have you come to plunder? Have you gathered your hordes to loot, to carry off silver and gold, to take away livestock and goods and to seize much plunder?" (v. 13).

## God Controls by Hook and by Crook

As one reads these two chapters, the strong declarations that God—in His sovereignty—keeps all of these recorded events and happenings under His absolute control commands our attention. Careful focus is kept upon the truth that God is in total control. Supporting that message is what I have called God's "I will" statements that appear approximately eighty times in the two chapters. Included in those "I will" assertions are assurances that God has full awareness of every action of the invaders: "You will come from your place in the far north.... You will advance against my people Israel like a cloud that covers the land" (vv. 15–16).

Although Gog and the nations with him regard the invasion to be all their idea and their doing, God demands credit for those very thoughts. God has used their thoughts to fulfill His sovereign plan to bring them to their time of facing His judgment: "I will turn you around, put hooks in your jaws and bring you out with your whole army—your horses, your horsemen fully armed, and a great horde with large and small shields, all of them brandishing their swords" (v. 4). Even mighty armies are weak in God's hands.

As I write these words, a picture from my childhood memories springs to mind. My father had a huge, powerful bull that became a threat to his safety and the safety of his sons. He once even started to charge toward my dad when he was walking among the cattle and caring for his herd of cows. Bulls, with their superior size and power, can be deadly.

My dad never said much about his own danger, but he was concerned. He and our hired hand went to work to soften the arrogance of that abusive bull. They lassoed the bull's front hoofs with one strong rope, and his rear hoofs with another strong rope. After fastening each rope to two separate tractors, they began to drive in opposite directions, causing the powerful bull to fall on his side and be stretched out upon the ground in a helpless format. There was considerable bellowing of protest by the bull for a few moments, but in his helpless condition, he soon quieted down.

My father then inserted a brass ring prepared for such purposes into the tender area of the bull's nose and fastened it securely. After appropriately releasing the bull from his helpless state, that powerful animal became like a meek pet to my dad. With a suitable leash attached to the ring, as a young boy, even I could lead that powerful bull anyplace he needed to go.

God uses a similar picture of His "hooks in the jaws" of Gog to illustrate His sovereign control over violent Gog and this whole consortium of invaders. God can humble the most powerful in a moment of time.

Biblical study concerning God's omnipotence, omniscience, omnipresence, holiness, and all of His transcendent attributes convinces believers that God is in total control of all that is. The very concept of God as the Creator and Sustainer of all things demands that He be truly in control of it all. Yet when one reads the narrative as God Himself presents in Ezekiel 38 and 39, the impact of seeing God's attributes at work in such graphic detail and action is a bit overwhelming. How wonderful in power, holiness, mercy, and justice is the Lord God Almighty.

## GOD WILL BRING JUDGMENT

There was a time when "hellfire and brimstone" kind of preaching was heard in nearly all Bible-preaching churches. In some situations there may have even been an unbalanced emphasis on judgment and hell, leading to a tragic neglect of proclaiming the gospel of God's love and mercy.

We do not have that problem today. It is rare, even in evangelical churches, to hear a sermon on hell and God's coming judgment. It certainly is not because those subjects are avoided in the Scriptures. God's judgments are the central theme of many of the Old Testament prophetic books. Much of Jesus' teaching during His earthly ministry focused on God's coming judgment (Matt. 24—25; Mark 13).

The New Testament book of Revelation describes God's coming judgments in graphic detail. A healthy correction of the neglect to speak of God's coming judgments is desperately needed. Consider how the apostle Paul admonished Timothy:

> Preach the Word; be prepared in season and out of season; correct, rebuke and encourage—with great patience and careful instruction. For the time will come when men will not put up with sound doctrine. Instead, to suit their own desires, they will gather around them a great number of teachers to say what their itching ears want to hear. They will turn their ears away from the truth and turn aside to myths. (2 Tim. 4:2–4)

Could it be that we are experiencing that time about which Paul warned Timothy? In our present state of spiritual decline, it may well be that God's people would not tolerate much, if any, teaching and preaching on hell and judgment. That must change. God will see to that.

When we live in a culture that legally sheds the blood of millions of unborn children upon the altar of a false god called "Right to Choose"; when our celebrities and politicians advance homosexual marriage and the larger homosexual agenda with all of its abominable perversions; when the greed of gambling becomes the leading form of national entertainment and a lucrative source for tax revenue for our politicians; when our courts and legal system craft ways to eliminate prayer, the Ten Commandments, and all other references to God from schools and national public life; when divorce and family breakdown has become the norm for marriages, brokenhearted children, and multiplied emotional disasters; when our leading scientists, educators, politicians, and courts battle to make the theory of evolution the only theory to be heard by our students, can there be any question but that God will judge? We need not say more.

When these conditions and many more of parallel kind prevail, we need to know God's judgments are on the way. These realities offend God. The same God who judges Gog of Magog will apply His holy judgments to our world. In fact, He is doing just that. Cultures and nations change, but God and our Lord Jesus Christ remain "the same yesterday and today and forever" (Heb. 13:8).

God is not reticent to talk about judgment. In His holiness and perfect justice, God is ready to take full responsibility for His judgments. In passages like Ezekiel 38 and 39, God brings His judgments to bear in miraculous display of those elements that He fully controls; no other source could be assigned responsibility. God wants His people and all humanity to know that He is a God of accountability and holy judgment. Chapter 38 closes with God's claim of responsibility: "And so I will show my greatness and my holiness, and I will make myself known in the sight of many nations. Then they will know that I am the LORD" (v. 23).

## No Questioning the Origin of Judgment

As Gog and the army of nations with him begin their invasion of Israel, they exude confidence of a quick victory. Their "hordes," their overwhelming numbers, and their vast assembly of military power cause them to gloat in anticipation of their total conquest: "I will plunder and loot and turn my hand against the resettled ruins and the people gathered from the nations, rich in livestock and goods, living at the center of the land" (v. 12).

As the invasion begins, God steps into the scene: "When Gog attacks the land of Israel, my hot anger will be aroused, declares the Sovereign LORD. In my zeal and fiery wrath I declare that at that time there shall be a great earthquake in the land of Israel" (vv. 18–19). This is an earthquake of God's direct judgment upon the invaders. It is so powerful and devastating that it will affect fish, birds, animal life, and all creatures, including all humanity: "All the people on the face of the earth will tremble at my presence. The mountains will be overturned, the cliffs will crumble and every wall will fall to the ground" (v. 20).[†]

The devastation wrought by God's earthquake of judgment is so traumatic that it results in confusion and chaos among the invading hordes: "I will summon a sword against Gog on all my mountains, declares the Sovereign LORD. Every man's sword will be against his brother" (v. 21). With soldiers dying all around them from the earthquake's shaking and the crumbling rocks, mass confusion among the invaders causes them to turn their weapons upon each other.

In the midst of that chaotic confusion, God injects His further instruments of judgment: "I will execute judgment upon him with plague and bloodshed; I will pour down torrents of rain, hailstones and burning sulfur on him and on his troops and on the many nations with him" (v. 22). A plague of divinely caused illness sweeps in upon the invaders. Flash floods from the "torrents of rain" sweep away many of the invaders. Giant hailstones and the burning sulfur of probable lightning origin finish off the carnage, and death is brought by this divine judgment of God's holy wrath. The judgment is so far-reaching that virtually all of the invading troops perish: "For seven months the house of Israel will be burying them in order to cleanse the land" (39:12). All of that death is not a scene we would desire to look upon. Birds, vultures, and flesh-eating animals begin to feed on the fallen bodies of the invading soldiers.

The judgment appears to extend even beyond the northern part of Israel where the invading troops attempt to launch their military conquest: "I will

---

† Some of us wonder if this might be the moment when the Islamic "Dome of the Rock" will be removed by God's direct judgment to make place for Israel to begin to rebuild the temple.

send fire on Magog and on those who live in safety in the coastlands, and they will know that I am the LORD" (v. 6). The "homelands" represented by the invading hordes appear to also experience God's fire and judgments falling at this same time upon them.

God is making sure that not just the invading troops but their homelands and the whole world get the message He is communicating. All of earth's inhabitants are accountable to God. Almighty God holds His right to execute holy judgment upon all of humanity at the time of His holy discretion.

## *The Purpose of Judgment*

Joel C. Rosenberg, a Christian believer of Jewish heritage, is an exceptionally gifted writer, communicator, novelist, and a devoted student of biblical truth. He is the best-selling author of several provocative novels that have captured the attention of numerous recognized media sources such as *ABC's Nightline, CNN Headline News*, and *The Rush Limbaugh Show*.

Rosenberg's novels are more than just novels. He includes not only scriptural comment but also speaks to the political and troubled conditions of our world from a prophetic perspective. His book *The Last Jihad* puts the reader inside the cockpit of a hijacked jet on a suicide mission of destruction. The amazing thing is that he wrote the novel nine months before September 11, 2001. His second novel, *The Last Days*, begins with the death of Yasser Arafat, published thirteen months before Arafat's actual death.[†]

Rosenberg's 2005 novel, *The Ezekiel Option*, provides the reader with his interpretation of Ezekiel 38 and 39. His competency as a novelist alone is worth the read, but so much of his explanation of Ezekiel 38 and 39 is supportive of my own understanding of the message of those chapters. I was particularly fascinated by one of his major conclusions concerning God's purpose in bringing His judgments upon the invaders. In the novel the lead character, Jonathan Bennett, has a trusted mentor, Dr. Eliezer Mordechai, who is a Jewish Christian believer and a devoted student of the prophetic Scriptures. As the story unfolds, Dr. Mordechai gives Bennett his under-

---

† This has led some to conclude that God is providing him with a unique touch of prophetic wisdom along with his biblical understanding.

standing of the major reason for God's judgment interventions upon the invading hordes described in Ezekiel 38 and 39. After a general explanation of God's judgment purposes to Bennett, Dr. Mordechai adds these pertinent words of explanation concerning these judgments:

> Judgment is just one part of God's plan. But so is salvation. God wants to catch people's attention, Jonathan. He wants to awaken them from their slumber. I have no doubt a day of great terror is coming. But a great spiritual awakening is coming as well. And it is possible that more people could become followers of Christ through this single event than at any other time in history. Millions. Possibly tens of millions, if not more.
>
> Think of it, Jonathan—true followers of Christ have always dreamed of the Rapture, when in the blink of an eye Christ will snatch them away from the suffering of this life into the glories of heaven. But what if there was a great spiritual awakening first? Would it not be just like God to do something like that first— before the Antichrist is revealed, before the Tribulation begins, before billions suffer and perish forever? (250)

When I first read these words, I was rather startled. They are on target with my own understanding of God's purpose for this visible display of His wrath. Even Dr. Mordechai's view of the timing just before the tribulation time and the beginning of the Antichrist's rule seems consistent with Ezekiel's prophecy to me.

There are a number of statements in the two chapters that appear supportive of such a purpose by God. Consider the following: "In days to come, O Gog, I will bring you against my land, so that the nations may know me when I show myself holy through you before their eyes" (Ezek. 38:16).

Almighty God has a singular intent to communicate to all people on the face of the earth concerning His judgments, His greatness, His holiness, and His power. As His judgment earthquake rumbles out its trembling message, the Creator states His desire that "all the people on the face of the earth will tremble at my presence" (v. 20). God desires, through the shocking events of His judgment described in these two chapters, for a holy "fear of God" to come afresh upon all of humanity. If repentance and revival is to happen, a holy fear of God must come home to people's hearts with compelling urgency.

Ezekiel 39:21 confirms how deeply God desires for the nations to hear what He is saying: "I will display my glory among the nations, and all the nations will see the punishment I inflict and the hand I lay upon them." The nations' mad rush toward sin and rebellion against God needs to be confronted to comprehend just how accountable to God they really are. God wants His justice and holiness to be presented before the eyes of the world.

In 38:23, the same communication is expressed in similar words: "And so I will show my greatness and my holiness, and I will make myself known in the sight of many nations. Then they will know that I am the LORD." These chapters make it clear that almighty God intends to use the judgments described to awaken a spiritual alertness upon all of humanity. It seems likely that this is a precursor to prepare the hearts of people for God's bringing of revival.

There is not much evidence of a holy fear of God in our world today. Arrogant acts of defiance of God are more in view. So much of the murderous violence, the hardness of human hearts to be open to hear the message of the gospel of Jesus Christ centers in a powerful religious bondage.

Those of us who work with spiritually oppressed people have come to know that a deep commitment to a counterfeit religious system grants much ground for the kingdom of darkness to rule in people's lives. I have heard my colleague Dr. Jim Logan say on numerous occasions, "The religious spirits are the worst kind. They are the most difficult to face in helping the spiritually oppressed find freedom!"

As we view the present world picture, this end-time invasive force appears to be made up of countries and people who espouse a religious system that is violently opposed to Christians and the nation of Israel. The loyalty to their religious system is so deep that young people are recruited by the hundreds and even thousands to turn themselves into suicide bombers. Their primary purpose is to kill the "infidels" to advance their own religious and political agenda and to earn a special reward of high-level ecstasy in the next life. To break through that kind of religious bondage requires God to use supremely convincing displays of His power and holy judgment. I see God's severe judgments as an expression of His love for the multitudes that are held in such a false religious system.

### God's Judgments That Involve Israel

The nation of Israel in its larger expression has long rejected their Messiah. And while, as already seen, there are increasing numbers of Jews who are embracing Christ as their long-awaited Messiah, those many generations of unbelief have created a wall of opposition in the minds and hearts of many Jewish people the world over. It is difficult to penetrate.

Messianic Jews (followers of Christ) still find it difficult to find acceptance, status, and equal opportunity within the nation of Israel. Many within the culture of Israel refuse to admit that such people should be able to claim that they are Jews. Yet, there are increasing numbers of believers in Christ who are present in Israel.

The Bible makes it clear that there is a day coming when, within a short period of time, the closed-minded position of unbelief in Jesus Christ by Jews will change. The apostle Paul wrote these words in Romans 11:26–27: "And so all Israel will be saved, as it is written: 'The deliverer will come from Zion; he will turn godlessness away from Jacob. And this is my covenant with them when I take away their sins.'" It is obvious if Israel is to be saved, there will be a time when Israel will begin to recognize on a nationwide basis that Jesus Christ is their Messiah. Many have associated this magnificent moment with the second coming of Jesus Christ.

The late Dr. John Walvoord expresses that view. The esteemed former president of Dallas Theological Seminary was an ardent, scholarly proponent of the "pre-millennial view" of Israel's future:

> Though the meaning of this passage has been debated, probably the best interpretation is to regard it as a national promise, namely, that at the time of the end when her period of suffering has been

fulfilled, Israel as a nation or Israel as a whole shall be delivered from her enemies. The salvation in view is not that of freedom from the guilt of sin, but deliverance from persecution and trial. This will be accomplished when the Deliverer comes out of Zion, an unmistakable reference to Jesus Christ. (112–13)

Although I have profited much from his writings and have high respect for Dr. Walvoord, I cannot accept his interpretation of Paul's statement, "All Israel will be saved." I have two main reasons. The first is that Paul ties the saving promise specifically into forgiveness of their sins: "And this is my covenant with them when I take away their sins" (Rom. 11:27). The saving of all Israel must include the removal of the guilt of sins. That's what salvation is all about.

The second reason I find Dr. Walvoord's explanation lacking is that this time when all Israel will be saved is not the end of Israel's sufferings. Rather, it seems to be the means God uses to prepare Israel for the terrible sufferings to be inflicted upon them by the Antichrist in the midst of the tribulation time. Their "salvation" will be God's part in making them ready to face martyrdom. Daniel 9:26–27 describes a coming time when, in the midst of the tribulation, the Antichrist breaks his seven-year covenant treaty with Israel and introduces a terrible slaughter of the Jewish people. According to Zechariah 13:8–9, as many as two-thirds of the Jews living in Israel will die at the hands of the Antichrist.

Ezekiel 38 and 39 appear to introduce Israel's salvation as part of God's purposes for His judgments upon the invaders. As already noted, a major purpose of the judgments is to bring a shocking awareness to all of the nations of the world concerning their accountability to God. A similar purpose of these judgments is to bring a message to the people of Israel. In Ezekiel 39:7, God states His purpose in the judgments related to what they communicate concerning Israel: "I will make known my holy name among my people Israel. I will no longer let my holy name be profaned, and the nations will know that I the LORD am the Holy One in Israel."

The events described in these two chapters appear to provide a pivotal turning point for the Jewish nation that has so long rejected Jesus Christ as their Messiah. "From that day forward the house of Israel will know that I am the LORD their God" (Ezek. 39:22). That statement holds special reference to Jesus Christ. In fact, He seems to be the speaker. Jesus said, "I am the way and the truth and the life. No one comes to the Father except through me" (John 14:6). If the people of Israel are to really know the One who said, "I am the LORD their God," they would have to know Jesus Christ. Jesus makes that quite plain.

The momentous events of God's judgment upon the invading hordes have a supernatural shock benefit to the whole house of Israel. A supernatural, God-authored change takes place within the hearts of the people of Israel. God's sovereignty makes Israel ready for an entire change in their national attitude toward God the Father and Jesus Christ, their Messiah.

God also uses these events of judgment to effect a rapid return of Jews to the land of Israel. "Therefore this is what the Sovereign LORD says: I will now bring Jacob back from captivity and will have compassion on all the people of Israel, and I will be zealous for my holy name" (Ezek. 39:25). God brings them back for a witness purpose to the nations: "They will forget their shame and all the unfaithfulness they showed toward me when they lived in safety in their land with no one to make them afraid. When I have brought them back from the nations and have gathered them from the countries of their enemies, I will show myself holy through them in the sight of many nations" (vv. 26–27). These verses depict a time of repentance and change, first in the hearts of the Israeli people, and then through their witness: God is able to show His holiness "in the sight of many nations."

The climax of what God does for Israel through His miraculous judgments upon the invaders is expressed in the closing two verses of Ezekiel 39: "Then they will know that I am the LORD their God, for though I sent them into exile among the nations, I will gather them to their own land, not leaving any behind. I will no longer hide my face from them, for I will pour out my Spirit on the house of Israel, declares the Sovereign LORD" (vv. 28–29). These words seem to portray revival for the nation that parallels what God did for His church at Pentecost when the Holy Spirit was poured out. When God says, "I will pour out my Spirit on the house of Israel," He seems to be promising a national revival within the nation that would be similar to the revival that came to God's people at Pentecost.

## THE BLENDING OF TWO ELEMENTS OF REVIVAL

What is revival? Revival is God's people earnestly accepting their responsibility to be "laborers together with God" in His sovereign plan to refresh and renew His people with heavenly, spiritual blessings in Christ Jesus. It means that God's own people recognize their sinful state of spiritual decline, enter into repentance for their lukewarm apathy, and begin to buy from their Lord all that He knows they need. Through persistent, doctrinal prayer, through earnest listening to God by immersing themselves in His Word, through seeing obedience to the Lord Jesus Christ as God's answer for their needs, they begin to pray with new levels of fervent waiting upon God.

Revival happens when God interjects Himself through His chosen means of powerful communication into the life of nations and people. God's power makes them ready to repent and receive His salvation. His love, mercy, and grace of cleansing forgiveness through the blood of Jesus Christ energize them. God floods His people with the power and fullness of the Holy Spirit, and they begin to move in obedient service with God and His plan.

In his classic book *The Pursuit of Holiness*,[†] Jerry Bridges used an example from the world of farming that is very helpful to understand the intimate bond between human responsibility and God's sovereign moving. Since holiness and revival are so close in meaning and goals, I have substituted the word *revival* each place where Jerry Bridges uses the word *holiness*. In doing this, his telling illustration will have its greatest impact to clarify the relationship between human responsibility and God's sovereign intervention toward revival as well as holiness.

---

† Jerry Bridges was one of the leaders of the Navigator's ministry team. This book has continued to impact the lives of many believers who desire a deeper intimacy and a higher level of obedience to God. It has much to say about what a God-authored revival will do in a believer's life.

A farmer plows his field, sows the seed, and fertilizes and culti-vates—all the while knowing that in the final analysis he is utterly dependent on forces outside of himself. He knows he cannot cause the seed to germinate, nor can he produce the rain and sunshine for growing and harvesting the crop. For a successful harvest, he is dependent on these things from God.

Yet the farmer knows that unless he diligently pursues his responsibilities to plow, plant, fertilize, and cultivate, he cannot expect a harvest at the end of the season. In a sense he is in a part-nership with God, and he will reap its benefits only when he has fulfilled his own responsibilities.

Farming is a joint venture between God and the farmer. The farmer cannot do what God must do, and God will not do what the farmer should do.

We can say just as accurately that the pursuit of [revival] is a joint venture between God and the Christian. No one can attain any degree of [revival] without God working in his life, but just as surely no one will attain it without effort on his own part. God has made it possible for us to walk in [revival]. But He has given to us the responsibility of doing the walking; He does not do that for us. (13–14)

Oftentimes the spark that God will use to ignite revival in the hearts of His people comes drifting into their lives from the furious blaze of His judg-ment. There is an ironic beauty that God can bring into our lives when we watch, awestruck, at His terrible justice. Passion is ignited among the faith-ful as they are forced to remember His definitive declaration, "I am the LORD their God."

*Chapter 4*

# RESISTANCE TO REVIVAL FIRE

*Now Ahab told Jezebel everything Elijah had done and
how he had killed all the prophets with the sword. So
Jezebel sent a messenger to Elijah to say, "May the gods
deal with me, be it ever so severely, if by this time tomorrow I do not make your life like that of one of them."*

*1 Kings 19:1–2*

After the powerful display of God's fire from heaven, of his power and
judgment, King Ahab rushed home and told his pagan queen Jezebel
everything that Elijah had done. Elijah had killed all the prophets … *her*
priests and prophets. Elijah had all 450 prophets of Baal and 400 prophets
of Ashera executed in the Kishon valley.

This was war; and Jezebel sent a messenger to Elijah with her unblink-
ing terms: You are as good as dead!

The stakes today are no less threatening for God's people. The subject of revival is a great threat to the kingdom of darkness. The Devil
knows that a revived and Holy Spirit–empowered church will glorify
God; renew and energize God's people for holy living; and produce an
explosive, worldwide outreach of salvation among the lost. Those God
entrusts with a burden and vision for revival need to utilize the protection God provides His people.

A careful study of Psalm 91 presents God's *sure stance for defeating darkness.* Memorizing this prayer for daily use provides believers with an essential
covering of protection from evil attacks. Understanding this psalm's message
needs top priority. It has a helpful message for the defeat of all our enemies,
but Psalm 91 provides us with particular insights concerning the overcoming

of the Devil and his kingdom. Supernatural evil always presents believers with a unique and formidable challenge. Our Lord wants us to know that He has provided us with His superior power and assurance of His victory.

In our English Bibles, the word "enemy" or "enemies" appears more than one hundred times in the book of Psalms. Depending upon your choice of translation and concordance, the numbers may vary slightly, but the fact that the psalms place a lot of focus upon the subject is important. When one considers other words in the Psalms that convey the same thought of opposition, hostility, antagonism, and a desire to harm, at least one hundred more references would need to be added to the one-hundred-plus direct references to enemies. Thoughts and words like *hate me, destroy me, evildoers, the wicked, adversary,* and like expressions appear repeatedly in the psalms. In one concordance the word "wicked" appears eighty-nine times, often referring to those who oppose God.

The point should be obvious. The Holy Spirit, through His inspiration and revelation to the psalmist writers, wants us to know that the subject of enemies needs serious and immediate consideration. Even though the Psalms belong in the category of ancient writings, the subject of enemies is very contemporary. In fact, it's a hot topic for these times when terrorism is in the forefront of world thought. The hate, violence, murder, litigation, ugly divorce battles, family chaos, and political infighting cry out this message: "Enemies abound!"

"Road rage" has been coined to describe the brutal, senseless, sudden violence happening on the roadways of our nation. And, as already stated, the enemy problem continues to heat up. Much enemy activity is raging through our country and world.

Most of us are familiar with the teachings of Scripture that divide our enemies into three separated spheres of battle: the *world,* the *flesh,* and the *Devil.* Careful study of the Psalms reveals that the full spectrum of these three enemies of the righteous are recognized and dealt with by these Old Testament theological poets. And for those of us who have been called by our Lord to enjoin the battle, it's important that we know our enemies.

## THE WORLD

Enemies in the world are many and perhaps the most obvious. Tangible, visible, physical enemies of the world system were often front and center in the Psalms. David, the warrior king, faced very physical enemies that were determined to capture and kill him. He prayed and wrote psalms about this kind of enemy.

In Psalm 7, it was Cush, a Benjamite, who was out to capture and tear him to pieces like a lion rips apart its victims. In several psalms, David wrote about Saul seeking to pin him to the wall with his javelin or hunting him down to kill him, forcing David to hide himself in deserts and mountain caves (Ps. 18; 57; 142). In Psalm 34, David was facing his enemy, Abimelech; in Psalm 52, it was Doeg the Edomite who had revealed David's hiding place to Saul; in Psalm 54, he faced the betrayal of the Ziphites; in Psalm 56, his capture by the Philistines is the focus of his enemy concern. David, the valiant warrior, had many tangible, visible, physical enemies to face on the battlefields of life. Even his own son, Absalom, tried to take David's life and wrest the kingdom from his father. He was doubtlessly a part of the enemy mix prayed about in numerous psalms, such as those recorded in Psalms 18, 102, and 143.

God's people need to recognize that this kind of enemy problem is greatly increasing in our day. Terrorists' brutality, religious enemies, government persecutions in some regions of the world, and violent criminal acts like road-rage incidents come near to us. We need to wear our armor and be mindful in prayer to be alert of worldly enemies and carefully appropriate our protection. Just as He did with David, God is able to provide a way of escape for His children, even when they are facing physical world threats from enemies who would effectively swear by their gods, "Your life is mine!"

## THE FLESH

As if the external world forces weren't enough to deal with, David also wrote psalms dealing with the battle within his own flesh. In Psalm 25:17, he writes, "The troubles of my heart have multiplied; free me from my anguish." Like all of us, David had an internal problem with spiritual heart trouble. Sins like lust, anger, selfish ambition, and thoughtless abuse of power roared into his life at times and almost destroyed him.

His lustful episode with Bathsheba and his proxy murder of her husband tells part of the story. Psalms 32, 51, and 143 reveal the depth of problems that David faced in dealing with his sinful, internal desires inherited from the fall of Adam. Our flesh is a formidable opponent for all believers. It can introduce terrible havoc and extremely destructive disasters into our lives. Christian believers must pursue careful biblical study to understand and use God's provided victory over this fleshly enemy. Failure to resist these lustful desires gives opportunity for Satan's kingdom to gain a place of advantage in believers' lives. Major defeats in this area in the lives of Christians is one of the profound evidences of the need for revival awakening to come to the personal lives of believers.[†]

## The Kingdom of Darkness

The third enemy dealt with in the Psalms also must be recognized to be a formidable foe. The kingdom of darkness represents a very real and present realm of supernatural opposition to God's people. Satan rules over a kingdom of spirit beings identified in Scripture as fallen angels or demons (Rev. 12:7–9). These spirit powers play a virulent role in much of the chaos and troubles of the earth.

Since this adversary dwells in a realm of existence that is not visible to human sight, the advantage this represents is very great. There is an invisible, yet very real foe of unusual power that is determined to do us harm. It is not the purpose of this book to develop extensive study concerning the kingdom of darkness. Much helpful material is available for those desiring to pursue such study.[††]

---

[†] I deal more carefully with this problem of spiritual war with our own flesh in my book *The Adversary at Home* Life Journey, Cook Communications Ministries, Colorado Springs, 2006.

[††] Some suggested beginning readings: Dr. Ed Murphy's *The Handbook for Spiritual Warfare*, Nashville: Thomas Nelson, 2003; Erwin W. Lutzer's *The Serpent of Paradise*, Chicago: Moody Publishers, 1996; Robert Lightner's *Angels, Satan, and Demons*, Nashville: W Publishing Group, 1998; and my own, *The Adversary*, Chicago: Moody Publishers, 1981.

## Sure Stance for Defeating Darkness

Our purpose in this setting is to focus upon a psalm that presents to believers a sure stance for defeating darkness. God has not left His people defenseless against the Devil. Satan and his kingdom do represent a powerful enemy, but God is infinitely greater. Sometimes in the Psalms it is difficult to separate out which enemy is being recognized by the text, because many enemy references reveal a composite problem. All three enemies appear to be a part of the mix of battle the psalmist includes in his prayer. It's that way with us, too. We cannot always readily recognize whether we are facing battle with the world, the flesh, or the Devil, but our victory in Jesus Christ is inclusive. He has defeated all of them.

There are times, however, when the enemy we face is more evident.[†] Our Lord Jesus Christ experienced such focused assault from evil powers against Himself, and He repeatedly warned us that what happened to Him will face His followers as well. In Matthew 24:9, He spoke this strong warning: "Then you will be handed over to be persecuted and put to death, and you will be hated by all nations because of me." Being a follower of Jesus Christ will bring times of spiritual battle into our experience. His wilderness temptation and His garden of Gethsemane battles both describe intensified, fierce spiritual battle with the Devil and his kingdom. The battle was so fierce in both of those situations that God the Father sent His holy angels to minister their strength to Jesus (Matt. 4:11; Luke 22:43). Focused spiritual oppression addressed against us from the kingdom of darkness can be intense and extremely difficult to face. Without God's enabling support it can drain our human strength.

As I have sought to deal with the spiritual assault from the Devil's kingdom, the Lord has directed me to seek relief in two primary ways. Both of which have proved very helpful. First, I have earnestly sought to solicit the prayer support of other believers. Although they failed Him, Jesus sought that supportive help from His disciples in Gethsemane.

---

† As I have been writing this book, I have sensed intensified spiritual oppression from the realm of darkness. I know Satan and his kingdom are addressing their spiritual opposition to what God has appointed me to do.

The second resource of help has been to arise numerous times in the middle of the night for times of personal, intensive, doctrinal prayer. Several references in the Gospels call our attention to the fact that our Lord Jesus Christ often left His place of ministry or rest to go alone to pray. Mark 1:35 states, "Very early in the morning, while it was still dark, Jesus got up, left the house and went off to a solitary place, where he prayed." Luke 9:12 records for us when He sought a place of mountainside solitude and prayed all night. In light of my own experience, I have wondered if those might have been times when our Savior was sensing the fierceness of spiritual battle and needed to be quietly alone with His Father. When the battle is great, alone times of prayer can bring relief and renewal.

### The Psalm 91 Foundation

Psalm 91 provides the foundational Old Testament passage to help God's people know how to defeat the attacks of the Devil and his kingdom. Just as Ephesians 6:10–20 presents New Testament foundations to help believers battle supernatural evil, God provided equally important truth in the Old Testament. These two passages have much in common. I often urge believers to commit both texts to memory. I have done so and have reaped measureless benefits for my own spiritual journey. Those committed to experiencing God's fire from heaven will need the foundations these passages convey to "fight a good fight!" Satan finds the subject of revival extremely threatening to his plans. He will fight against it with all the deceptive power available to him and his army. That's a given.

Scholars are not in agreement concerning the human author of Psalm 91. The best tradition seems to have assigned it to Moses. There are two primary reasons for this view. The first is that it follows Psalm 90 with the trusted author designate: "A prayer of Moses the man of God." It was a common practice for psalms authored by such a man to be followed by another psalm authored by the same person. That would mean Psalm 91 also belonged to Moses.

A second reason for assigning it to Moses has to do with some internal evidence in the psalm that fits him. Psalm 91 maintains a profound appreciation for God's names that fits the enlightenment Moses had for the names of God (Ex. 6:2–3; 34:5–7). The fact that Psalm 91 deals with confronting supernatural evil also fits Moses exposure to Pharaoh's "wise men and sorcerers, and the Egyptian magicians" (Ex. 7:11). That's all a part of the supernatural realm of evil.

As Moses and Aaron displayed God's power with Aaron's staff by turning it into a snake when Aaron threw it on the ground, we read that these sorcerers and magicians "did the same things by their secret arts." That illustrates the Devil's counterfeit power at work. It is revealing and even a bit humorous that Aaron's staff, which had become a snake, "swallowed up their staffs" (Ex. 7:10–12). There was no question remaining. Satan's power is at best an imitation of God, and God's power is infinitely superior.

Another bit of internal proof that supports Moses' authorship concerns the testimony of the psalmist recorded in Psalm 91:9–12. This passage seems to fit the experience of Moses in his house that last night in Egypt when the death angel visited judgment upon the Egyptian households by bringing death to each family's firstborn son. In obedience to God's instructions, Moses and all those in his "tent" were safe. The blood on the top and each side of the doorframe of Moses' house and those of Israel's people was there.

The Lord uses very interesting terminology when He informs Moses of the place of safety He will provide: "When the LORD goes through the land to strike down the Egyptians, he will see the blood on the top and sides of the doorframe and will pass over that doorway, and will not permit the destroyer to enter your houses and strike you down" (Ex. 12:23).

Revelation 9:11, using both Hebrew and Greek words, assigns to Satan the name "destroyer." The judgment upon the Egyptian firstborn was God's judgment, but the "agent" or angel by which the Lord carried out these judgment deaths probably was "Destroyer," the name of the fallen angel Satan. As Erwin Lutzer points out in *Serpent of Paradise*, "The devil is just as much God's servant in his rebellion as he was God's servant in the days of his sweet obedience. Even today, he cannot act without God's express permission; he can neither tempt, coerce, demonize, nor make so much as a single plan without the consent and approval of God. As Martin Luther so aptly explained, the Devil is God's devil" (102).

Our heavenly Father in His sovereign control of all things can and does use the Devil to accomplish His will and purposes. A careful study of passages like Matthew 18:21–35 seems to lend strong support to such truth. In the parable, the unforgiving servant had his master turn him "over to the jailers to be tortured, until he should pay back all he owed." Many Bible students understand the "jailers" to be describing the discipline that may come from demonic work under the watchful control of the Master. The unforgiving servant needed to come to the place where he would see the necessity of forgiving the offender who owed him unpaid debt. An unforgiving heart was not acceptable to his Master.

And that is key to our understanding the battle we must enjoin as we anticipate God's revival. Whether the enemy's battalion is the world, our own flesh, or literal enemy spiritual forces, God is the Master of it all. The battle could not even be enjoined without His permissive bidding.

## Chapter 5

# GOD'S SURE-FIRE
# PROTECTION PLAN

*Elijah was afraid and ran for his life. When he came to Beersheba in Judah, he left his servant there, while he himself went a day's journey into the desert. He came to a broom tree, sat down under it and prayed that he might die. "I have had enough, LORD," he said. "Take my life; I am no better than my ancestors." Then he lay down under the tree and fell asleep.*

*1 Kings 19:3–5*

*He who dwells in the shelter of the Most High will rest in the shadow of the Almighty. I will say of the LORD, "He is my refuge and my fortress, my God, in whom I trust."*

*Psalm 91:1–2*

A broom tree seems a far stretch from the shelter of the Most High. But Elijah was afraid and on the run. Where was the fire now? Where was the leader who had commanded God's judgment upon his enemies? At the end of his rope, fearful unto death, at the bottom of the barrel … Elijah falls asleep under the tree … he rests in the shadow.

Psalm 91 also begins by describing one who rests in a shadow—the shadow of the Almighty. And while Elijah clearly and disappointingly has stumbled in his faith after a moment of powerful revival, he finally echoes the psalmist—he cries out to his Lord, his refuge, his God. The psalm lifts our eyes to see and understand more of the transcendent loftiness of the God of the Bible—the God whom Elijah momentarily lost sight of. The Holy Spirit does that by leading the psalmist to focus upon some of the biblical names for God that are unfolded for God's people in the Old Testament Scriptures.

Elijah needed that perspective. And likewise God wants us to know that the surety of our victory over supernatural evil rests in our understanding more of His person.

## SURE OF A SAFE, RESTFUL DWELLING PLACE

The message of Psalm 91 recognizes that God's people do face a battle with supernatural evil. The Devil is our enemy. He and his kingdom come close to do battle against us. As we will see in the development of the psalm, we encounter a "fowler" (Satan) who has plans to snare God's people and do his deadly work against them. As we face such a foreboding prospect, the psalmist lets us know where we must begin to meet such a challenge. We must begin with God.

The psalmist introduces us to God. In these two verses, he focuses attention upon four different Old Testament names for God. Getting to know God is not an easy assignment. The whole of the Bible introduces us to Him as an infinite, transcendent, personal being. Left to us, His person is so above and beyond the reach of human understanding that "knowing Him" expresses an exceedingly stretching desire.

Philosophers, theologians, poets, and godly saints of the past may help us to know about Him, but truly knowing Him goes deeper. It conveys a personal, relational intimacy. Ultimately, the process of knowing God requires a personal relationship with Jesus Christ. Jesus said to His disciples, "If you really knew me, you would know my Father as well" (John 14:7).

Philip's response was, "Lord, show us the Father and that will be enough for us." The Lord Jesus answered Philip with a question: "Don't you know me, Philip, even after I have been among you such a long time? Anyone who has seen me has seen the Father" (John 14:7–9). In John 10:30, Jesus described the intimacy between Himself and the Father in these words: "I and the Father are one." It is impossible to know God the Father the way He wants us to know Him without coming to know Jesus Christ as one's personal Savior and Lord.

We need to know, however, that knowing Jesus Christ is just our beginning place. Psalm 91 helps us enlarge our knowledge of God. By focusing our attention upon four of God's Old Testament names, the Lord assists us to know and grow in our understanding of who He is. His names help us come closer to Him and more confident in times of battle.

### The Shelter of the Most High (Elyon)

The psalm opens with an inviting statement to a person of faith. We can have a part in choosing to dwell ("choosing to abide" might be a good New Testament meaning) in the provided "shelter" of "the Most High." Before we look at the Hebrew name translated Most High, it is beneficial to meditate for a moment on the "shelter."

What is this provided shelter? The truth of both the Old and New Testaments quickly focuses our attention upon the only shelter God has ever supplied for the righteous. This can only be the person and work of Jesus Christ. The Old Testament's sacrificial system, the writings of the prophets, and numerous pronouncements of God focused upon a coming prophet, priest, and king who would be "the shelter of the Most High." Jesus Christ is God's provided dwelling place of shelter for His people. There is no other. The shelter includes His person and His work. His death, burial, and resurrection, the very heart of the gospel as defined for us in 1 Corinthians 15:1–5, are all wrapped up in this reference to God's provided shelter.

The name of the One providing this "shelter" contributes much to our getting to know God and why our dwelling place is so adequate, safe, and secure. "The Most High," Elyon, the highest of all the high, provides this shelter. After we have done our best to understand His highness, we are compelled to leave such noble effort with this echo of truth reverberating in our hearts: "He's higher than that!"

This Old Testament name for God forces us to struggle with transcendent, superlative, measureless concepts. That's as it should be. Understanding God as an infinite being and who He is in His fullest dimension remains beyond the human reach of comprehension. Finite man, even though redeemed, remains limited in capacity to grasp the realm of the Infinite One.

Kay Arthur's book *Lord, I Want to Know You* has timeless value for those wanting to know God on the biblical, practical, and personal levels. The book's study guides provide help to better understand God's names in their biblical settings. She states that Elyon elevates God's transcendent highness as "the name that designates God as the sovereign ruler of all the universe" (15). Elyon in His total sovereignty rules over all the affairs of humanity and the nations. He's the One who has final and total control over everything.

Arthur reminds us that God even brought Babylon's powerful King Nebuchadnezzar to recognize Elyon's sovereign control of everything. After Nebuchadnezzar recovered from God's imposed discipline of insanity, God used this conceited king to state this lofty truth about His name, Elyon:

> Then I praised the Most High; I honored and glorified him who lives forever. His dominion is an eternal dominion; his kingdom endures from generation to generation. All the peoples of the earth are regarded as nothing. He does as he pleases with the powers of heaven and the peoples of the earth. No one can hold back his hand or say to him: "What have you done?" (Dan. 4:34–35)

If God could humble arrogant King Nebuchadnezzar and turn him into such a proclaiming prophet of truth, the Most High's sovereignty is wonderfully displayed. Our provided shelter is secure to withstand the most powerful blasts evil can muster.

### Resting in the Shadow of the Almighty (Shaddai)

The second Hebrew name for God in Psalm 91 focuses our attention upon God's almighty strength and power. This name relates to God's omnipotence to provide protection for His people. *Shaddai* is another superlative, measureless name. God's almighty power is infinitely beyond all other power. The Devil's power and that of his entire kingdom shrinks to nothingness when compared to Shaddai's power. God's power stands alone. Stretching to comprehend the meaning and message of our text will serve to enlarge our quest to know God.

Shaddai expresses more to us than just God's infinite, almighty power. Some scholars emphasize that the name, especially in its compounded form of

*El Shaddai,* does communicate God's might and power to execute His judgments upon all that deserves His justice and wrath. It's good to know that God's holy justice and divine wrath will, in His perfect timing, banish all evil forever from His presence and that of His redeemed ones. The Devil and his angels will ultimately face Shaddai's power, which will cast them into the lake of fire that God in His judicious wrath has prepared for them (Matt. 25:41; Rev. 20:10).

God's name, Shaddai, as it is used in Psalm 91, also conveys a comforting dimension of God's almighty power. He provides a protective covering for God's people. It is fascinating to me that our text shows us that those who are dwelling in the shelter of the Most High will find a place of restful protection in "the shadow of the Almighty." There is important truth to note in this biblical picture. To be in Shaddai's shadow means that the One casting the shadow is very close to you. It also means He is between you and the source of the blast, the heat, and the oppression that is trying to get at you.

The picture conveyed is one of the hovering, watchful presence of Shaddai, always between you and your enemy. He keeps Himself between you and the "fowler" and all of his destructive schemes. The protection is so thorough and "Almighty" that even in times of great battle, He provides a secure, quiet place of restful comfort. There is rest in His shadow.

When God first revealed Himself as Shaddai in the Bible, He used a compounded form of this wonderful name: He is El Shaddai, God almighty. The setting of this revelation conveyed this concept of a protective covering. His almighty name was revealed to Abraham during what must have been a time of uncertainty and confusion in Abraham's life. God's almighty power conveyed to Abraham a message of encouragement and comfort that he greatly needed to hear:

> When Abram was ninety-nine years old, the LORD appeared to him and said, "I am God Almighty [El Shaddai]; walk before me and be blameless. I will confirm my covenant between me and you and will greatly increase your numbers."
>
> Abram fell facedown, and God said to him, "As for me, this is my covenant with you: You will be the father of many nations. No

longer will you be called Abram, your name will be Abraham, for I have made you a father of many nations. I will make you very fruitful; I will make nations of you, and kings will come from you. I will establish my covenant as an everlasting covenant between me and you and your descendants after you for the generations to come, to be your God and the God of your descendants after you. The whole land of Canaan, where you are now an alien, I will give as an everlasting possession to you and your descendants after you; and I will be their God." (Gen. 17:1–8)

The biblical context following this introduction to God's almighty name reveals that Abraham had been struggling with his mind and emotions concerning God's covenant calling recorded in Genesis 12:1–3. Possibly he was hearing taunts to his mind from Satan and the realm of darkness concerning these earlier promises from God. I gain that insight from the fact that when God told him that he would be a father of Isaac at a hundred years of age and that Sarah would be his son's mother at the age of ninety, Abraham laughed. He even went so far as to suggest to God that maybe He should consider using his existing son, Ishmael, instead of the promised son (Gen. 17:15–18). As we ourselves sometimes do, he appears to want to "help God out"; to make it easier for God to fulfill His promises. El Shaddai did not need such assistance.

Abraham's thinking and reasoning were quickly corrected. He heard God's message firm and clear. God almighty, El Shaddai, would do just what He promised; and as the Scriptures record, He did it all. Abraham was able to "rest in the shadow of the Almighty." Shaddai would accomplish what to Abraham appeared impossible.

Kay Arthur assigns the primary meaning of Shaddai as: "The All-Sufficient One" (35–40). That meaning certainly includes this protective-covering concept. Although I prefer to keep the focus of God's almighty name upon the larger concept of His omnipotence, the protective presence and comfort of that infinite power as "The All-Sufficient One" are most appropriate. There is tenderness and loving provision wrapped up in Shaddai that God wants His people to grasp.

## *My Refuge and My Fortress* (Jehovah)

The third Old Testament name for God used in Psalm 91 is the name *Jehovah*. It's from the Hebrew word *havah,* which means, "to be." This name introduces us to the very essence of God's being. He is the "I AM" one (Ex. 3:13–15). He is self-existent in His being in the absolute sense of those words. Jehovah is not dependent upon anything but Himself for His being, His essence of life, and His eternal existence. Those words express truth that remains beyond our full grasp, but the concepts they express contribute to our capacity to know Jehovah.

Some have defined this name as God's personal name. Jehovah (*Yahweh* in its more accurate Hebrew transliteration) is God's very high and holy name. To help us recognize Jehovah's name in our English Bibles the translators assist us by having it always appear in full capital letters. Thus, He is "LORD." God Himself provides the best insight concerning the meaning of Jehovah.

In what surely was one of the most singular moments of the Old Testament, Jehovah defines His name for Moses. In his anger and frustration over Israel's flagrant sins, Moses had thrown down and broken the original stone tablets upon which God had written the Ten Commandments. God's discipline and judgment hung heavy over the people for their idolatry with the golden calves and their sinful revelry. Moses fervently interceded for the people with God. The crisis brought God and Moses very close together. God said to Moses, "I will do the very thing you have asked, because I am pleased with you and I know you by name" (Ex. 33:17). What a profound moment that was for both God and Moses.

God called Moses back to the mountain where He defined His name for Moses. Just as God knew Moses by name, He desired for Moses to know Him by His name, Jehovah. The details of that momentous event are recorded in Exodus 34:4–8:

> So Moses chiseled out two stone tablets like the first ones and went up Mount Sinai early in the morning, as the LORD had commanded him; and he carried the two stone tablets in his hands. Then the LORD came down in the cloud and stood there with him and proclaimed his name, the LORD. And he passed in front of Moses, proclaiming, "The

LORD, the LORD, the compassionate and gracious God, slow to anger, abounding in love and faithfulness, maintaining love to thousands, and forgiving wickedness, rebellion and sin. Yet he does not leave the guilty unpunished; he punishes the children and their children for the sin of the fathers to the third and fourth generation." Moses bowed to the ground at once and worshiped [the LORD].

How does Jehovah want us to know Him? He wants us to see Him as the compassionate One. He has feelings of sympathy and sorrow for us in our failing, sinful ways. He is gracious, bestowing upon us favor that we really do not deserve. Jehovah declares Himself to be patient, slow to anger, and His love has an abounding outflow toward His people. He's faithful. He can always be trusted to honor and keep His Word, His promises, and His covenants. Thousands benefit from His outflow of love in His offer of forgiveness for deeds of wickedness, rebellion, and sin. That's who Jehovah is. What encouraging truth to seal in our minds and hearts.

In this revelation of the meaning of His name, Jehovah also presents Himself as the judicious and holy One. He does not simply dismiss our sins as an indulgent father might do for his rebellious, sinning child. Our Holy God of justice and truth cannot do that and remain holy and just. The sins of the guilty demand a judicious settlement before a holy God. (This text also gives hint of the generational consequences of mankind's sinful deeds.†)

As wonderful as it is that Jehovah defines the meaning of His name in this text, more insight and understanding is much needed. If we had to leave it here, we would be left rather helpless and hopeless concerning what we must have from Jehovah to rescue sinners and heal our failing, sinful ways. We dare not forget the context in which the psalmist introduces these Hebrew names for God. We must keep focused upon the "shelter" introduced in 91:1. We have concluded that the only shelter God has ever

---

† We will not deal with the reality of generational consequences in this book, but those interested in pursuing study on the subject will find helpful insights in chapter 2 of *The Adversary at Home,* Life Journey, Cook Communications Ministries, Colorado Springs, 2006).

provided for safety and escape from the consequences of our sins is the Lord Jesus Christ. He's Elyon's provided "shelter." He is our protection. As the refrain of the old hymn concludes, "O, Jesus is a Rock in a weary land, a shelter in the time of storm."

Jesus Christ is not only Jehovah's provided shelter; it is also proper to recognize that because He is one with the Father, He fulfills all the implications that flow out to us from Jehovah's name. His name too is Jehovah. As we get to know Jesus Christ through reading the Gospels, we can readily see that Jesus indeed is "the compassionate and gracious God, slow to anger, abounding in love and faithfulness, maintaining love to thousands, and forgiving wickedness, rebellion and sin" (Ex. 34:6–7). Those words describe the essence of His earthly ministry, but we must not miss the fact that He also resolved the judicious, holy aspects of Jehovah's name that required Him to punish the guilty: "Yet he does not leave the guilty unpunished" (v. 7).

Jesus Christ took the place of the guilty. He paid the full price Jehovah's holy justice demanded. Second Corinthians 5:21 states this truth so concisely: "God made him who had no sin to be sin for us, so that in him we might become the righteousness of God." He not only removes the guilt of our sins, but He also makes us to "become the righteousness of God." Jesus Christ is our complete and perfect "shelter."

In Ephesians 1 the apostle Paul states such important truth about the perfect shelter Jesus Christ provides: "Praise be to the God and Father of our Lord Jesus Christ, who has blessed us in the heavenly realms with every spiritual blessing in Christ. For he chose us in him before the creation of the world to be holy and blameless in his sight" (vv. 3–4). "In him we have redemption through his blood, the forgiveness of sins, in accordance with the riches of God's grace that he lavished on us with all wisdom and understanding" (vv. 7–8).

After introducing us to this third Hebrew name for God, the psalmist shares a brief testimony, and in so doing provides us with some added insights concerning Jehovah's "shelter." "He is my refuge and my fortress." (Ps. 91:2). In the simplest terms, a refuge is a protected place set apart by the provider to protect the hunted.

In my days as an avid hunter, I learned to respect and honor the game refuge provided by the state for the hunted game. You could hunt up to the refuge fence, but you could not cross into the refuge area. Violation of the refuge would subject one to fines, arrest, or other severe penalty. Confiscation of one's hunting weapon is a common penalty for such a breach.

It is noteworthy that the psalmist declares Jehovah Himself to be his refuge. He does not just provide a place of fenced-in refuge for His own. Jehovah desires intimacy, personal relationship, and a flow of fellowship with His servants in His protective care.

A fortress speaks for itself. It affords more protection than a refuge and usually denotes some kind of military presence. It's often pictured as a place of walled-in safety; closed gates; and watchful, alert guards. A fortress provides the highest level of protection for the hunted. This fortress is more than walls of stone with human guards and warriors. The psalmist knows Jehovah Himself to be his fortress, and what a fortress He is.

If indeed we are correct in concluding Moses to be the author of this psalm, he had much personal experience of knowing Jehovah to be his fortress of protection. As Pharaoh and his army pursued Moses and the people of Israel, Jehovah kept Himself between the pursuers and Israel in the visible cloud by day and pillar of fire by night. Through Moses, Jehovah spoke to the frightened people: "Do not be afraid. Stand firm and you will see the deliverance the LORD will bring you today. The Egyptians you see today you will never see again. The LORD will fight for you; you need only to be still" (Ex. 14:13–14). Moses had learned the lesson King Solomon later wrote in his proverbs: "The name of the LORD is a strong tower [fortress]; the righteous run to it and are safe" (Prov. 18:10).

Jehovah is our fortress of safety. As we face the spiritual battles of life, this is such important truth for believers to know. In the great spiritual battles of the Reformation, Martin Luther learned and walked in the truth of knowing Jehovah to be his fortress. These words from Luther have importance for those who desire to fight for their revival:

Observe this for your comfort: here these enemies are never called our enemies, or those of Christendom, but the enemies of the Lord Christ.... For Christ, who sits above at the right hand of the Father, cannot be attacked, they cannot hurt one hair on His head, much less drag Him down from His throne. Still they are properly called His enemies, not ours. For the world and the devil do not attack and plague us because of secular matters or because we have merited or caused it. The only reason for it is that we believe this Lord and confess His Word. Otherwise they would be in agreement with us, and we would be at peace with them. For this reason He must deal with them as enemies who attack His Person. Everything that happens to the individual Christian, whether it comes from the devil or from the world—such as the terrors of sin, anxiety and grief of heart, torture, or death—He regards as though it happened to Him. Thus He also says through the prophet Zechariah (Zech. 2:8): "He who touches you touches the apple of My eye." And in Matthew 25:40 we read: "As you did it to the least of these My brethren, you did it to Me." And to Paul, while he traveled from Damascus in order to bind Christians and hand them over to the tribunal, Christ speaks from heaven (Acts 9:4): "Saul, Saul, why do you persecute Me?" Again (Acts 9:5): "I am Jesus, whom you are persecuting." (1040–41)

### *My God, in Whom I Trust* (Elohim)

The fourth name for God in Psalm 91 is the Hebrew word *Elohim*. This is the primary Hebrew word translated "God" in the Old Testament. *Elohim* has been a fascinating word for biblical scholars to study. Although it is usually translated in a singular form, "God," the "—*him*" ending is definitively plural, indicating more than one. The first appearance of this Hebrew name for God is in the first verse of Genesis: "In the beginning God [Elohim] created the heavens and the earth."

Some pagans and polytheistic proponents of their concept of many gods in our universe have pointed out that this text could be more accurately translated, "Gods created the heavens and the earth." Serious biblical scholarship has never considered such translation valid or even worthy of argument. Conclusive texts like Deuteronomy 6:4—"The LORD [Jehovah] our God [Elohim], the LORD is one"—have served to close the door on such fallacious thought. Yet, the plural ending of Elohim does leave room to prayerfully ponder its significance.

The most accepted insight concerning the significance of this "singular-plural" word in Genesis 1:1, designating God as the Creator of the heavens and the earth, relates to God's triune being. From the clear teachings of the whole of Scripture, it can be conclusively demonstrated that God the Father, God the Son, and God the Holy Spirit were each uniquely involved in the whole of creation. We should never build our doctrine of the Trinity on God's name, Elohim, but it is significant that the first verse of the Bible provides an open door of encouragement to those of us who love and worship our God in His triune being.

The psalmist declares Elohim to be our God in whom we trust. As we study biblical teaching concerning our sure stance for defeating darkness, we will see much evidence that God the Father, God the Son, and God the Holy Spirit uniquely provide our protection and freedom from the rule of darkness. We are never more secure than when we know we are under the watchful care of the Father, Son, and Holy Spirit.

## SURE OF A PROTECTED, COMFORTING HIDING PLACE

> Surely he will save you from the fowler's snare and from the deadly pestilence. He will cover you with his feathers, and under his wings you will find refuge; his faithfulness will be your shield and rampart. (Ps. 91:3–4)

For the most part, "fowlers" were not admired sportsmen of the ancient world. There are valid reasons for their negative image. To fair-minded people, their hunting techniques for capturing targeted fowl seemed ruthless, cruel, and too painful for the birds. *The International Standard Bible Encyclopedia* mentions the practice of taking a captured fowl, sewing its eyelids together, and causing the bird to sound forth cries of distress. Those desperate screeches of the suffering fowl attracted other birds of that species to the vicinity of the bound bird. With the helpless bird in range, the concealed fowler would have opportunity to catch incoming inquisitive birds. In addition to the snare, fowlers used a stick weapon somewhat like the boomerang. As the targeted bird came within range, the skillful fowler would hurl his weapon to stun the bird and knock it senseless or break its legs. The victim was then easy prey.

Through the prophet Jeremiah, God reveals numerous reasons why He is allowing Jerusalem and the people of Judah to come under the siege and eventual captivity of Babylon. As we consider the "fowler" in Psalm 91, one of God's pronouncements has much relevance: "Among my people are wicked men who lie in wait like men who snare birds ["fowlers" in some translations] and like those who set traps to catch men" (Jer. 5:26).

The "fowler" of Psalm 91 is bent on capturing human beings. This fits many of the biblical descriptions concerning the Devil and his work. The apostle Peter said it well: "Be self-controlled and alert. Your enemy the devil prowls around like a roaring lion looking for someone to devour" (1 Peter 5:8). Our Lord Jesus Christ defines the thief's (the Devil's) agenda this way: "The thief comes only to steal and kill and destroy" (John 10:10). Thus, there remains little question that the psalmist's "fowler" introduces the Devil and his evil work into the psalm.

Like the fowler, the Devil has a reputation for being ruthlessly cruel and brutal toward those he "snares." Our text declares that the fowler has "deadly pestilence" in mind for those he captures. Killing and death are always parts of the Devil's purpose and work. He majors in death. Concerning the murderous intent of His critics under the Devil's control, the Lord Jesus declared, "You belong to your father, the devil, and you want to carry out your father's desire. He was a murderer from the beginning, not holding to the truth, for there is no truth in him" (John 8:44). What a bold and revealing declaration. The more our culture and world focus on "death," the more evidence we have that the Devil's lies and murderous agenda are at work.

The Psalm 91 introduces us to a level of battle with supernatural evil that must be taken seriously. This is not a battle that we can resolve by our own efforts.

We need someone to save us: "Surely he will save you." The One who saves us is the God of His names: Elyon, Shaddai, Jehovah, and Elohim. He is the One who saves us from the "fowler" and his pestilent, cruel agenda of suffering and death.

There will be a battle for our revival. We need our Savior to bring us there.

### He Will Cover You with His Feathers

The psalmist pulls from the realm of nature a graphic picture of God's work of saving His own from the fowler. He provides them a comforted, protected hiding place. Those privileged to have grown up in a rural setting will immediately visualize this picture. We are helped to see a hen putting her newly hatched chicks under her feathers. This brings into view one of my fondest memories of growing up on a farm. Although my father tried to prevent it, his hens loved to find a hidden spot to build a nest. The hen would fill her hidden nest with her eggs and sit on them until they hatched. That was always such a memorable event. The hen would appear with her chicks, strutting with pride as she introduced them to the world. They commanded her constant attention. She had a certain cluck that signaled a place to find food. The chicks would scamper to the place where her cluck and scratching called them.

The hen had another cluck that signaled danger for her chicks. An approaching storm, a threatening animal, or gathering darkness would trigger that special cluck. As she sounded that alarm, the chicks would scurry into her presence. Fluffing her feathers, the hen would settle down on her brood. Using her beak, she would make sure that each chick was safely tucked under her feathers. She was there for the duration. No matter what danger might come her way, she would not leave.

The only time I can remember my dog failing to meet a challenge was in that situation. I tried to get him to go near a hen to test her resolve to protect her chicks. He put his tail between his legs and started to slink away. I was impressed. There was something about that look in the hen's eye that made him fearful.

Perhaps most of us have read stories of prairie fires that swept over the spot where a nesting hen had her chicks under her protecting feathers. The fire-blackened prairie now showed only a lump of the hen's charred carcass remaining. As investigators push aside the carcass, little chicks would some-times run out. The hen wouldn't leave. She died protecting her brood.

The Gospels record these words of our Lord Jesus Christ: "O Jerusalem, Jerusalem, you who kill the prophets and stone those sent to you, how often I have longed to gather your children together, as a hen gathers her chicks under her wings, but you were not willing" (Matt. 23:37; Luke 13:34). As the people of Jerusalem passed up His presence and His caring love for them, one can feel the tears in the heart of our Lord Jesus Christ. His emotions seemed similar to when He wept over the city at the time of His triumphal entry:

> As he approached Jerusalem and saw the city, he wept over it and said, "If you, even you, had only known on this day what would bring you peace—but now it is hidden from your eyes. The days will come upon you when your enemies will build an embankment against you and encircle you and hem you in on every side. They will dash you to the ground, you and the children within your walls. They will not leave one stone on another, because you did not recognize the time of God's coming to you." (Luke 19:41–44)

Jesus Christ compassionately loved Jerusalem and its entire people. He longed to put them under the comfort of His feathers and the protection of His wings.

As He was dying on the cross, Matthew records for us the words many of the people of Jerusalem were crying out:

> Those who passed by hurled insults at him, shaking their heads and saying, "You who are going to destroy the temple and build it in three days, save yourself! Come down from the cross, if you are the Son of God!" In the same way the chief priests, the teachers of the law and the elders mocked him. "He saved others," they said, "but he can't save himself! He's the King of Israel! Let him come down from the cross, and we will believe in him. He trusts in God. Let God rescue him now if he wants him, for he said, 'I am the Son of God.'" (27:39–43)

He didn't come down. Like the hen taking the fire rather than abandoning her chicks, Jesus took the fire. He stayed on the cross. He could have come down, but His love would not permit Him to do so. He needed to be able to cover us with His feathers and keep His people under the refuge of His wing. He would not come down from the cross.

### His Faithfulness Will Be Your Shield and Rampart

"It is good to praise the LORD and make music to your name, O Most High, to proclaim your love in the morning and your faithfulness at night" (Ps. 92:1–2).

Praising the Lord for His love and His faithfulness needs to be included in our daily routine of worship and prayer; the psalmist calls for our morning focus upon God's love and our evening focus upon His faithfulness. Both of these character attributes reveal God to us, which is the beginning of revival.

An important element to our protected, comforted hiding place from the fowler's snare focuses upon the faithfulness of the One whose name is Elyon, Shaddai, Jehovah, and Elohim. The imagery of the feathers and protecting wings brings beautiful truth to help us understand, but our "Protector" is the God of these transcendent names. It's His faithfulness that provides God's people their *shield* and *rampart*. Both of these words convey military significance, reminding us that we are in a battle. The shield conveys the truth that the fowler's deadly arrows will be coming at us. The apostle Paul lists the "shield of faith" to be a part of the believer's armor. "In addition to all this, take up the shield of faith, with which you can extinguish all the flaming arrows of the evil one" (Eph. 6:16). How reassuring to know that this shield of God's faithfulness is big enough and strong enough to extinguish the whole arsenal of missiles the fowler will use against us.

The rampart speaks of the protection, the fortification, the bastion, the safe hiding place of our living fortress. A rampart was usually an irregular stone formation at the top of the walls of the fortress. As the enemy's arrows and other destructive missiles were hurtling at the intended target, the defender could step behind the rampart and be in a protected hiding place. The faithfulness of our God is the believer's rampart.

During all my years of ministry, this truth has provided much comfort and assurance. Since being a part of a ministry designed to help spiritually oppressed people, this has been especially true. There are times when the arrows fly your way at a furious pace. They are targeted not only at you but also at those associated with you. In those kinds of situations, I can recall numerous times when the Lord called me aside to pray. Those petition times would be expressed in words like these: "Loving Lord Jesus Christ, the sense of evil oppression and the arrows of opposition are coming at me and those around me with near overwhelming force. You have declared Your faithfulness to be our shield and rampart. I deliberately hide myself and everyone targeted in this spiritual assault from evil powers behind our Shield and Rampart. I ask You, Lord Jesus Christ, to hide us there and protect us from this spiritual storm. In the name of my Lord Jesus Christ, I look to You for rest and quiet safety."

After claiming such protection, it has been wonderful to see how the Lord has honored such petition. Sometimes associates, who did not know of my petition, would make statements like, "I was having a difficult time with a sense of spiritual oppression against me today. My counselee even remarked about the sense of battle, but suddenly the oppression lifted and we had a real breakthrough!"

When the Jezebels of this world are breathing down our necks, when we find ourselves casting glances backward as we run for our lives, when the sun beats down upon us mercilessly and we cry out to the Lord to just let us die, that's when God's shade, His resting place, revives us. Revival often is fostered in God's protected refuge.

Praise the Lord. His faithfulness is our "shield and rampart!"

## Chapter 6

# GOD'S SURE-FIRE VICTORY PLAN

*All at once an angel touched him and said, "Get up and eat." He looked around, and there by his head was a cake of bread baked over hot coals, and a jar of water. He ate and drank and then lay down again.*

*The angel of the LORD came back a second time and touched him and said, "Get up and eat, for the journey is too much for you." So he got up and ate and drank. Strengthened by that food, he traveled forty days and forty nights until he reached Horeb, the mountain of God. There he went into a cave and spent the night.*

*1 Kings 19:5–9*

*You will not fear the terror of night, nor the arrow that flies by day, nor the pestilence that stalks in the darkness, nor the plague that destroys at midday.*

*Psalm 91:5–6*

God never abandoned Elijah. He was watching over him under that broom tree. Elijah was in the shadow of more than a tree in a wilderness—he was in the shadow of the Almighty. Despite all of Jezebel's ravings, God was in control, and His victory was certain. Elijah just needed to be refreshed … revived.

So God provided. He sent an angel, in fact. And he cooked for him, gave him drink, and then he let him rest more. Nowhere is there any sign of objection from God or his servant over Elijah's need for retreat. He let him rest, and He actually provided for His prophet. Undoubtedly, the angel of the Lord even made for good company.

And then Elijah was strengthened. He was revived, and he set out on a forty-day journey to meet the Lord at Horeb. No longer did Elijah fear the terror of the night, and we have no indication that he was watching his back for arrows that might fly at him in the day from Jezebel's guard.

Elijah had come back to rest in the God he knew—God who was always his faithful protection; God who sent fire from heaven, who protected His servant, and who provided the means and resources not just to survive, but to be victorious.

## SURE OF NIGHT-AND-DAY STRATEGIES

As in other biblical texts, the "fowler's" oppressive tactics are shown for what they are in the form of psalm. The agenda of this supernatural, evil enemy is exposed. Important truth concerning the nature of the battle is revealed. It is always important to study the kinds of weapons and strategy that our Enemy will employ against us. These two verses provide insights concerning four different tactics our Enemy repeatedly uses in his strategy of assault that would squelch any hope of revival.

### You Will Not Fear the Terror of Night

Fear is the opposite of faith. Just as exercising our faith toward the Lord and His promises pleases Him, fear activates and pleases the plans of the Devil to devour us. Satan majors in fear tactics. His roar like a lion (1 Peter 5:8) is designed to paralyze those he targets with fear.

Some time back I had occasion to watch on the Discovery Channel a special filming of the tactics used by birds of prey to stalk their intended victims. They use two primary weapons: One is the element of surprise and the other is paralyzing fear. These powerful hunters of the sky often swoop down in swift silence on unsuspecting prey and snatch away a targeted fish, rodent, or rabbit in their talons. The victim had no awareness that danger was anywhere near.

At other times these birds of prey stalk their victims with such skill and power that the victim to be devoured is paralyzed by fear. One in-flight sequence showed an eagle pursuing a targeted grouse, the size of a large pigeon. When the grouse became aware that the great eagle was in pursuit, he went into evasive, desperate moves trying to avoid capture; but the eagle was not to be denied. As the great eagle came closer, the grouse obviously panicked. He seemed to go into a dead fall and almost turn on his back in paralyzing fear. In a midair display, the eagle set his deadly talons into the neck and side of the grouse, and the battle was over. The hunter devoured the hunted. Satan employs his devouring tactics in like manner. He wants to paralyze us with such fear that we will forget to resist him with our weapons of warfare.

Overcoming fear in spiritual battle involves the "will" of a person: "You will not fear." The proper exercise of our will requires the foundations of doctrinal truth as set forth in this psalm. We must know that our faith rests in the One whose names are Elyon, Shaddai, Jehovah, and Elohim. God's infinite power and loving promises assure us that we need not panic in fear when the Devil and his kingdom target us. In His name, authority, and infinite power, we can obey His command to resist the Devil and force him to flee.

"You will not fear the terror of night." The Devil and his emissaries often come against God's people during the night: horrific nightmares, ghostly apparitions, fearful sounds, or even physical sensations may be a part of this "terror of night" evil attack.

### You Will Not Fear the Arrow That Flies by Day

The Devil and his kingdom do not turn off their efforts to oppose God's people simply because the day has dawned. The "fowler" shoots his "arrows" at God's own throughout each day that we live. This is the reason we should all be sure to put on God's provided armor daily: "In addition to all this, take up the shield of faith, with which you can extinguish all the flaming arrows of the evil one" (Eph. 6:16).

New Testament truth blends powerfully with this Psalm 91 promise that the Devil's evil arrows will come flying at us every day that we live. Putting on and claiming the protection of each part of the believer's armor needs to be as much a part of our routine as brushing our teeth or putting on our physical clothing. It greatly honors God when we take our battle against evil seriously. Somehow the kingdom of darkness seems to know when to hit us. Satan knows when we are most vulnerable; when we have neglected our walk of obedience by failing to appropriate God's protection for that day.

"You will not fear ... the pestilence that stalks in the darkness." The psalmist reminds us that the Devil is a "stalker." Those victimized by the crime of stalking know the terror of such pursuit. In our country, we have federal laws that can put convicted stalkers behind bars. The Devil's emissaries, in that supernatural and unseen realm where they do their evil work, will follow us, watching for an opportunity to do their disruptive deeds.

"Pestilence" is often associated with contagious diseases, but it also conveys the more general idea of anything that is harmful, pernicious, annoying, or troublesome. The Devil's agenda makes sure that this kind of harm stalks us in the darkness. Our Lord Jesus Christ declared, "This is the verdict: Light has come into the world, but men loved darkness instead of light because their deeds were evil" (John 3:19). The evil stalker seeks to take advantage of this world's evil inclinations by use of his agenda of harmful plans.

"You will not fear ... the plague that destroys at midday." Increasingly the message is made clear in these two verses from Psalm 91. Morning, noon, and night the Devil and his demons have God's people in their sights to do us evil. They attack us emotionally and psychologically with fear and terrors in the night; they seek to harm us physically with their arrows that fly by day; they seek to attack our health with their stalking of God's people with pestilence in the darkness and destructive plagues at midday. Evil is committed to do their work on a ceaseless, round-the-clock strategy of attack.

Former president and current missionary of the Romanian Missionary Society, Josef Ton, wrote his doctoral thesis on a subject that is now a book: *Suffering, Martyrdom, and Rewards in Heaven*. It is a remarkable, scholarly work. Dr. Ton provides readers with some of the most thorough coverage of the history of martyrdom available today. In the chapter that covers the history of martyrdom among the Anabaptists, he presents insights concerning their worldview:

In order to better understand the Anabaptist theology for martyrdom, we must understand the way they interpreted their own world and the way they interpreted history. The Anabaptists returned to the earlier Christian concept of the two worlds or two kingdoms in conflict. One kingdom is this "world," which is governed by "the prince of this world," that is Satan; this kingdom consists of people separated from Christ, without the life of God. The other is the "kingdom of God," whose citizens are people born from above and united with Christ. The two worlds interpenetrate and coexist, although they have different laws, principles, and goals. These two worlds, the kingdom of darkness and the kingdom of light, are engaged in a life and death war; this war is also a cosmic battle in which every individual born on this earth is a participant, having no choice but to choose a side and fight accordingly. The victory of the kingdom of God is certain, but it cannot be accomplished without the suffering and martyrdom of its members. With this worldview in mind, the Anabaptists recognized that they had a great responsibility to this cosmic and historic war. (399)

The Anabaptist worldview shows a harmony with the Psalm 91 picture of the battle between light and darkness. We are in a major conflict. The Devil and his kingdom are committed to promote their opposition to God, His people, and the rule of righteousness and truth. The Devil's agenda is always on display—morning, noon, and in the darkness of night. The victory of righteousness is sure, but the battle is very real. We who would be spiritually revived must know we are participants in that battle.

## A Sure Eye for Fallen Victims

A thousand may fall at your side, ten thousand at your right hand,
but it will not come near you. You will only observe with your eyes
and see the punishment of the wicked. (Ps. 91:7–8)

The obvious questions to be answered concerning God's truth expressed in these verses are: Who is represented by these thousand who fall by our side?

Who are the ten thousand at our right hand? Within the context of the psalm, they can only represent the fallen victims of the fowler. They represent the wounded, the hurting, and the deceived victims of the brutal agenda of the powers of darkness.

Despite our inclinations otherwise, our Lord wants His people to see them. They are all around us, everywhere. The prophet Joel speaks of them in this graphic terminology: "Multitudes, multitudes in the valley of decision! For the day of the LORD is near in the valley of decision" (3:14). That's how our Lord Jesus Christ sees the victims of the fowler. They are in the "valley of decision"; they are ripe for God's harvest through His love, mercy, and grace.

### What Catches Jesus' Eye

During His earthly sojourn, Jesus called upon His disciples to open their eyes of spiritual perception and see these victims of the fowler. While His disciples went into the village of Sychar to purchase needed provisions, Jesus remained to rest at Jacob's well until they would return. While waiting there, the Lord Jesus had a remarkable encounter with a Samaritan woman who came to draw water from the well. His ministry to her had a life-transforming impact.

She seemed to have experienced regeneration and a renewed life from that brief dialogue and ministry of love from the Lord Jesus. She was so ecstatic by what had happened to her that she overflowed with excitement. She left her water jar at the well and rushed back into the village, calling out to the people: "Come, see a man who told me everything I ever did. Could this be the Christ?" (John 4:29).

As she was departing from the well, Jesus' disciples returned. They expressed surprise that Jesus had been talking to a Samaritan woman. Not only was she a woman of great failures, but she was also a Samaritan—a racially impure caste to the Jewish culture. In the eyes of Jews, Samaritans were a people below the level of their consideration. The disciples seemed to share that perception and thought Jesus shouldn't be talking to her.

The Lord Jesus used that occasion to teach His disciples an important lesson concerning the fallen victims of the fowler. As He continued His remarks, the woman made her way back to the well with a large number of people who were responding to her exciting testimony. They wanted to see the person who had changed the woman's life so quickly. As the Samaritans were coming toward Him, Jesus concluded His lesson to the disciples with admonishing words: "Do you not say, 'Four months more and then the harvest?' I tell you, open your eyes and look at the fields! They are ripe for harvest" (v. 35).

### In the Spirit of Corrective Vision

Like many of us have done with others, Jesus' disciples had missed seeing the Samaritans, these "fallen victims" of the fowler, as fields ready to harvest. But they most certainly were ripe. "Many of the Samaritans from that town believed in him because of the woman's testimony, 'He told me everything I ever did.' So when the Samaritans came to him, they urged him to stay with them, and he stayed two days. And because of his words many more became believers" (vv. 39–41). His disciples never forgot that lesson. The Holy Spirit prompted the apostle John to keep the message before us through his gospel record.

The Holy Spirit wants us to hear the same today: There are thousands and tens of thousands of fallen victims of the fowler. Certainly God's people are assured of a place of protection from the fowler's attack: "It will not come near you" (Ps. 91:7). God puts a protective covering over His people who obey His calling. But why does He do that? It certainly is not so we can strut about, basking in our good fortune to not be down there with all of those "Samaritans" who are such sinful failures. Like our Lord Jesus Christ explained to His disciples, He wants us to see the fallen ones as fields ready to harvest!

As he looked toward the coming of the Messiah, the prophet Isaiah captured the essence of our Lord's earthly ministry to fallen people in these graphic words:

The Spirit of the Sovereign LORD is on me, because the LORD has anointed me to preach good news to the poor. He has sent me to bind up the brokenhearted, to proclaim freedom for the captives and release from darkness for the prisoners, to proclaim the year of the LORD'S favor and the day of vengeance of our God, to comfort all who mourn, and provide for those who grieve in Zion—to bestow on them a crown of beauty instead of ashes, the oil of gladness instead of mourning, and a garment of praise instead of a spirit of despair. (61:1–3)

These prophetic words communicate to our hearts. The Lord wants us to see hurting, fallen people in all of their need: "You will only observe with your eyes and see the punishment of the wicked" (Ps. 91:8). The fowler's victims are experiencing the Enemy's destructive work. Because of the consequences of being deceived by the Devil's lies, they are helpless to recover. They need God's rescue. Being able to identify and turn from their sins is an important part of helping them get up from their flattened condition, enter into repentance, and move into God's mercy and healing love.[†]

A loving approach to fallen victims should always recognize that truth, but the real purpose of seeing them for what they are is to pour God's healing oil into their injuries, to bind up the wounds of the hurting, and to set the captives free.

## SURE OF ANGELIC REINFORCEMENTS

If you make the Most High your dwelling—even the LORD, who is my refuge—then no harm will befall you, no disaster will come near your tent. For he will command his angels concerning you to guard you in all your ways; they will lift you up in their hands, so that you will not strike your foot against a stone. (Ps. 91:9–12)

We have come to an important break in the narrative of the psalm. The psalmist's message shifts from giving forth the biblical, objective truth to that of sharing his own personal, subjective testimony. He wants all to know that his expounded message concerning Elyon and Jehovah has brought refuge into his own life.

---

† My colleague and good friend Dr. Jim Logan wrote an important book on this subject of repentance and healing titled *Reclaiming Surrendered Ground* (Chicago: Moody Press, 1995).

As much as Elijah could testify to the ministering work of the angel of the Lord, which brought about his own physical and spiritual revival, the psalmist seems to be saying, "If you will do as I have done, you too will experience Jehovah being your refuge. He will be your protection from the harm and disaster of the fowler's plans. You may even experience the activity of holy angels on your behalf."

## Testimonials Affirming Angelic Intervention

The apostle Paul used this same kind of personal-testimony approach in his teaching of truth: "Even though you have ten thousand guardians in Christ, you do not have many fathers, for in Christ Jesus I became your father through the gospel. Therefore I urge you to imitate me" (1 Cor. 4:15–16). In chapter 11, he repeats the counsel: "Follow my example, as I follow the example of Christ" (v. 1). He gave similar admonitions to both Thessalonian and Philippian believers (Phil. 3:17; 1 Thess. 1:6).

Seeing great truth being lived out in the life of another person is a powerful way to communicate. Jesus spent three years of His earthly life communicating in that manner with His disciples. The apostle Paul followed his Lord's example and instructed the Corinthians to have a similar understanding: "You yourselves are our letter, written on our hearts, known and read by everybody. You show that you are a letter from Christ, the result of our ministry, written not with ink but with the Spirit of the living God, not on tablets of stone but on tablets of human hearts" (2 Cor. 3:2–3).

As the psalmist moves from a format of teaching truth to that of sharing his personal testimony, he refers back to the lofty names of the Lord that he introduced in those opening verses: "If you make the Most High [Elyon] your dwelling—even the LORD [Jehovah], who is my refuge" (Ps. 91:9). In essence he is saying, "This is what I have done in my life." He has come to know Elyon/Jehovah in a growing, personal relationship, and this has brought meaningful protection to him. Dwelling in fellowship with Elyon/Jehovah has brought to him a place of protected refuge. With assurance he knows that this has kept him from the intended harm of the fowler: "Then no harm will befall you, no disaster will come near your tent" (v. 10).

The fowler, Satan and his hosts, has a deadly and powerful agenda to snare God's servants (v. 3). This agenda includes the use of fear and terror in night attacks, hurtful arrows that target us during the day, a stalking presence of evil powers seeking to harm us in the darkness, and planned plagues of harm with intention to utterly destroy us (vv. 5–6). The picture of the deadly power of the fowler's success is further exacerbated by portraying the victims who have fallen by the thousands and tens of thousands all around us (v. 7).

The psalmist's testimony shines like a beacon of hope into this dark scene of enemy activity. He declares that in this place of Jehovah's protected refuge, no fowler-caused harm could personally befall him. The second level of refuge is even more reassuring. This shelter concerns his tent and seems obvious to be a reference to his house, his home—including his wife, his children, and all of those under the protective covering of his authority and responsibility.

### Angels in Your Tent

This is a huge area of concern for every servant of the Lord. The Devil often seeks to attack those under our protective care. During my many years of pastoral ministry, I observed this strategy of the fowler numerous times. When he wanted to attack me, he would often focus his oppressive assault against my wife or my children.

If I observed oppressive activity against those in my "tent," it always signaled me to check my own walk of yielded obedience to my Lord. If I were walking in some manner of disobedience, the fowler would be quick to take advantage of my sin. He can only violate Jehovah's place of promised refuge when my own choices would grant him a place of opportunity. (Ephesians 4:25–28 seems to be providing us a warning us concerning such matters.) When I would let the Lord deal with my own heart and make things right with Him, the wall of asylum for those in my "tent" would quickly return.

If I am correct in assigning Psalm 91 to Moses, this personal testimony might well relate to his experiences in dealing with the reluctance of Pharaoh and the Egyptians to release the people of Israel to fulfill God's plans. The enemies' plans to harm Moses and those he led were not successful. As mentioned above, that would be particularly true of that last plague when death came to every home in Egypt that did not have the protection of the blood of the lamb in its place. Moses and all the people of Israel were safe in their "tents." The destroyer could not enter the tent of those who had claimed Jehovah's place of refuge provided by the blood in its proper place on the door of entrance.

An important part of our "tent" of protection relates to the assignment of God's holy angels to guard His people from the evil agenda, activities, and intentions of fallen angels: "For he will command his angels concerning you to guard you in all your ways; they will lift you up in their hands, so that you will not strike your foot against a stone" (Ps. 91:11–12). Angels have an important function within the fulfillment of God's plans for His people. Although this is not an appropriate place to launch into an extended biblical study of angels, the psalmist's inclusion of their ministry assignment in these verses does require more than passing mention.[†]

### Calling in for Angelic Support

Angels occupy a major place of importance in biblical emphasis. They are mentioned 273 times in 34 of the Bible's 66 books. Since we are considering their capacity to protect God's people, some pertinent facts concerning angels deserve our mention: God created all of the angels (Col. 1:16); they report directly to God (Job 1:6; 2:1); angels do not marry (Matt. 22:30); and angels are mentioned in terminology that suggests they are innumerable (Deut. 33:2; Matt. 26:53; Heb. 12:22).

Although angels are stronger than men (2 Peter 2:11), they are not omnipotent (Jude v. 9; Dan. 10:13); although they possess great intelligence (Dan. 9:21–22; 10:14; Rev. 19:10; 22:8–9), they are not omniscient (Matt. 24:36); and although they can travel very swiftly (Dan. 9:21;

---

† Those desiring more extensive, sound, doctrinal information on angels will find these books helpful: C. Fred Dickason, Angels: Elect and Evil (Chicago: Moody Publishers, 1995); Mark I. Bubeck, *Preparing for Battle* (Chicago: Moody Publishers, 1999), especially pp. 69–82.

9:21; Rev. 14:6), they are not omnipresent (Dan. 10:12). Although they can manifest to the physical sight of humans (Luke 1:11–20; 2:8–15), for the most part, as spirit beings, they remain invisible to human sight (Num. 22:21–31). References such as these bring comfort to know that they are part of our defense team.

The Scriptures clearly set forth that angels have both heavenly and earthly duties. They participate in worship, praise God in the heavenly scene, and are constantly present in readiness to do God's will (Ps. 29:1–2; 104:4; Rev. 4:8; 19:4; Dan. 7:10). Their primary function and ministry on the earthly level seems to be summed up for us in Hebrews 1:14: "Are not all angels ministering spirits sent to serve those who will inherit salvation?"

That's an amazing assertion. All of the holy angels participate in ministry and in the serving of the redeemed. There are many Scripture references supporting this wonderful pronouncement. Here are a few to encourage our hearts: Angels ministered to Elijah (1 Kings 19:5–9); they protected Elisha from the Syrians (2 Kings 6:15–17); in the events surrounding the birth of Christ, angels ministered to Zechariah (Luke 1:11–30), to Mary (vv. 26–33), to Joseph (Matt. 1:20), and to the shepherds with their sheep (Luke 2:8–12). As the church was being launched, angels ministered to the apostles (Acts 1:10–11), to Philip (8:26), to Cornelius (10:5–6), to Peter (12:6–10), to John (Rev. 17:1; 21:9), and to the apostle Paul (Acts 27:23–24).

The psalmist understood the truth later expressed in passages like Hebrews 1:14. For the redeemed who are dwelling in God's provided shelter, God assigns His holy angels to guard them in all of their ways. That is so reassuring. These guarding angels are attentive enough to lift us in their caring "hands" lest we strike our foot against some stone and stumble.

It is very proper and honoring to God to ask the Lord to keep His holy angels attentive to our security and the safety of each one in our "tent." As we look back upon our lives, many of us can remember times when we were miraculously protected. In a time of reflection upon such matters, I once counted nine different times when I was exposed to a potential accident happening that probably would have snuffed out my life. I know God's holy angels were there in their guarding presence.

## Beware the Infiltrators

We would be remiss not to mention some cautions associated with this consideration of angels. Since angels are supernatural beings that minister from
the spirit realm, we must guard against deception. The major reason for this
caution is knowing that some angels are fallen angels. Revelation 12 unfolds
a scenario of the Dragon (Satan) who swept a third of the "stars" out of sky
and "flung them to the earth" (v. 4). Many biblical scholars see this apocalyptic language describing a scene where one-third of the created angels
followed Satan in his rebellion against God. These fallen angels (more commonly called demons) carry out the Devil's work.

But there are more than the fallen angels among the ranks of demonic
infiltrators. Humans have joined their ranks to practice and employ the same
deceptive tactics.[†] The passage in 2 Corinthians 11:1–15 is one of the strongest
New Testament warnings concerning false teachers and "super-apostles" (v. 5).
The climax of Paul's warning comes in verses 13–15:

> For such men are false apostles, deceitful workmen, masquerading as
> apostles of Christ. And no wonder, for Satan himself masquerades as an
> angel of light. It is not surprising, then, if his servants masquerade as ser-
> vants of righteousness. Their end will be what their actions deserve.

In both the Old Testament and New Testament, the Devil and his fallen
angels frequently intrude into the realm of humanity as "angels of light."
This fact brought disaster to both Israel and Judah. Fascination and intrigue
with the supernatural spirit realm of darkness always introduces a malady of
spiritual disaster into human lives and cultures. Biblical history shouts out
that message. Even the fine body of believers at Colosse needed to be warned
concerning false teachings about angels (Col. 2:18). Christian believers too
can be deceived by "masquerading angels of light."

---

† As I am writing these thoughts, the newscasts abound with references to the newest Harry Potter book.
Well over one hundred million copies of the six Harry Potter books have been sold in the United States
alone. Apart from J. K. Rowling's ability to write well, which has made her one of the world's richest
women, what is this phenomenal interest in these books saying? There is no denying that much of the
attraction must be in how these books focus on witchcraft, sorcery, magic, curses, spells, and so many other
things that belong to the spirit realm of darkness. Books such as these, targeting youth, are promoting
interest in what the Word of God profoundly condemns (Deut. 18:10–13; Eph. 5:6–14).

Before we leave this subject of the protective ministry of God's holy angels, a few general cautions are in order:

Other than prayers to God, do not seek to communicate with the supernatural realm of spirit beings.

Do not regard all supernatural happenings as being necessarily from God. Deceiving spirits seek to use such things to deceive and draw people into their influence and control.

Do not "order" angels to do your bidding. Such abuse of the believer's authority opens the door for deceiving spirits to intrude and obey your commands to deceive.

Avoid participating in practices that are common fare to the realm of the occult. Indiscriminate laying on of hands, even in prayer, is not a good practice, since occultists transfer their "gifts" to others by such means. Avoid deep meditation practices that are not focused upon meditating on the Scriptures for instruction and understanding of the Lord and His will.

## SURE OF OUR ULTIMATE WEAPON

You will tread upon the lion and the cobra; you will trample the great lion and the serpent. (Ps. 91:13)

Satan seemed to know that Psalm 91 was about his destructive work as the fowler. As Jesus began His earthly ministry, the Devil quoted this psalm in his third attempt to get our Lord Jesus Christ to do Satan's bidding:

The devil led him to Jerusalem and had him stand on the highest point of the temple. "If you are the Son of God," he said, "throw yourself down from here. For it is written: 'He will command his angels concerning you to guard you carefully; they will lift you up in their hands, so that you will not strike your foot against a stone.'" (Luke 4:9–11)

Jesus taught us much about resisting the Devil by quoting Deuteronomy 6:16 as His answer: "Do not test the LORD your God." His response forced the Devil to leave Him "until an opportune time" (Luke 4:13).

The Devil can quote the Scriptures and use them to tempt us. As in the case just quoted, he is clever to distort its message, but he often uses Scripture to create false guilt, fear, hopelessness, and despair in the hearts of God's people. It always amazes me to see how often the Devil torments people by telling them that they have committed the "unpardonable sin" or that they have failed to "believe right" when they first came to know Jesus Christ as their Lord and Savior. He tells them they are not really saved.

Through my years as a pastor and counselor, I always urged those under such attack to use the moment to reaffirm their total faith in the finished work of our Lord Jesus Christ. A verbal affirmation like this glorifies the Lord and is always appropriate: "Lord Jesus Christ, I use this moment of attack to affirm again that my only hope for eternal life is that You died and shed Your precious blood to cleanse me of my sins and to robe me in Your righteousness. My only hope is You, Lord Jesus Christ, and I resist this accusing attack of the Devil on my faith in Your precious name." That kind of assertion turns an attack of our enemy into a triumphant moment of declaring your faith and resisting the Devil's work. He will soon come to see that his negative attack is becoming a glorifying moment for our Lord Jesus Christ.

It is noteworthy that in quoting Psalm 91 in his temptation of Jesus, the Devil conveniently stopped short of quoting verse 13. Satan would not like to call any attention to the fact that our Lord Jesus Christ has vanquished, decimated, and crushed the Devil and his work by His death and resurrection:

Since the children have flesh and blood, he too shared in their humanity so that by his death he might destroy him who holds the power of death—that is, the devil—and free those who all of their lives were held in slavery by their fear of death. For surely it is not angels he helps, but Abraham's descendants. For this reason he had to be made like his brothers in every way, in order that he might become a merciful and faithful high priest in service to God, and that he might make atonement for the sins of the people. Because he himself suffered when he was tempted, he is able to help those who are being tempted. (Heb. 2:14–18)

Through His incarnation, His cross, and the full scope of His finished work, the Lord Jesus effectively trampled upon and defeated the fowler. And the victory of our Lord Jesus Christ is our victory. It is through our union with Him in the triumph of His victory that we too participate in the "treading" and "trampling" of our defeated evil Enemy. As the apostle Paul brought his deep doctrinal study set forth in the book of Romans to a close, he left this triumphant message with them: "The God of peace will soon crush Satan under your feet. The grace of our Lord Jesus be with you" (16:20).

That's also the message of Psalm 91. As God's people walk in the truth of who God is and what He has provided for our safety, we participate in what God is doing to bring down evil and exalt righteousness. The battle against evil provides opportunity to develop a growing intimacy and appreciation of who God is and the wonder of His provisions for His people.

A military person once said in my hearing: "One of life's most exhilarating moments in battle comes when you realize that you have been targeted and the bullet missed." Many readers will know that experience. You have been in war's battles and have experienced literal bullets whizzing by you but missing your targeted person. Although I have never experienced that in a physical war, I have experienced it numerous times in the spiritual battles of life. The Devil and his kingdom shoot at believers with a fearsome tenacity. They intend to rob freedom, to kill and destroy God's people. Psalm 91 has reinforced that acute awareness. However, the message God wants His people to carry from this psalm concerns Him. Even when we are being targeted, He provides His protection. That, too, provides a spiritual exhilaration of assurance, comfort, and rest.

## SURE IN OUR FELLOWSHIP WITH GOD

"Because he loves me," says the LORD, "I will rescue him; I will protect him, for he acknowledges my name. He will call upon me, and I will answer him; I will be with him in trouble, I will deliver him and honor him. With long life will I satisfy him and show him my salvation." (Ps. 91:14–16)

Psalm 91 climaxes by Jehovah Himself interjecting a direct word concerning the message the psalmist has declared to God's people. One almost senses that Jehovah is so pleased with the truth shared in those first thirteen verses that He had to add His own special words of instruction and assurances.

In so doing, God reveals some insights about who these people are that "dwell in the shelter of the Most High" (Elyon) and "rest in the shadow of the Almighty" (Shaddai). They are people who love the Lord. "Because he loves me," says the LORD, "I will rescue him."

Jehovah provides us with an amazing level of assurance. This is the One who told Moses how to answer questioning Israelites concerning the authority of his leadership:

> Moses said to God, "Suppose I go to the Israelites and say to them, 'The God of your fathers has sent me to you,' and they ask me, 'What is his name?' Then what shall I tell them?" God said to Moses, "I AM WHO I AM. This is what you are to say to the Israelites: 'I AM has sent me to you.'" (Ex. 3:13–14)

Jehovah has total authority and absolute sovereignty. In Psalm 91:14, we see "I AM WHO I AM" saying "I will rescue him!" When "I AM" says "I will," you have Jehovah introducing a level of assurance that is absolute. People who love the Lord have a dwelling place of absolute assurance of rescue from the fowler's efforts to destroy them.

### Those Who Love the Lord

Who are these people who love the Lord? Since "God has poured out his love into our hearts by the Holy Spirit, whom he has given us" (Rom. 5:5), we know that they are people in whom the Holy Spirit dwells. In New Testament truth, this means that they are the people who have been made righteous by Christ's saving grace (vv. 6–11).

God wants His people to be certain of their love for Him and tell Him of their love. God desires this relational intimacy and communion of fellowship between the redeemed and Himself. Our love is not as mature and perfect as it will one day be in God's redemptive plans, but His Holy Spirit has planted love for God into the believer's heart. That's why it is very important to personal revival that we express our love often to Him.

Lovers of God are people who are growing in their knowledge of God. "I will protect him, for he acknowledges my name" (Ps. 91:14). Psalm 91 elevates the importance of God's name to a very high level. As we have already seen, His name reveals to us who He is. He wants us to know Him.

Each of the four Hebrew names for God shared in this psalm reveals deeper insights to us concerning God's Person. As with our imperfect love, our understanding of the infinite, transcendent, and superlative wonder of God revealed in His name will remain limited in this life. Only in our glorified state will those limitations be completely removed. As the apostle Paul explains, "Now we see but a poor reflection as in a mirror; then we shall see face to face. Now I know in part; then I shall know fully, even as I am fully known" (1 Cor. 13:12). By His Word and the ministry of the Holy Spirit, it is within God's purposes that His people should keep growing in knowledge of who He is. This text helps us see how very important that is to God.

Lovers of God are likewise people who pray. "He will call upon me, and I will answer him" (Ps. 91:15). Prayer is the major way that communion and fellowship flow between the Lord and His people. Prayer is important to God. "Pray continually," Paul admonished the Thessalonians (1 Thess. 5:17). God loves that instruction. People who dwell in the shelter of the Most High promised in Psalm 91 are those who maintain an open line of communication flowing between them and their Lord.

Everything in life is to be handled through this constant flow of prayer. When we need answers, God says, "I will answer him." When we are praying and trouble comes, we can know that God affirms, "I will be with him in trouble." When we are praying and hard-pressed by evil attacks, God proclaims, "I will deliver him." When we are praying and need a sense of self-worth and appreciation, God declares, "I will … honor him." Having honor from the Lord flows from a continuing flow of prayer communication.

The level of promised victory recorded in Psalm 91 has a close affinity with Ephesians 6:10–20. It is significant that both of these foundational passages concerning victory over evil powers close with a focus upon what I call the "all-ness" of prayer. "And pray in the Spirit on all occasions with all kinds of prayers and requests. With this in mind, be alert and always keep on praying for all the saints" (Eph. 6:18).

Finally, lovers of God are people who find deep satisfaction in both life and death: "With long life will I satisfy him and show him my salvation" (Ps. 91:16). Very near to the heart of our God is the joy and satisfaction of His people. When a believer walks in the truth set forth in Psalm 91, the Lord promises satisfaction in the length and the value of the life He provides. To be satisfied with the quality and duration of life God gives to us is indeed a reward, but the promise goes even beyond this life.

The conclusion of the psalm seems to be saying, "When this life is over, I will show him my salvation." The Hebrew word for salvation is fascinating. It's the word *Yeshua!* That's also the Hebrew word for Jesus. Our Lord is looking forward to that wonderful day when He will be able to show us His *Jesus.* His glorious *salvation* is the Person of our Lord Jesus Christ, and we will see Him as He is. When we first see our Yeshua, He may well appear much like the apostle John saw Him:

> I saw seven golden lampstands, and among the lampstands was someone "like a son of man," dressed in a robe reaching down to his feet and with a golden sash around his chest. His head and hair were white like wool, as white as snow, and his eyes were like blazing fire. His feet were like bronze glowing in a furnace, and his voice was like the sound of rushing waters. In his right hand he held seven stars, and out of his mouth came a sharp double-edged sword. His face was like the sun shining in all its brilliance. When I saw him, I fell at his feet as though dead. Then he placed his right hand on me and said: "Do not be afraid. I am the First and the Last. I am the Living One; I was dead, and behold I am alive for ever and ever!" (Rev. 1:12–18)

What a beautiful description of our Yeshua! This is the One our Lord is waiting to show us in all of His glory and victory. May it be soon that we will see Him.

*Chapter 7*

# GOD'S FIRE
# ACROSS THE LAND

*Humble yourselves, therefore, under God's mighty
hand, that he may lift you up in due time. Cast all your
anxiety on him because he cares for you.*

*1 Peter 5:6–7*

On Christmas Day 1989, surprising, dramatic history was made in
Romania when a dictator died. As reported in *Newsweek*, the
Romanian people felt both relief and bitterness toward the man.

> All over Romania, people let out a collective sigh of relief and bitterness
> when the visible proof of [Nicolae] Ceausescu's downfall and death was
> broadcast last Tuesday, a day after his execution on Christmas night.
>
> "The antichrist is dead," murmured a man who watched the
> broadcast in Bucharest, the capital.
>
> "He died too easily," complained a soldier in the city of Timi
> soara, where the popular uprising against Ceausescu's hated dicta-
> torship began.
>
> "I would have kept him in a cage in the public square," said a
> Bucharest hotel manager, "so that people could spit on him and
> pelt him with stones." (Watson, 16)

The news media covered the dictator's last days from the political and
military perspectives, but they missed the real story. The bitterness mentioned in *Newsweek* was not the predominant characteristic. The spiritual
struggle between light and darkness was. Without that dimension the
account is tragically incomplete.

Living in such a repressive, brutal police state usually would produce a seething caldron of hate and bitterness in the hearts of the people. Instead the people of Romania largely protested with grace, dignity, and the courage to die for their beliefs. Why?

I think I found an answer three years earlier during a visit to Romania. The people's courage comes from a strong faith and visible displays of God's protection. During my visit to then-communist Romania as part of a four-man team sent to teach and encourage the body of believers there, I saw how God's Spirit was already powerfully at work in that land.[†]

## GOD'S SPARKS OF REVIVAL IN A LAND

Romania's revolution is a story of triumph through spiritual renewal. The sparks of that spiritual revival that occurred in 1986 were ignited by the prayers of a people who knew God's power and sought it. The praying people who acted in the power of the Holy Spirit drove the democratic movement that toppled communism. Their actions, recounted in this chapter to show how renewal can move a nation, are best summarized by the apostle Paul, in his commendation to another church years ago:

> You welcomed the message with joy given by the Holy Spirit. And so you became a model to all the believers in Macedonia and Achaia. The Lord's message rang out from you not only in Macedonia and Achaia— your faith in God has become known everywhere. (1 Thess. 1:6–8)

Prior to Ceausescu's execution, the Reverend Josef Ton had a significant spiritual impact as the pastor of the Second Baptist Church in Oradea, Romania. His successes so threatened the communist authorities that they exiled him under threat of imprisonment if he remained in his pastorate. Immediately following the death of Ceausescu, Josef Ton returned to his beloved homeland. During the previous eight years in exile, he had been serving in Illinois; there, as president of the Romanian Missionary Society, he had proclaimed the gospel via overseas radio.

---

† For a specific recounting of the story of God's miraculous work through His oppressed church, as we witnessed it firsthand, read appendix C, "Romania and Spiritual Renewal."

During that time I was honored to develop a personal friendship with Ton. Soon after he arrived, he sent me a video briefing of the overthrow. I am indebted to him and his firsthand accounts from the spiritual perspective for much of what I am able to report here. The breaking of the bonds of Ceausescu's communist rule in Romania becomes a parable illustrating how believers can rise up in spiritual renewal to undermine evil spiritual influences in their own cultures.

At the Second Baptist Church of Oradea, Dr. Nick Gheorghita described how his people were fervently praying. Then he added, "I am believing God for the renewal the church is experiencing here to erupt in a great spiritual revival. I believe it will jump through the wall that separates East and West and will spread throughout Europe and the world."

Could Dr. Nick's vision be in the process of fulfillment? God has previously used suffering churches to initiate revivals. The very first church at Jerusalem, born on Pentecost when the Holy Spirit came, was quickly subjected to oppression. Yet the first church prayed, studied Scriptures, partook in spiritual fellowship; and its members shared what they had (Acts 2:42–47). The result was the oppressed church in New Testament times exploded and "turned the world upside down" (Acts 17:6 KJV). Perhaps in these "final days" of history, God in His grace will do it again.

As we look at the developments in Romania, we can find several principles at work, principles that are active in every spiritual awakening that has revived Christ's church in cultures near and far.

### Ingredients That Break Bondage

Though the makings that bring spiritual power and contribute to revival are not new, I believe Satan attempts to keep them clouded, especially in the West. But when we (the four-man team) visited the church in communist Romania, we saw them operating strongly among the Romanian believers, and the force of the impact will not soon be forgotten. Those ingredients include (1) fervent prayer, (2) joyful worship, (3) refinement of persecution, (4) courageous faith, (5) hunger for God's Word, and (6) a strong bond of fellowship.

I communed with the Lord about my preaching to the believers in Romania, and I felt the Holy Spirit's leading to make prayer the subject of my first message. As things turned out, I was somewhat embarrassed—the teacher became the student.

The first service we attended was at 6:00 on a Friday night. We arrived shortly before that to find a small, humble church building. Nestled in the midst of the surrounding newly constructed apartment buildings, it appeared insignificant. Conditioned to the American scene, we wondered where the people were. To our thinking, few cars meant few people.

Dr. Nick, the lay-pastor of that church since Ton's exile, interrupted our thoughts with, "Look at them come! Look at them come! Isn't that a great sight?"

Suddenly, our American-conditioned minds understood. Instead of cars entering a parking lot, people were walking, converging from every direction upon that house of worship. Small groups and large groups, wearing happy, smiling faces, poured in from everywhere, expecting spiritual food.

## 1. Flames of Fervent Prayer

We were ushered into the pastor's study where we gladly joined deacons and leaders of the church in a circle of clasped hands, and several lifted up prayers for the service. The language barrier didn't hinder the passion of our prayers at all. Leaving the office, we were led through crowded aisles. The people who were standing there pressed together to make room for us. A chorus of *"pachay, pachay"* (peace, peace) hummed in our ears. Many reached out to touch us or to grasp our hands, and we felt their sincere love. A breath of spiritual ecstasy swept over us. As we moved to the platform, our inner excitement grew.

The people were singing a familiar hymn, "To God Be the Glory," and we followed Dr. Nick's example and reverently knelt before our Lord in silent prayer. After a few moments, we rose to our feet and began to sing with the people. We sang in English; they sang in Romanian.

I looked out over the sea of joyous faces. They had no hymnbooks— each was singing from memory. Their radiance told of their love for Christ. The scene was invigorating, almost overwhelming. I had never witnessed such a service.

After the hymn ended, the pastor called the church to prayer. Many of the people went to their knees, and a quiet hush enveloped the body. The pastor asked for men in a given area to lead in prayer. Without a moment's hesitation, a man began to pray with great fervency. Though I could not understand his words, my eyes filled with tears as he prayed. "When these people began to pray, it was like the thunder of heaven," Dr. Michael Chandra, one of our team members, recalled later.

Ushers extended a microphone toward the praying person's voice, enabling everyone to hear. Interjections of *"AH-meen! AH-meen!"* rippled through the congregation, adding a melodious touch to the prayer. As quickly as one prayer ended, another began. Though we could not understand their language, we heard their cries. These people knew how to pray, and they loved to pray.

The pastor shifted the prayer participation to another area of the church where the women were seated. The response from the women was equally instantaneous and electric. They prayed as fervently and effectively as the men.

After several had prayed, the giant choir that filled the entire balcony sang "God, the All Merciful!" The spiritual impact of their music was deeply moving. As soon as the choir ended, the church was at prayer again. By this time there was no longer room to kneel in the packed aisles, so the congregation stood as the same pattern of prayer flooded forth from the young people.

Three times during the two-and-a-half-hour service these prayer interludes were interjected into the worship. At least forty minutes of the service time was devoted to these impassioned, participating intercessions.

The scene reminded me of two New Testament verses that describe the power of righteous praying:

The prayer of a righteous man is powerful and effective. (James 5:16)

After they prayed, the place where they were meeting was shaken. And they were all filled with the Holy Spirit and spoke the word of God boldly. (Acts 4:31)

I have focused much of my ministry on prayer, but by the time I was introduced to speak on my chosen topic, I felt like a novice. Yet as the interpreter delivered my thoughts to the people, I sensed unusual freedom and power to preach. The prayers of the people had unlocked my lips. I now knew that our miraculous procession through the border checkpoint had had a much deeper prayer base than just the prayers we had offered as we rode in our car (see appendix A, "Romania and Spiritual Revival").

Prayer is the life's breath of the Romanian believers, and the flow of corporate prayer from these committed believers testifies of their vital, individual, private prayer lives. Satan's program cannot stand before a praying people of such obvious, sincere fervency. Prayer breaks the bondage of darkness.

Significantly, God promised such spiritual healing to Israel centuries ago. Americans can have it today. The promise depends on humble, sincere prayer: "If my people, who are called by my name, will humble themselves and pray and seek my face and turn from their wicked ways, then will I hear from heaven and will forgive their sin and will heal their land" (2 Chron. 7:14).

## 2. Blazing, Joyful, Genuine Worship

The second element that brings spiritual power and revival to a culture is worship. "Ascribing worth-ship" is one definition of worship. In biblical worship, God is the audience, and the worshippers offer their adoration to Him. Love flows from each believer's heart toward the heavenly Father and the Lord Jesus Christ by the enabling of the Holy Spirit. True worship requires sincerity from hearts that are clean before God.

Anne Ortlund, in her helpful book *Up with Worship*, wrote,

> Not often do churchgoers find themselves in the Presence. But when they do—all is changed.
>
> They may destroy their idols, as in Genesis 35:2. They may, as a group, promise to obey all of God's Word, as in Exodus 24:7. They may have a great musical time, as in 2 Chronicles 5:11–14. They may be moved to weeping, as in Nehemiah 8:9. They may just have a

wonderful "ball" enjoying God! In Nehemiah 8:6 they said, "Amen," lifted their hands toward heaven, and then bowed and worshiped with their faces toward the ground. In any case, they are moved to move! (3)

Ortlund has captured several of the aspects of the joyful worship we observed in Romania: full of spontaneity and participation; hymns sung from memory; upturned faces focused in worship toward God and expressing joy; music reaching out with a forceful message of biblical truth, yet communicating spiritual warmth; and rapt attention to Scripture reading. As God's Word was read, quiet expressions of *"AH-meen, AH-meen"* sounded like water cascading down a mountain stream.

"I couldn't understand their language, but I surely understood their worship," recalled another of our team members, Dr. Charles Hamm, after that Friday night service.

To these believers, God is everything. They have no hope but Him. He remains the focus of their joy and the recipient of their praise. They long for His presence. Suffering had lifted their worship to a high and holy level.

Such in-depth worship was a vital key to the strength of the believers in the Romanian uprising.

## 3. The Refining Fires of Persecution

The third component in escaping from bondage is accepting persecution. Such persecution is part of the refining process that purifies our devotion to God. When the Lord Jesus Christ addressed Himself to the church at Laodicea, He counseled those "poor" believers to receive healing by purchasing from Him "gold refined in the fire ... white clothes to wear ... and salve to put on your eyes, so you can see" (Rev. 3:18).

"Gold refined in the fire." What a descriptive statement of divinely superintended suffering and persecution. Bruce Shelley wrote in *Church History in Plain Language* that one of the reasons the gospel spread in such an extraordinary way during its early years was that persecution publicized the Christian faith.

Martyrdoms were often witnessed by thousands in the [Roman] amphitheater. The term *martyrs* originally meant "witness" and that is precisely what many Christians were at the moment of death.

The Roman public was hard and cruel, but it was not altogether without compassion; and there is no doubt that the attitude of the martyrs, and particularly the young women who suffered along with the men, made a deep impression. In instance after instance what we find is cool courage in the face of torment, courtesy toward enemies, and a joyful acceptance of suffering as the way appointed by the Lord to lead to his heavenly kingdom. There are a number of cases of conversion of pagans in the very moment of witnessing the condemnation and death of Christians. (50)

One key to deliverance from spiritual bondage is to accept persecution in the name of Christ. We Christians should not see ourselves as victims when persecution comes but view it as a way to grow closer to God and to purify our commitment. God will honor such devotion.

Perhaps Christian believers in Romania had suffered more than in any other communist-era country. Many have read of the pain and tortures suffered by Richard Wurmbrand and other believers in the early days of the communist takeover in that country. One would be naive to say that such persecution has not hurt the advance of the church. Yet the benefits of persecution are evident, just as Shelley wrote about the early church.

One of those benefits is the refinement our Lord Jesus Christ spoke of in His message to the church at Laodicea. Persecution burns away the sinful, worldly dross that limits our usefulness to the Lord. A lack of separation between Christians and the world, expressing itself in questionable practices, is not tolerated in the lives of believers who are going through persecution.

This "gold refined in the fire" had given them spiritual power and effective witness, which was seen particularly in their resolute devotion to their faith while showing kindness toward their persecutors.

## 4. Unquenchably Courageous, Confident Faith

"And now, compelled by the Spirit, I am going to Jerusalem, not knowing what will happen to me there. I only know that in every city the Holy Spirit warns me that prison and hardships are facing me." (Acts 20:22–23)

Words like those, spoken by Paul in the face of brutal persecution, show courageous, confident faith that moves everyone who hears them. Such faith is the fourth ingredient in breaking spiritual bondage in a country.

Josef Ton had been arrested because of his bold witness and open challenge to the communist system. The dedicated pastor then endured threats, long interrogations, and painful beatings. Eventually, he was ordered to leave Romania or go to prison. When Ton was given that ultimatum, he had already endured pain for his Lord Jesus Christ and was prepared to face prison if necessary. But he felt confusion, so he sought out Dr. Nick for advice.

Ton respected his good friend's wisdom. And Dr. Nick's counsel seemed wise indeed. In essence the doctor said, "Josef, if you stay here, at best you would continue to have a congregation of 2,500 people to preach to every Sunday. If you go to the West and broadcast back to Romania, you will have a congregation of millions."

That advisement liberated Josef to see God's plan. He courageously accepted his exile, and God rewarded him. For eight years he beamed a broadcast into Romania over Radio Free Europe. Millions of people listened every Sunday afternoon to the Bible-preaching ministry of Josef Ton.

Ton's departure had a far-reaching impact for Dr. Nick as well. This Christian physician with a respected medical practice was also a weekend preacher. Eventually, the leaders of the Oradea church sought God's guidance regarding their next pastor and then extended a call to Dr. Nick. He was a gifted expositor of God's Word, and his wise, fervent preaching had made him a favorite supply for the church. At first, Dr. Nick turned down the call. In the process of time, though, and through the persuasion of the church leaders, God showed Dr. Nick he should accept. The people of the church were overjoyed, and God's blessing was quickly seen in weekly conversions to Christ and increasing attendance growth.

Dr. Nick could appear only on Sundays though. As a medical doctor, he must remain a medical doctor, the authorities told him. They would not allow him to be a Baptist pastor. They did everything in their power to keep that from happening. It soon became obvious that the church needed him full time, but the communist authorities simply refused him permission to move to Oradea.

Now Dr. Nick Gheorghita would need a courageous, confident faith. In the government's power play to keep him from Oradea, they confiscated his internal passport. Such a passport was required at all times, or he was subject to arrest, imprisonment, or heavy fines. Without the internal passport he could not move to Oradea or even travel there to preach and pastor the church. Both were now illegal.

The church was brokenhearted. Would they never be able to have Dr. Nick as their pastor? They prayed and wept that week the news came.

Dr. Nick struggled over what to do as well. Should he give the whole vision up and return to his former pattern of medical practice and weekend ministry? The prospect of imprisonment, severe fines, and possible torture was not easy to face. Sunday drew near, and the tension mounted. Dr. Nick felt it was a lost cause. Then the Lord used his wife to help release him from the intimidation.

"Nick," she said, "God has called you to pastor the Second Baptist Church of Oradea. You have accepted that call. You are their pastor. Those people are counting on you. You cannot let them down, even if it means jail."

Sunday morning arrived, and the deacons, unsuccessful in trying to get permission for Dr. Nick to come, resigned themselves to having one of their own preach. Then the phone rang. It was Mrs. Gheorghita. "Paul," she said, "you meet the train. God has arranged a speaker for you. 'Silas' is coming."

Deacon Paul Negrut left for the train station wondering whom this "Silas" might be. Deep in his heart he hoped his beloved pastor was coming. The train pulled into the station and finally he saw "Silas"—yes, Dr. Nick himself—and tears accompanied their embrace. They both knew full well the price this step might exact.

At the church, the people, not knowing of Dr. Nick's coming, had gathered in extra numbers—crises brought them together. They began singing the hymns under a cloud of sadness. While they were singing, Dr. Nick started pressing through the crowded aisles toward the platform, and suddenly everything changed. A holy hush fell on the people. Most of them started to cry. *"Ah-meen, ah-meen!"* echoed throughout the church. Their pastor had come! He loved them enough to face prison.

Even more dramatic, Dr. Nick conducted a funeral that Sunday afternoon for an important government official. The man's wife was a member of the church. Many communist officials attended the funeral, and they knew that Dr. Nick did not have his internal passport. As he spoke in a dynamic message, Dr. Nick contrasted what Jesus Christ and Karl Marx could do for a dead man. Such fearless faith ignites the confidence of the persecuted and confounds persecutors. Those officials didn't know what to do—but they did not arrest him.

Eventually, Dr. Nick was permitted to move to Oradea and served for many years there as one of his country's most gifted pastors. If revival comes to our world, his bold faith and his courageous people will have been a part of the fire that started it.

If revolutionary revival is to come to us, the same faith and courage must become motivating fires in our hearts as well.

## 5. The Hunger for God's Word

One of the most important keys to any revival awakening that will break Satan's bonds is biblical balance. Revivals by their very nature tend to promote extremism, and that can lead people off on a tangent that distorts biblical balance. J. Edwin Orr's lifetime study of evangelical revival awakenings has convinced him of the danger of extremism. He warns that nearly every past revival or spiritual awakening cooled when an extremist tangent appeared. Sometimes it was an "organization extreme," sometimes a "nationalism extreme," or a "glossalolic (tongues speaking) extreme," or a "signs and wonders extreme."

Significantly, the post-Pentecost revival that ebbed and flowed for many years in New Testament times featured believers who "devoted themselves to the apostles' teaching and to the fellowship, to the breaking of bread and to prayer" (Acts 2:42). This biblical balance carried a four-fold emphasis: (1) study of the Word ("the apostles' teaching"); (2) body life ("fellowship"); (3) worship ("the breaking of bread"); and (4) prayer.

Notably, the first emphasis for good balance was "the apostles' teaching." Through the apostles God gave the new-covenant revelation to His people. The apostles taught the Old Testament Scriptures, recalled the teachings of the Lord Jesus Christ, and recorded the Holy Spirit–authored new revelation in various writings and epistles. For those first-century believers, the apostles' teaching was equivalent to what we treasure now as our New Testament. They heard the Word of God—they devoted themselves to "the apostles' teaching."

When it's dark, really dark; when the situation is desperate; when you need hope and there is none visible; when people are hurting and the Enemy seems in full control; there is only one source for real hope and comfort: the Word of God.

Perhaps that explains why such an appetite has continued in Romania for the Word of God. Conversely, it also explains why the atheists, the pagans, and the satanic movements do everything they can to stamp out the Scriptures.

When we attended the Monday night youth meeting at the church in Oradea, we noticed that very few of the young people had Bibles. Prior to the uprising, it was hard to get a Bible in Romania. Despite the constant desire of the churches for more Bibles, the government kept a tight restraint on the number that could be published. Some Bibles were smuggled into Romania, but it was dangerous, often led to arrests, and at best was a limited answer because there were never enough.

During that Monday night meeting, one of the apprentice pastors was teaching the young people a Bible lesson from Nehemiah. Clearly, his teaching methods were not up to date. He read from handwritten notes in a dry monotone. He had no overhead projector or even a chalkboard to help emphasize the ideas. Yet as we watched for more than twenty minutes, we were amazed. More than four hundred young people hung on every word. Most were writing notes at a furious pace, trying to retain every word they could of the book of Nehemiah.

They obviously hungered for God's Word.

The one hope for us in this dark time is that we will hear the Word of the Lord. Only the Word has the power to save us in this late hour.

## 6. The Welding of Christian Fellowship

The sixth element necessary for revival in a land is genuine Christian fellowship. In Thessalonica, the persecution of Christian believers was particularly severe. When Paul was there, Jewish rejecters formed a mob and led a riot to oppose him preaching the gospel message. Under cover of darkness, Paul and Silas fled to Berea. The militant opposition from Thessalonica was so intense that they followed Paul and Silas and stirred up a riot in Berea, too.

That militancy created the climate in which the church of Thessalonica had to live and function. It was tough to be a Christian in that city and to be part of that church (2 Thess. 1:4–10).

An understanding of the persecution and suffering of the believers at Thessalonica will greatly deepen our appreciation of this New Testament epistle, especially when we see that one of the major messages of the book is the importance of Christian fellowship and closeness. Today we sometimes call it "body life" or church *koinonia*, based on the Greek word that "denotes 'participation,' 'fellowship,' especially with a close bond" (Kittel, 798).

Paul continually refers to this vital bonding of fellowship in the suffering Thessalonian church. It was so precious to him that he did not want to leave them and miss it. He speaks of this in some of his most deeply moving words:

> But, brothers, when we were torn away from you for a short time (in person, not in thought), out of our intense longing we made every effort to see you. For we wanted to come to you—certainly I, Paul, did, again and again. (1 Thess. 2:17–18)

Paul found great comfort in the bonding of their fellowship, in the "body life" of that church.

## BODY LIFE

True spiritual fellowship—when fellow believers listen and uphold each other through words of comfort, prayer, and biblical truth—is a mighty way to repulse satanic influence that would thwart revival. I remember seeing throngs of happy people gather in the churches of Romania for prayer, worship, and instruction. They came together because they needed to be together. We felt the bonding power in every gathering of the church. Such conditions produce revival warmth.

This body life was recognized by the communist authorities as deadly to their goal of stamping out the church. That's why they opposed church gatherings with such a vengeance and why they bulldozed church buildings. They didn't want the people to be together.

We marveled at the believers' courage, but Dr. Nick stated repeatedly, "The communists fear us much more than we fear them."

When the church is in spiritual health, its body life is one of the most potent ingredients it has going. The writer to the Hebrews speaks eloquently of the need for fellowship:

> Let us hold unswervingly to the hope we profess, for he who promised is faithful. And let us consider how we may spur one another on toward love and good deeds. Let us not give up meeting together, as some are in the habit of doing, but let us encourage one another—and all the more as you see the Day approaching. (10:23–25)

During our final night in Romania, we went to Dr. Paul Negrut's home. There we saw extended body life in action. Different groups were meeting in every room. In one, Drs. Hamm and Chandra examined people who had come for medicine, and they consulted over the difficult cases. In the kitchen, a one-to-one discipling relationship was underway. In another room, Dr. Paul's wife conducted a small group Bible study. In still another room, those who had come for medical treatment visited with each other.

Hans Finzel (another one of our team members and my son-in-law) and I looked for a place to settle but were "pushed" out by yet another group, so we went for a long walk. As we walked the streets of Oradea, we talked and prayed and marveled together over the church. Despite the oppression and opposition, this church was alive and well on the Romanian portion of planet earth.

As it turned out, we were right. This church and dozens of others like it were at the forefront of the Romanian miracle of Christmas 1989. They had prayed and worshipped faithfully. They were ready when God chose to move to confront the powers of darkness in their land.

*Chapter 8*

# WHERE TO BEGIN: PERSONAL RENEWAL

*When I heard these things, I sat down and wept. For some days I mourned and fasted and prayed before the God of heaven. Then I said: "O LORD, God of heaven, the great and awesome God, who keeps his covenant of love with those who love him and obey his commands, let your ear be attentive and your eyes open to hear the prayer your servant is praying before you day and night for your servants, the people of Israel."*

*Nehemiah 1:4–6*

How does a believer who recognizes the need for a revolutionary revival begin to lift himself, his society, and his culture toward it? What can believers do to experience personal spiritual renewal that can lead to national revival?

The answers to these questions can be found in prayer—prayer that is personal, heartfelt, and focused on the greatness of God. Only when we come to the right source—a powerful God—can we hope to find personal renewal that can lead to national revival.

## COMING TO THE RIGHT SOURCE

Several years ago our growing congregation at Fruitdale Baptist Church desperately needed a larger building. The architect had drawn up beautiful plans for a new sanctuary, and everyone was excited and ready to go. We had one major problem—no money and little prospect of finding any. Our church body had just extended itself in a major effort to clear the mortgage on our existing building. As their young pastor, I could not ask them now to enter another building fund drive.

What to do? We examined sales of bonds, professional fund drives, and denominational assistance. A major lending institution told us our track record was not good enough to warrant their loaning us the amount we needed. If they did make the loan, the interest level would have to be high because such a loan would be a major risk to them. The door seemed closed, but we prayed. We needed the building to keep the work moving, so we kept knocking on more doors.

Our local bank had never given a church loan and had turned us down earlier even for consideration. Sensing God's leading, I returned to our bank and asked the vice president if I could present our case to the loan committee. Her reply was less than positive, but she agreed to check it out. Much to my delight, the bank agreed to the presentation.

I'll never forget getting ready for that day. I assembled a carefully worded prospectus. Financial reports and projections of growth were meticulously charted. The artist's concept of the new building was framed and in hand. Documents were ready to place in the hands of the loan committee, officers, and board representatives. I practiced and practiced presenting my case. I prayed, and others prayed, that I would be granted wisdom.

At the time I was only thirty years old and in my first full-time pastorate. Aware of my youth and inexperience, I dressed conservatively for the occasion—I wanted to appear as mature and dignified as possible.

Finally, the hour came. I dried my moist, anxiety-soaked hands, entered the room, and for about forty minutes poured out our case and answered each of their questions with as much wisdom as I could. They would let me know their decision in a few days.

The waiting was not easy. Days passed and I wondered if that might mean bad news. Eventually, the vice president phoned. "I have good news for you," she said. "Your church can have a loan for fifteen years at 6 percent interest." The amount approved was for more than we'd requested—just in case it might be needed!

"I guess you know," she continued, "this is very unusual for our bank. The presentation of your case with such responsible candor made the difference. Congratulations!"

Something else made the difference. I had come to the right source. I had presented the needs of our church body to the people in the bank who could help us resolve our need. Careful preparation and my best efforts were vital to my approach.

That's also the beginning point for the rescue of our culture. We must come to the right source. As believers, we have the privilege of presenting the needs of those around us to the One who can help us resolve those needs. The very concept of finite, failing humans being able to address and influence the infinite, almighty Jehovah staggers the mind. Yet that's what prayer is.

Prayer is serious business. We need a proper attitude—of reverence and carefulness—recognizing that prayer is the most important work we can do in this world. To have audience with almighty God concerning things important to Him and to us puts every other human endeavor far down on the list.

As Ronald Dunn wrote, "Prayer is not a religious exercise—it is a human necessity." He added,

> Prayer means that I never have to say, "There's nothing I can do." I can always do something ... I discovered that prayer is the secret weapon of the kingdom of God. It is like a missile that can be fired toward any spot on earth, travel undetected at the speed of thought, and hit its target every time.... Satan has no defense against this weapon; he does not have an anti-prayer missile.... We do not pray by default—because there's nothing else we can do. We pray because it is the best thing we can do. (19–20)

## FINDING THE INTERCESSORS

To be God's means of revival in our culture, we must begin by observing God-authored principles in claiming a city, state, or nation for our Lord Jesus Christ. One principle is: Preparation is made through serious intercessors. God always works this way in the affairs of humanity.

The coming of the Holy Spirit on the day of Pentecost was preceded by serious intercession. Before that time, God had His 120 disciples shut away in prayer for ten days in the upper room. The prayers of the psalmist and the prophets reveal that Christ's birth was also preceded by much prayer. Simeon and Anna carried this intercession on through the time of His birth and His temple dedication (Luke 2:21–38).

Nehemiah was God's sovereignly chosen instrument to bring renewal to Jerusalem, yet he didn't even start until after he presented his case to the heavenly Father. At least four months of careful, travailing prayer preceded those beginning steps that led to revolutionary revival (December–April; Neh. 1:1; 2:1).

This principle does not change. Revolutionary revival will not visit any culture without previous, fervent intercession. Apart from impassioned prayer, our nation can never expect the revival we need to save our culture from disaster. As we look at Nehemiah's story, I hope that message comes through.

We must note that the prayer needed does not flow from aimless, emotional wishes. It must show a prepared, purposeful, God-honoring pattern. Nehemiah's prayers had that. There is a dignity, a majesty of greatness, about his praying. My preparations to present my case to the bankers paled compared to the care Nehemiah showed in his approach to the God of Israel. Let's note the characteristics of his praying. In doing so, we can find a pattern for praying for our culture in the late twentieth century.

## CHARACTERISTICS OF PRAYER THAT WILL SAVE A CULTURE

### 1. Prayer Will Be Both Private and Corporate

Prayer that saves a culture often begins as private prayer. Nehemiah began by praying alone: "When I heard these things, *I* sat down and wept. For some days *I* mourned and fasted and prayed before the God of heaven" (1:4).

We usually do our greatest praying alone, when God is our only audience. A genuine sincerity and a true measure of our burden begin to emerge. There's no one to impress when we're alone. As Jesus told His followers,

"When you pray, go into your room, close the door and pray to your Father, who is unseen. Then your Father, who sees what is done in secret, will reward you" (Matt. 6:6).

Those words of our Lord Jesus focus upon this private aspect of prayer, and He observed the same principle Himself: "Very early in the morning, while it was still dark, Jesus got up, left the house and went off to a solitary place, where he prayed" (Mark 1:35).

In my own experience, the Word of God has become practical as I've prayed it back to God. I've learned more about God and His ways through my private shut-away times with Him than I've learned from any other source. Private prayer has been the greatest delight of my whole Christian experience.

A key reason that private prayer is effective for cultural revival is its impact on personal renewal. Private prayer provides opportunities for significant personal spiritual growth. It is of paramount importance to revival as it becomes a wellspring from which refreshing waters flow out of our lives to others.

Corporate prayer is equally as important. Though we have little insight into how it developed in Nehemiah's time, it definitely was present. "O Lord, let your ear be attentive … *to the prayer of your servants* who delight in revering your name" (Neh. 1:11). At some time during those months of Nehemiah's private prayer, he linked up with others who shared his "delight in revering" God's name. This corporate prayer indicates a time of sharing with others who had a similar burden for the rescue of Jerusalem.

For many years, I felt restricted when I prayed with others. When they were listening to what I was saying, it was hard for me to be open and honest before God. I much preferred just being alone with Him. Eventually, I sensed His rebuke for that preference. I saw, in the cry of the disciples, "Lord, teach us to pray," that corporate prayer is just as essential to God's plan as private prayer.

When believers meet to pray, the liberty comes and the hindering of spiritual progress is broken. Revival demands both private and corporate travail before God.

## 2. Prayer Will Flow Out of the Need

Prayer that saves a culture responds to a need. Nehemiah listened to the sad report about the Jewish remnant, and then he cried. His brother told him, "Those who survived the exile and are back in the province are in great trouble and disgrace. The wall of Jerusalem is broken down, and its gates have been burned with fire." When Nehemiah heard this report, he "sat down and wept."

Nehemiah felt the need of his city. No doubt he expected a better report. Zerubbabel's returning remnant had done much to rebuild the temple. Ezra had reestablished worship and had led in an earlier time of spiritual renewal. But now this—broken walls, burned-up gates, and his people experiencing "great trouble and disgrace" (1:3–4). The city's awful need began to penetrate Nehemiah's security of a good job and a nice home.

The need has to come close to us personally before we'll do much about saving a culture. We must keep fresh the urgency of our culture's needs each passing day. If we read newspapers and watch closely, we feel the need. I remember the words of a Denver teenager some years ago, as recounted in an Ann Landers article:

> I live in a well-to-do suburb in Denver. Within the last four years I have seen ten classmates die from drug overdose or suicide. Five classmates became pregnant. Dozens of my friends became addicted to cocaine. At least double that number are beer drunks. Several have told me that their parents get bombed or stoned every night. A few weeks ago, a junior high kid went on a shooting rampage and killed three people. Divorce and unemployment are so common that I am considered lucky by my peers because my parents are still married and working.

Can you feel his need—our needs—that reveals the broken walls and burned-up gates that once protected American culture?

Syndicated columnist Cal Thomas once told James Dobson on a "Focus on the Family" radio broadcast that aberrant sexual behavior is winning approval in our culture. He cited a municipal law in San Francisco, "the domestic partnership law," which granted homosexual and heterosexual couples who are not married the right to live together and to receive the benefits from the state and city that are normally reserved for heterosexual married couples. Under this new law, insurance benefits, hospitalization coverage, and other benefits from government-supplied money for married couples will now go also to recognized homosexual partners and unmarried heterosexual couples.

The San Francisco ordinance, the first in the United States, has been followed by proposals from other city councils, and other cities seem sure to follow. Similar national legislation may not be far behind.

The arrogance of man in flaunting his rebellion and sin before a holy God seems to know no bounds. During the program, Dobson read a copy of a proclamation declaring "gay/lesbian pride week" in Milwaukee. The document, signed by the mayor, read,

> WHEREAS, Milwaukee's gay/lesbian community has become a growing force in the cultural and political life of this city, and
>
> WHEREAS, Milwaukee's gay/lesbian community will come together during the period from June 16–27, 1989, to celebrate Milwaukee's gay/lesbian pride week, and
>
> WHEREAS, the theme of this year's gay/lesbian pride week is "Stonewall 20, a generation of pride,"
>
> NOW THEREFORE, I, John O. Nordquist, mayor of the city of Milwaukee, do hereby proclaim the period from June 16–27, 1989, to be Milwaukee gay/lesbian pride week throughout the entire city of Milwaukee. We are proud of who you are.

Thomas said that if Mayor Nordquist had tried to put out a proclamation for a day of "fasting, humiliation, and prayer" as Abraham Lincoln did in 1863, he immediately would have been in court answering charges of violating church-state separation.

Broken walls, burned-up gates, people in great trouble and disgrace: That's what sin is doing. If it's to change, someone has to see the need.

Many in Nehemiah's day saw the need only on a superficial level. Nehemiah's brother and the other men could see the need in a "wring your hands in despair" kind of mode. They could recite the problem in graphic details, but apparently the need did not touch them personally like it did Nehemiah. He saw it. He felt it, and the "great trouble and disgrace" moved him to prayer. The saving of a culture, even a spiritually corrupt culture, is in the wind when that happens.

### 3. Prayer Will Focus upon the Greatness of God

Prayer that saves a culture recognizes the sole source of deliverance: almighty God. Nehemiah had a high view of God. During his four months of prayer for the saving of a city, he must have lingered long and often at this point of worship. That's what prayer is meant to accomplish in each of our lives. Worship is our highest calling. Nehemiah worshipped the Lord: "Then I said: 'O LORD, God of heaven, the great and awesome God, who keeps his covenant of love with those who love him and obey his commands, let your ear be attentive and your eyes open to hear the prayer your servant is praying before you.'" (1:5–6).

Worship is loving God. It's recognizing His majesty. It's seeing Him as Jehovah, the God of heaven. Worship is bowing before "the great and awesome God" and staying there long enough to glorify Him, to marvel over who He is and what He does.

In *Don't Just Stand There, Pray Something,* Ronald Dunn asked, "Why does God delight in answering prayer? Why does Jesus commit Himself to act when we ask?" Then he answers his own question: "That the Father may be glorified in the Son (John 14:13 KJV) … Here is the supreme motive of all praying … not that we get what we ask for, but that God is glorified in our getting it" (53–54).

People who have God's vision to save a culture, to see revival come, are not in a hurry. They have embarked upon a venture of entering into God's sovereign will and plan. They take time to tune in to God, to know God.

An important part of revival praying is simply loving God. The intercessor must see that this God to whom he prays is mighty enough and sovereign enough, with sufficient knowledge, wisdom, mercy, grace, and power, to turn the most hopelessly rebellious to Himself. As the prophet Daniel described the rebellion of the antichrist against God, he added this closing statement: "But the people who know their God will display strength and take action" (11:32 NASB).

This is a prerequisite for the intercessors who help save a culture or a nation. They must know God.

The better we know the God of heaven, the great and awesome God, the greater will be our display of strength sufficient to take action. How important it is to take time to seek earnestly to know God and allow Him to reveal Himself to us.

## God's Natural Attributes

Doctrinal praying has become one of life's richest experiences for me. Doctrinal praying in worship is praising God for what we're learning about who He is. His attributes, found in the Scriptures, tell us about His person. Doctrinal truth about God lifted from His Word is not something to be filed away for future reference. His name and His attributes become the springboard for extended meditation and worshipful prayer.

When we linger over lofty truths about God, such as those shown below, through prayerful worship, they become part of us. Here are several to thank God for during extended times of private prayer. As we pray, God can begin to fill us with awe about Himself.

- God is omnipotent (Job 42:2; Jer. 32:27).
- God is omniscient (Ps. 139:1–6).
- God is omnipresent (Isa. 57:15; Ps. 139:7–10).
- God is eternal (Lam. 5:19).
- God is immutable (Ps. 102:25–27).
- God is transcendent and beyond man's comprehension (Isa. 55:8–9; Rom. 11:33–36).
- God is absolutely sovereign (Dan. 4:34–35).

## God's Moral Attributes

God relates with His creation through His moral attributes; His are several revealed in the Scriptures:

- God is holy (Isa. 47:4).
- God is righteous (Ps. 89:14).
- God is just (Deut. 32:4).
- God is wise (Job 12:13; Dan. 2:20–23).
- God is loving, merciful, and patient (Jer. 31:3; Rom. 5:8; 9:14–16; 2 Peter 3:9).
- God is good and gracious (Ex. 33:19; 34:6; Ps. 106:1; Rom. 5:8).
- God is truthful and faithful (Deut. 7:9; Titus 1:2).
- God is wrathful and jealous (John 3:36; Rom. 1:18; Ex. 34:14).

Satan is always busy manipulating us to doubt God in some way, as he did Eve. He wants us to question God's goodness or wisdom or one of His other attributes. God's character and attributes are never to be measured by our circumstances or by the things we see over a short span. If we know God by His attributes as they are divinely revealed in His Word, we will always know that He is loving, good, kind, etc. His very nature means that He could never be anything but what His attributes make Him—a great God.

## Praying What We Learn Back to God

Written prayers have great value. The Bible has many of them for our learning process. I find it of great benefit to read the prayers that I have taken the thought and time to write out. I love to memorize as many of the prayers of Scripture as I can. It's a wonderful worship time to then pray them back to God out of my own heart.

I encourage you to write prayers to God extolling His attributes and acknowledging your sins. Written prayers can be of vital help in learning how to pray. Of course, they are not a substitute for expression of prayers in our own words; they are a means of learning, developing, and growing in our prayer practice. Below is the first of several "Prayer Patterns for Revival," sample prayers you can use to focus your mind and heart on God's goodness and to confess your needy condition before Him. You may want to recite these prayers as part of your approach to drawing close to Him in prayer.

Much praying that goes on in evangelical Christianity is superficial—even shallow. I hope that doesn't sound critical or judgmental. Rather, I trust it will motivate and stimulate you to prepare yourself more fully to approach God. The unlearned, innocent, meek cry of a newborn child of God means just as much to Him as any well-thought-out prayer. Yet, if after years of being Christians, we approach God with only neophyte understanding, that must be very sad for our loving heavenly Father. God certainly expects more from our praying as we learn more of Him. Lord, teach us to pray!

## REVIVAL PRAYER PATTERN: TEACH ME TO KNOW YOU

*Loving heavenly Father, I come before You in this time of prayer to open my heart to You about the brokenness and need I see about me. I see great needs in my own heart, in my family, among my fellow believers, and in my culture, community, and world. Teach me to care and to pray about those needs as Your servant Nehemiah learned to pray. I long to honor You as the "God of heaven, the great and awesome God," whose greatness is sufficient to meet the urgent needs of this day. I long to love and worship You, heavenly Father, as You are worthy to be worshipped. I do love You; not as perfectly as I will one day, but I do love You and worship You now. Teach me to know You. Even as I worship You this moment, grant me new insights into Your greatness and sufficiency. As I speak to You, please speak to me.*

*Thank You, heavenly Father, that You are omnipotent, almighty, and sovereign. I praise You that it was no threat to Your sovereign omnipotence to create Satan and all of the angels who fell, even though You foreknew they would rebel against You. Thank You, also, that it was no threat to Your sovereign omnipotence to create man in Your own likeness and image, even though You knew man would fail the test and would sin. I sense comfort and assurance from such a great and awesome God who could keep it all within His sovereign oversight and controlled limits. I rejoice that even the great needs of this day are no threat to Your omnipotent power and sovereign design.*

*I pray for a revolutionary revival to come from Your sovereign hand, and I affirm that Your omnipotence is sufficiently strong to bring it to pass. I affirm that Your omnipotent power is sufficient to humble the most hostile arrogance of man in a moment of time. I affirm that Your omnipotence is able to bring to nothing the most careful strategy and plan of Satan and his kingdom.*

*By faith I hold Your omniscient knowledge and Your total awareness in perspective as I pray. Thank You that there is no wickedness or sin that escapes Your knowledge. Thank You that the cross and redemptive work of our Lord Jesus Christ was sufficient to enable You to forgive the wickedness of man. I praise You that in Your omniscience You were able to apply His atoning blood to cleanse away the guilt of all my sins; none were missed. I hold Your omniscient understanding over the tragic conditions of the wicked rebellion of our age and ask You to humble us and bring us to repentance before You.*

*I worship You in the wonder of Your omnipresence. With the psalmist I acknowledge, "Where can I go from your Spirit? Where can I flee from your presence? If I go up to the heavens, you are there. If I make my bed in the depths you are there." Thank You that You are present wherever the dawn rises. In all of the extremities of space and in all of Your creation, You are there. Thank You that You inhabit eternity itself.*

*I rejoice that Your presence is as much with us in our day as it was there in the revival awakenings of history. I ask You to unveil Your presence among us. I invite You to draw near to us that we might experience the brokenness and the awareness of our sinful need that Your presence brings. I affirm that revival comes as people become broadly aware of the near presence of our holy God. I hold Your mercy and Your grace before You as providing sufficient ground for the fulfillment of the cry of my heart.*

*I exalt Your unchanging perfection in all that You are; that You are the same yesterday, today, and forever. Thank You that Your promises are trustworthy. I believe that if Your people unite with You in the wonder of Your person and seek Your face in humble prayer, You will hear. I affirm my desire to turn from all my wicked ways, and I cry out to You to hear from heaven, to forgive our sins, and to heal our land. In Your immutable, sovereign plan, I look to You to effect all that is necessary to bring us to revival.*

*I exalt Your justice, heavenly Father. I rejoice that You will one day banish all* evil forever from Your presence in Your perfect plan of holy wrath. I also rejoice to see Your justice and truth displayed in loving mercy at Calvary. I acknowledge that Your holy wrath was requited by the atoning sacrifice of the Lord Jesus Christ. Thank You for being willing to place upon Your own Son the judgment that we, who have received Your grace instead, deserved. The wonder of that escapes my full capacity to understand. Yet I know that Your justice, shown in such mercy and grace, remains at the very core of my prayer for revival. I ask for Your justice to draw near to us. I acknowledge that our culture deserves what came to Sodom and to the earth in Noah's day. I plead rather for the justice that came at Pentecost.

Thank You that many of those same people who cried out for Christ to be crucified cried out at Pentecost in broken repentance, "What shall we do? What shall we do?" Do it again, oh God. Judge us not with wrath as You did Sodom, but judge us with terrible conviction of sin until repentance flows down before You in rivers of tears.

You are wise and truthful, and faithful to Your Word of truth. I marvel and wonder after Your patient endurance with us. I acknowledge that I ask of You a hard thing. Thank You that You remain transcendent above all of the chaos upon this earth. I rejoice that, in the infinite greatness of Your highness and loftiness, You abide in the divine stillness of Your perfection.

I hunger and thirst for Your righteousness. I know it will necessitate a revolutionary revival for such righteousness to touch our culture in large degree, but in Your greatness, You can bring it to pass. As I worship You in Your greatness, I claim the Word of Your promise in the book of Isaiah: "For this is what the high and lofty One says—he who lives forever, whose name is holy: 'I live in a high and holy place, but also with him who is contrite and lowly in spirit, to revive the spirit of the lowly and to revive the heart of the contrite.'" I ask that You would bring the truth of that loving promise to reality in my life and my culture. I affirm that there is sufficient merit in the name and finished work of our Lord Jesus Christ to accomplish even more than I ask. It is in His name I pray. Amen.[†]

---

† The author grants permission for the seven prayers in this book to be reproduced without charge, up to twenty copies, for convenience in usage. The prayers must include the following credit line: © 2007, Mark Bubeck, from *Fire from Heaven*, Victor, Colorado Springs. All rights reserved. The seven "Prayer Patterns for Revival" are also available in booklet form. Instructions for ordering large quantities (more than twenty copies) appear after the contents page at the beginning of this book.

*Chapter 9*

# FEELING GOD'S BURDEN

*Restore our fortunes, O LORD, like streams in the Negev.
Those who sow in tears will reap with songs of joy. He
who goes out weeping, carrying seed to sow, will return
with songs of joy, carrying sheaves with him.*

*Psalm 126:4–6*

G eorge was a hard-driving executive, a successful owner of his own
business, and tireless in his pursuit of excellence and efficiency.
Employees who did not share his zeal for hard work often received fierce
tongue-lashings complete with salty language. Though a professing
Christian, George's faith had not brought the change of life God intended.

One day a Christian friend happened into George's office and overheard
one of his angry tirades. George was embarrassed by this exposure. "Sorry,
Stu. It's just one of those bad days in the office," George explained.

Stu recognized George's spiritual need. He had fought the same problem in his own life, and the Lord had set him free. Stu told me about his
concern for George, and we discussed how we could help him. We both were
close to him, so we proposed a weekly, early-morning discipleship time for
the three of us to share. Prayer, Bible study, and Scripture memorization
would be our format. George eagerly accepted. We said nothing to him
about his anger.

Several weeks passed. The spiritual hunger grew in all our hearts, and as
we memorized the Word followed by the times of prayer, good fruit appeared
in each of our lives.

## A PRELUDE OF BROKENNESS

Some of the psalms spoke deeply to George. We considered memorizing

Psalm 19; so we read through it, each reading a few verses. Finally George read aloud the last three verses:

> Who can discern his errors? Forgive my hidden faults.
>
> Keep your servant also from willful sins; may they not rule over me.
>
> Then will I be blameless, innocent of great transgression.
>
> May the words of my mouth and the meditation of my heart be pleasing in your sight, O LORD, my Rock and my Redeemer. (vv. 12–14)

As he read the Scripture, George experienced a deep brokenness, and he began to weep. Being a strong leader, he felt embarrassed by his crying, yet Stu and I also were moved by what God was doing and began to shed tears with him. We started to pray, and all went well until George's turn came.

His emotions were suddenly overwhelmed. Deep, broken sobs rolled up from the depths of his being. "I'm so sorry. I'm so sorry!" was all he could pray.

His confession and the feeling of wholeness that followed brought George and us great joy. When George, Stu, and I eventually went our separate ways, each felt a deep gratitude for the Lord's special presence with us.

George returned to work, but God was not finished. George was reading Andrew Murray's *Absolute Surrender*, and he'd stay at his desk with that and his Bible most of the day. He felt deep repentance, and sometimes he'd leave the office and go to the private retreat of his car. There he felt free to let his emotions flow. Humbling tears and deep sobs of repentance accompanied the transformation God was effecting within him.

This process of God's grace went on for several days. God was at work, preparing a chosen vessel for an anointed ministry.

## A TRANSFORMED LEADER

Whether you're a man or a woman, tears are a beautiful token of repentance as they arise from a sincere heart. Stu and I had witnessed a great transformation of George's life. From his encounter with God, George developed a strong commitment. In his midfifties, he eventually sold his business and retired. He became a wise spiritual leader in our local church, and he prayed for enlarged service for his Lord.

Through God's sovereign working, George received a position on a leading evangelical mission board with more than five hundred missionaries. He has served there many years, managing retirement monies for the missionaries, and he has traveled the world, counseling and helping missionaries regarding their personal and field financial needs.

As we've seen, prayer that confronts Satan's rule and rescues a culture keeps in touch with God in His greatness. However, our concept of God's greatness must not come from a well containing only intellectual awareness of truth. It must arise from feeling God's own burden for His creation. Our understanding of God's greatness must affect our deepest feelings. Then we can move in unity with God's will into actions that change things.

We must feel the deep burden that God feels. The spiritual rebuilding of burned-up gates and broken walls requires a people who can weep over the ruins. When God prepares to use someone greatly, He must first bring him to a place of personal brokenness, as He did with George. This leads us to another element of revival prayer.

## PRAYER THAT SAVES A CULTURE EXPRESSES GOD'S BURDEN

Nehemiah experienced a similar brokenness before the Lord. As God prepared him for the rescue of a broken culture, He let Nehemiah feel His own burden.

> When I heard these things, I sat down and wept. For some days I mourned and fasted and prayed before the God of heaven. Then I said … "Let your ear be attentive and your eyes open to hear the prayer your servant is praying before you day and night for your servants." (Neh. 1:4–6)

Like Jesus Himself, we need to feel and understand the longing of God's heart for hurting people. Jesus was emotionally affected by the blindness and brokenness of the culture of His earthly sojourn. When He made

His triumphant entry into Jerusalem, He "saw the city, he wept over it and said, 'If you, even you, had only known on this day what would bring you peace—but now it is hidden from your eyes'" (Luke 19:41–42).

Today, the broken walls and hurting people of our fallen culture surely merit the tears of our Lord flowing from His burdened people. Nehemiah expressed his burden in four ways that we would do well to follow: through tears, mourning, fasting, and consistent, continual prayer.

### Nehemiah Wept

"I sat down and wept." Nehemiah's sorrow expressed more than compassionate, human tears. He felt the burden of his Lord. He shed the tears of God.

There are plenty of examples of superficial emotionalism around today, but not many tears of God. This broken, hurting world of wounded people needs such tears. God's Spirit enables intercessors to feel His burden. Earlier, God used Babylon to discipline His people, but He had taken no pleasure in the hurt of those He loved. At least three times in Ezekiel, God states,

> As surely as I live, declares the Sovereign LORD, I take no pleasure
> in the death of the wicked, but rather that they turn from their
> ways and live. Turn! Turn from your evil ways! Why will you die,
> O house of Israel? (33:11; see also 18:23, 32)

God weeps when He must deal with man's rebellion and rejection. Revival praying requires that God's people feel the emotional burden of our loving Lord.

### Nehemiah Mourned

"For some days I mourned." Nehemiah felt God's burden even more deeply. Such mourning ties in closely to the work of the Holy Spirit, who groans on our behalf:

> In the same way, the Spirit helps us in our weakness. We do not

know what we ought to pray for, but the Spirit himself intercedes for us with groans that words cannot express. And he who searches our hearts knows the mind of the Spirit, because the Spirit intercedes for the saints in accordance with God's will. (Rom. 8:26–27)

The Greek word for *groans* is similar to the Hebrew word Nehemiah used for *mourn*. For days Nehemiah felt the mourning, the groaning of God for the hurt of His people.

Today, most of us run from groans and mourning. If they come from a human condition and hang on "for some days," we may need our pastor or counselor, or we may even need to seek psychological help. But when the mourning is of the Lord, there is nothing wrong with letting it go on "for some days." Revival praying needs people who are willing to share God's groans for our broken world. The Holy Spirit will share His groaning burden with us if revolutionary revival is to occur.

### Nehemiah Fasted

"For some days I ... fasted and prayed before the God of heaven." Fasting is a secret, private expression of longing for God to intervene. More than he wanted the comfort of food, Nehemiah hungered for God to save His people.

A word of care needs to be interjected here. People who are thinking of fasting should study the biblical approach to fasting. Fasting is to be done in private, without desire for recognition, and only for a short period of time. Proper medical consideration needs to be given as well. God's people must not harm their health through some unwise practice of this Christian discipline.[†]

On the other hand, fasting does have New Testament endorsement. Our Lord Jesus Christ honored the discipline, and the apostle Paul practiced it (Matt. 9:15; Acts 9:9; 13:2–3; 14:23; 2 Cor. 11:27). The broken spiritual walls in our culture warrant prayer and fasting.

---

† See Arthur Wallis's *God's Chosen Fast* (Fort Washington, PA: Christian Literature Crusade, 1986).

### Nehemiah Prayed Day and Night

"Your servant is praying before you day and night for your servants." We know what it is to go without sleep to study, to pay our bills, to work, to enjoy a concert, to socialize, or to file our tax return. Nehemiah went without sleep to pray. The burden of the Lord touched his tears, his feelings, his desire for food, and even his desire for sleep.

When prayer takes on the deeper dimensions of God's burden, one can expect some sleepless nights. Sleep is temporarily replaced by the need to pray. Our responsibility is to yield to Him, to make ourselves available. We may even need to confess our coldness and lack of interest in these deeper levels of prayer.

But Nehemiah did more than feel God's burden for a wayward culture. He repented of personal and corporate sins. That's another truth of revival prayer.

## PRAYER THAT SAVES A CULTURE EXPRESSES REPENTANCE OF SIN

In his prayer Nehemiah told God,

> I confess the sins we Israelites, including myself and my father's house, have committed against you. We have acted very wickedly toward you. We have not obeyed the commands, decrees and laws you gave your servant Moses. (1:6–7)

After Nehemiah cried over the physical rubble of the fallen Jerusalem wall, he was ready to do something about it. He repented, and then rebuilding could occur. Similarly, after we weep over the spiritual rubble, we must do something about removing it.

In the rubble of the broken walls of Jerusalem, there were some salvageable, usable materials. That's true of most rubble, even that of our sinful failures. Much of it just has to be removed. The hurtful damage of sin must be taken away. Yet lessons are learned and insights are gained; humility and brokenness emerge, and God uses what He can of it to rebuild spiritual walls.

That is repentance: getting rid of useless matter so God can start to rebuild with what is left. For Nehemiah, as for us, the repentance takes place on three levels: personal, familial, and cultural.

## The Repentance Was Personal

"I confess the sins we Israelites, including myself ... committed against you." Most of us can see the failures around us, but it's quite another matter to acknowledge the wrongs within ourselves. Spiritual pride keeps them hidden. We experience true repentance when we are broken enough to weep over our own sins.

There is a personal yearning to recognize and expose sin fully. Thus David urged God, "Search me, O God, and know my heart; test me and know my anxious thoughts. See if there is any offensive way in me, and lead me in the way everlasting" (Ps. 139:23–24).

Revival is intensely personal. That's why its beginnings bring us such brokenness over our own sins. In American churches, carnality is rife among believers, and cleansing cannot come until we acknowledge our need in repentance as Nehemiah did. If we want true revival to come, we must clean up our act.

Personal repentance must become important to us. That's the place to start. As king of Israel, David was not afraid to humble himself by admitting his sinful bent. When Nathan confronted the king about his adultery, David confessed his sin to God: "Surely I was sinful at birth, sinful from the time my mother conceived me. Surely you desire truth in the inner parts; you teach me wisdom in the inmost place" (51:5–6).

## The Repentance Had Family Dimensions

"I confess the sins ... my father's house [has] committed against you." Next to ourselves, we are most responsible for our families. Family sins are rampant in our culture. Neglect of family devotions, a lack of caring for one another, and wrong family entertainment are among the things that can turn our mates and children from God. Sexual abuse among family members has reached alarming levels and, along with physical and verbal abuse, does great harm within a family.

What does one do with such sin? No matter how family sin may have affected you—whether abuse (physical, verbal, or sexual), strife, or abandonment, you cannot harbor resentment or hatred toward those family members who violate you. To do so only adds to the already burning fire of destruction.

How can we avert the continuing damage of family sin? I don't want to oversimplify the problem, but in the final analysis we must do what Nehemiah did. We must repent of our family's sins. Such repentance does not excuse the perpetrator, and acceptance of Jesus Christ as Savior and Lord can never erase his guilt. Yet, great good can come when a violated person prays as Nehemiah did: "I confess the sins my family member committed against You."

Many find liberating relief by pouring out such repentance for the hurtful things family members have done to them. God is honored in the open honesty of such confession. That kind of praying by even one family member also can bring hope for more of the family to participate in the repentance. God's sovereign hand will begin to move in that family when just one person begins to deal with the family's sin.

### The Repentance Was Cultural

"I confess the sins we Israelites ... have committed against you," Nehemiah prayed. "We have acted very wickedly toward you. We have not obeyed the commands, decrees and laws you gave your servant Moses."

In America, such wickedness in our society has led to a sin-ridden culture. Change can come in part by Christians working in the legal and political arenas to turn the tide. Such efforts are part of our being "light" and "salt" in a dark, decaying world. Yet I'm convinced we'll never really correct our cultural wickedness by marches, or by legal or political efforts. The most urgent ingredient in cultural change is what Nehemiah entered into—what I call "intercessory repentance."

The sins of our culture are a terrible affront against a holy God, and someone must continue to express repentance for them. God has already told us how He deals with cultural sins like ours when there is no repentance. He lets the sin become its own judgment.

Ask yourself these questions:

- Who will express sorrow to God for the wickedness of the rampant drug and alcohol addiction if I don't?
- Who will confess the murderous, violent tearing apart of little unborn babies in legal abortion procedures if I don't?
- Who will repent of the pornography, the vile cursing, the sexual promiscuity, the divorce scandal, and all the rest of it if I don't?
- Who will repent of the increasing openness of Satan worship and ritualistic violence if I don't?

Repentance begins with believers who care, and it is related to the weeping and groaning mentioned earlier.

If there remains only silence in our land for our cultural wickedness, we cannot expect anything but "God giving us up" to deeper and deeper levels of destructive sin. Repentance on the broad spectrum doesn't come first—deep repentance by a few believers does. In contrite intercession for their culture, believers lay hold of God's grace and mercy.

Nehemiah did that, and he included himself and his family in identifying with his culture's sins. When revival finally came to the city, the tears and repentance flowed freely from all the people. In Nehemiah 8:9, we learn that the planned celebration turned to a time of great sorrow. God was working deeply among His people, and His work would not be denied. In chapter 9, the repentance from the people rolls out like it did previously from Nehemiah.

> Those of Israelite descent had separated themselves from all foreigners. They stood in their places and confessed their sins and the wickedness of their fathers. They stood where they were and read from the Book of the Law of the LORD their God for a quarter of the day, and spent another quarter in confession and in worshiping the LORD their God. (9:2–3)

As people draw near to God and He to them, there always follows a longing to be clean.

*Chapter 10*

# BELIEVING GOD'S PROMISES

*For no matter how many promises God has made, they are "Yes" in Christ. And so through him the "Amen" is spoken by us to the glory of God. Now it is God who makes both us and you stand firm in Christ.*

*2 Corinthians 1:20–21*

B
ut, Dad, you promised!" eight-year-old Matthew whined. His little sister, Marcie, shook her head in agreement, waiting for Dad to change his mind and take them to the circus. But their father, who agreed six months earlier to treat them to the Ringling Brothers and Barnum & Bailey show when it came to town, looked at his schedule, saw he would have to be out of town that weekend, and shook his head.

"I'm sorry, kids. But I had no idea when I said yes that this week would be so busy. You can go with Mom, though."

But Mother wouldn't go without Dad coming along, and the children wanted Dad to come anyway. Father had forgotten his promise, and now a suddenly busy schedule made him the target of pleas and tears. Little Marcie began to cry, and Dad knew then he should never have made such a promise.

Unlike a father's promises to his children, which a dad sometimes forgets, ignores, or is unable to keep, God's promises are certain. He will never disappoint, for His words are true and reliable. Clearly Nehemiah realized this. As he prayed, he recalled the Scriptures, even though he lived in a foreign land. Some believe his words of prayer reveal his studies in Deuteronomy 30, Psalms 106 and 107, and perhaps some of the prophetic writings of both Isaiah and Jeremiah.

Remember the instruction you gave your servant Moses, saying, "If you are unfaithful, I will scatter you among the nations, but if you return to me and obey my commands, then even if your exiled people are at the farthest horizon, I will gather them from there and bring them to the place I have chosen as a dwelling for my Name."

They are your servants and your people, whom you redeemed by your great strength and your mighty hand. (Neh. 1:8–10)

Effective prayer is always in close harmony with everything God reveals in His Word about His will and plan. Nehemiah's prayer was within that harmony.

## PRAYER APPROPRIATES GOD'S PROMISES

Prayer that saves a culture often will include Scriptures that contain God's promises. Praying God's Word back to Him pleases God and is powerfully effective. Moses drew upon God's promise when he tried to intercede for his people who had sinned by setting up a golden calf as the god who had brought them out of Egypt. Animal sacrifices to this idol and celebrating through sexual orgy were all part of their great sin. God's anger was aroused to the point of severe judgment; He threatened to destroy the people and make Moses, not Israel [Jacob], the leader of "a great nation" (Ex. 32:9–10).

Moses' response illustrates the kind of praying necessary to bring a revolutionary revival to our day:

But Moses sought the favor of the LORD his God. "O LORD," he said, "why should your anger burn against your people, whom you brought out of Egypt with great power and a mighty hand? Why should the Egyptians say, 'It was with evil intent that he brought them out, to kill them in the mountains and to wipe them off the face of the earth'? Turn from your fierce anger; relent and do not bring disaster on your people. Remember your servants Abraham, Isaac and Israel, to whom you swore by your own self: 'I will make your descendants as numerous as the stars in the sky and I will give your descendants all this land I promised them, and it will be their inheritance forever.'" Then the LORD relented and did not bring on his people the disaster he had threatened. (vv. 11–14)

This is what I call "doctrinal praying." Moses pleaded back to God the promises that God had made to Abraham, Isaac, and Jacob. God was exceedingly displeased with Aaron and the people, and Moses appropriated the valid ground that touched God's mercy and grace. That mercy and grace is not based upon our emotional desires or finite reasoning; rather, it flows from who God is and what He has revealed about Himself.

God never brings revival because we deserve it. God brings revival because we understand His promises, claim them, and persistently keep them before Him as we wait upon Him.

What unique promise from God will lead His intercessors to claim revival awakening in our day? I do not know. However, the conditions of the church today are much like those of the Laodicean church described in Revelation 3, so we might find the promise in 3:17–20. (Remember, despite its popular use, verse 20 is not a call to spiritual salvation but spiritual revival given to the proud and complacent church in Laodicea.)

We, too, have to confess our spiritual pride, our rich materialism, and our self-satisfied complacency. We have to acknowledge truthfully that we are "wretched, pitiful, poor, blind and naked," and that we are powerless to do anything about it.

In faith we need to buy from our Lord Jesus Christ His "gold refined in the fire," His "white clothes" to cover our nakedness, and His eye "salve" to remove our spiritual blindness. We need to plead the truth of His knocking at the door of His church and of our personal lives. We need to claim His promise that when we open the door, He will come in with a revolutionary revival of His presence.

## PRAYER INCREASES IN ITS EXPECTATION

Prayer that saves a culture will grow in expectancy. In fact, as we pray, faith and expectations build. To anticipate God's people to build up to the level of boldness that Nehemiah displays, we need a period of time. Read

Nehemiah 1:11—2:10 to see the magnitude of his expectations. Let this list of what Nehemiah was looking for encourage you to ask God to build faith in your own heart.

- He expected God to sovereignly touch the Persian king Artaxerxes Longimanus so that despite the king's heathen outlook, he would look with favor upon Nehemiah's request (1:11).
- Despite his lowly position as a cupbearer, Nehemiah trusted God to use his inconcealable grief and his despondency to prepare the king for a good decision (2:1–2).
- He was bold enough to share with the king his brokenhearted concern for the conquered city of his forefathers (v. 3).
- He expected the king to put him in charge of an expedition to return to Jerusalem to rebuild and fortify it (vv. 4–5).
- He expected God to motivate Artaxerxes to supply him with safe-conduct letters, materials with which to build, and all the other things he would need for such a giant undertaking (vv. 6–8).
- He expected to be successful in rebuilding walls, rehanging gates, and reestablishing a valid government, despite all the enemies and hazards that Satan could throw at him (vv. 9–10).

To believe God for revolutionary revival in our nation is a challenge equal to the one Nehemiah met by showing his expectant faith. From a human perspective, there is much against revolutionary revival ever happening. Evil has laid its foundations deep and is on a bold revival march of its own.

The church, ridiculed and even ignored by most people, seems unable to rise to the challenge. This noble body looks insipid and weak to its critics. The "shakers and movers" of our day have given up on the church—and for good cause. Media notoriety has long made a mockery of well-known Christian leaders. Prayer meetings in the churches flounder in attendance. Many mainline denominational churches are pulling back in certain areas of ministry. Regular church-service attendance is dropping, and funds are shrinking. Where will we find an expectant faith like that of Nehemiah? Where can we turn for hope and help?

## FAITH AND PRAYER

### *Faith That Is Rooted in God's Word*

Our prayers can rest on an expectant faith when we look beyond people to the absolutes of God's Word. Biblical faith is not emotional desire, presumption, or pure conjecture. Faith that God honors always rests solely on the correct application of the promises of His Word.

Paul writes, "Faith comes from hearing the message, and the message is heard through the word of Christ" (Rom. 10:17). The writer of Hebrews adds that faith—"being sure of what we hope for"—was "what the ancients were commended for" (11:1–2). In fact, each of the many illustrations of faith given in Hebrews 11 is directly traceable to the foundational promises that God has given.

Nehemiah's confidence in what God would do had biblical foundation as well. He didn't act on the basis of some sentimental desire to see his homeland restored, nor was he counting on the king to fulfill his dream because of his and the king's close association. It was much deeper than any human conjecture. From man's reason there was no probability that his plans would ever succeed. His faith was in God's Word and in God's Word alone.

Faith must always rest upon our knowledge of God's purpose and will as revealed in His Word. Sometimes people feel they have received some special promise from God in an experience or through a "prophecy" or "word of knowledge." Such "special revelations" must be viewed with a critical eye. If the "promise" cannot be supported from God's written revelation, we should quickly discard it and put no faith in it.

Some seem to feel that if they believe hard enough and if they maintain a positive viewpoint, they can manipulate God and make miraculous things happen. Faith is not a human exercise in striving to believe. Rather it is based upon a surety that one is praying in harmony with God's will and plan.

### *Faith That Doesn't Quit*

Faith that rests on biblical truth doesn't back away when evidence and adversity say that what we're asking cannot happen. It digs in at such times and remains quietly confident and aggressively active. Peter spoke of this truth in these words:

> In this you greatly rejoice, though now for a little while you may have had to suffer grief in all kinds of trials. These have come so that your faith—of greater worth than gold, which perishes even though refined by fire—may be proved genuine and may result in praise, glory and honor when Jesus Christ is revealed. (1 Peter 1:6–7)

As we pray for revival, we must remember Peter's counsel that "all kinds of trials" will come, but we are to prove our faith. Satan will deluge us with obstacles, disappointments, and difficulties of every kind. The obstacles will seem to say, "No revival for you. Things are only getting worse," but we must know that faith has no root in the appearance of things. If revival is to come, it can only exist because it's all of God, and it's all of grace. We must be ever acknowledging in our own minds that God is in charge.

Faith rests in knowing God and in our acknowledging that He remains God. It doesn't retreat and quit when nothing seems to be happening. And faith is empowered by the power in us and His promises working through us. One can step out in faith on this great promise:

> His divine power has given us everything we need for life and godliness through our knowledge of him who called us by his own glory and goodness. Through these he has given us his very great and precious promises, so that through them you may participate in the divine nature and escape the corruption in the world caused by evil desires. (2 Peter 1:3–4)

## REVIVAL PRAYER PATTERN: REPENTANCE AND INTERCESSION

*Loving heavenly Father, I come again to worship You in the wonder of who You are. I approach You in the merit and worthiness of our Lord Jesus Christ. I open my whole being to the controlling work of Your Holy Spirit. I invite Him to express His interceding and His groaning through my prayers in the ways that He may choose. I yield to You, heavenly Father, all of the faculties and capacities You* have placed within me to be used for Your glory. I open my mind, will, and emotions to You that You might share with me Your burden for the church and for the lost around me.

I rejoice that my Lord Jesus Christ could weep over the people of Jerusalem as they passed up His presence and His caring love for them. Cleanse me of the coldness and indifference that keeps me from shedding tears for the rebellious sin of today. Share with me His tears. Allow me to feel the mourning of Your Spirit's groaning for my broken world. Grant me Your divine intervention expressing in me a willingness to fast and to spend time in extended sessions of prayer. Help me see those times when I awaken in the night as opportunities to cry to You for a revolutionary revival to visit Your church. What I pray for myself I pray also for a large number of other believers whom You are calling to a deeper prayer burden.

I confess my sins to You, dear heavenly Father. Wash me clean in my Savior's precious blood from all that offends You. I recognize within my person a fleshly condition that can be rebellious in Your sight. Thank You for informing me of this fact in Your Word. I affirm that in my union with Christ in His death I am dead to the rule of that fleshly condition. I desire the new nature You effected within me to be in charge through the power of my Savior's resurrection. Thank You for having made this new creation in righteousness and true holiness, so I can love You deeply and serve You fully. May Your Holy Spirit enable me to manifest before You and others the fruit of His full control. In the name of the Lord Jesus Christ, I bind Satan and his host from interjecting any interference in my prayer.

I bring to You, heavenly Father, the sins of my family, the church, and the culture in which I live. What great wickedness takes place in our homes. Thank You that it's not hidden from You. I repent of it for my family, other Christian families, and non-Christian families. You establish the home, and it's very dear to You. Forgive us for the way we too often talk to each other in anger and unkindness. How broken You must be over the physical, verbal, and sexual abuse that is too much a part of the families in our culture. I not only confess this wickedness, but I also ask You to intervene and change it by Your mighty power. Show us our sins and grant us the grace of repentance.

I recognize that the sins of our nation and culture are an abomination in Your eyes. I repent for our culture of the terrible abuse of our sexuality. The *misuse of this God-given gift is a curse upon our times. I apologize to You, heavenly Father, for the abomination of pornography and the wide audience that makes it profitable. Turn our hearts from this perversion. You intended that our sexual desires should glorify Your name within the bonds of marriage. May this take place in our culture.*

*I repent before You, loving God, for the violence against innocent people that has invaded our culture. My heart grieves as Yours surely does for those millions of unborn babies that have been destroyed by legalized abortions. I repent for our legislators and court judges and for the people who let it go on. Forgive and change the violence displayed in the entertainment media, in the inner city, and in the drug scene. I apologize for the burgeoning market for drugs and other intoxicants. My heart grieves for the cursing and vile talk that streams forth from people's mouths.*

*I see spreading through our culture a plague of fascination with the spirit realm of darkness. It poisons our little children in the themes of their toys, games, and cartoons. It permeates our entertainment media. It subtly is becoming a part of the business and educational world through various pagan themes. Growing hosts of people are so deceived that they are returning to the ancient pagan prac-tices of overt idolatry. How terribly this dishonors You, O Lord. I cry out against it in prayer, and I repent for them of this awful wickedness. I ask You to bring a revival awakening so intense that these things will be crushed by Your omnipo-tent power.*

*Forgive us for all our wickedness, O God. The sin of our land is so great. Religious sins of unbelief, legalism, and self-righteous pride abound. Greed, cov-etousness, gluttony, gossip, and spiritual indifference are almost as common to believers as to the lost. We desperately need a holy revival from You to confront our sins and bring us to humble repentance and spiritual renewal.*

*My hope, heavenly Father, is in the promises of Your Word. Thank You for Your compassion for us in our sinful ways. In our arrogant lifestyle, we say to You, "I am rich; I have acquired wealth and do not need a thing." I repent of that. I confess that, as believers, we show our wretched, pitiful, poor, blind, and naked condition. I accept that analysis by my Lord Jesus Christ as applying to my fel-low believers and me.*

*Thank You that our Lord Jesus Christ has invited us to come and buy from Him gold refined in His disciplining fires. I want that gold for me and for Your church. I ask for the white clothes that my Lord Jesus Christ promised would cover our nakedness. Anoint our eyes with the eye salve that enables us to see things as our Lord Jesus Christ sees them. I open the door of my life to my Lord Jesus Christ. I invite Him to come to me, to the church, and to our day, giving us a mighty sense of His holy presence. May His nearness break us over our sins until we flee to the cross for cleansing by His blood. May this revival for which I pray bring to saving faith multitudes that are not yet in our Savior's fold. Heavenly Father, move everything out of the way that hinders the coming of revival. Cause revival to affect churches, legislators, courts, businesses, education, government, and all that is before You. Will You not revive us again?*

*I lay all of this before You, heavenly Father, basing every request on the merit and worthiness of our Lord Jesus Christ alone, and His finished work. I ask that You build a faith within me and countless other believers. Build a faith that is growing and contagious and that rests totally upon Your will and plan for us in this day and upon the foundation of Your Word and the finished work of our Lord Jesus Christ. Amen.*

*Chapter 11*

# MAKING IT HAPPEN

*So neither he who plants nor he who waters is anything, but only God, who makes things grow. The man who plants and the man who waters have one purpose, and each will be rewarded according to his own labor. For we are God's fellow workers; you are God's field, God's building.*

*1 Corinthians 3:7–9*

Revivals usually begin with only a few people. In the two previous chapters, we saw that the saving of Jerusalem began with the prayers of Nehemiah and of the few who were burdened along with him. They experienced revival in their own lives first, and the movement could have stopped there. But to be widely effective, revival movements must reach out.

In our culture, paganism—from Wiccan-nature and goddess worship to outright devil worship—continues to pervade and rise in popularity in virtually every region of the country. Regarding the latter example, a high-ranking former satanist states that the "traditional satanists" have targeted four major areas of society for infiltration: the judicial, the legislative, the entertainment media, and the public educational system. Today's occultists include medical doctors, court justices, schoolteachers, lawyers, business people, government officials, military people, and even pastors.

To reverse this widespread satanic strategy will require a spiritual revival of massive dimension. Only God's methods can break the bonds of satanic power. Large groups of believers must understand and accept God's approach to revival.

## SHARING A REVIVAL BURDEN

One thing Christians must realize in today's threatening environment is that a person's deep burden for revival and divine intervention should not be carried alone. Satan's subtle assaults would soon cause him to crumble. We must bear these burdens together.

Note how the revival movement of Nehemiah's day involved the people of the entire city. Excitement and commitment built until they were all participating.

In more recent years God has granted other revival awakenings in diverse places, keeping an example before His people of what revivals can do. They encourage us. They also bear testimony that we must have a broad base of those who enter into the burden in order for revolutionary revival to visit our whole culture.

The Holy Spirit can arouse people to involvement. His powerful force is able to speak individually to those who belong to Him and who must be awakened to join the cause. If the Lord's people in our nation unite to seek His intervention, God will visit us with the greatest revival the world has known. The very gates of hell are no obstacle when Christ wills to build His church (Matt. 16:18).

Let's take a brief look at a revival that took place in the 1970s at a college here in America, and then we will discuss how to bring revival to where you are.

## THE ASBURY REVIVAL

Revival awakening flowed through several college campuses in 1970, beginning at Asbury College, a Christian liberal arts college of Methodist roots, and its graduate school, Asbury Theological Seminary, both in Wilmore, Kentucky (near Lexington). A small group of students began getting up thirty minutes earlier each day to gather for Scripture reading and prayer in search of a new touch from God. God granted meaningful experiences to those involved in this new discipline, and word of it spread through the student body. Group meetings to pray for spiritual awakening became common for both faculty and students.

On February 3, about one thousand students made their way to the 10:00 a.m. chapel service. As the students entered, an unusual air of expectancy accompanied the casual chatter. The dean of the college, scheduled to be the chapel speaker, laid aside his planned message and began to share with the students some of his personal experiences with God.

A holy hush settled upon the audience. When the dean invited the students to tell what God was doing in their hearts, they responded quickly. Many of them were immediately on their feet, giving fervent testimonies that reflected God's inner-heart searchings. Tears of concern and repentance began to flow.

The typical clichés common to many testimony services were absent. Instead, intense, contagious sincerity characterized humility and brokenness before the Lord. Robert Coleman reported, "Everyone sensed that something unusual was happening. God seemed very near" (18).

As the allotted time for chapel ended, one of the professors made his way to the platform. He invited any student who desired to pray to come to the altar. The student body began to sing "Just as I Am," and the response was instant and massive. The presence of God was strong, and all other interests seemed suddenly unimportant. The bell sounded for classes to begin, but no one left the chapel. Faculty and students alike realized God was at work. Students lined up to share testimonies. Confessions were made. Old hostilities between individuals melted away. God's presence and love immersed them all.

At lunchtime the dining hall remained empty. Spiritual hunger supplanted physical hunger.

Classes were suspended indefinitely. Prayer, testimonies, music, and Bible readings became a continuing part of the spontaneous participation. Some left the auditorium service at the dinner hour, but shortly the auditorium began to fill again. At times its 1,550 seating capacity was not sufficient. Word spread to the nearby seminary and to the townspeople concerning what was happening. People stood along the walls and crowded into the aisles and doorways. Everyone wanted to be a part of what God was doing.

The 450 seminary students were so challenged by God's visitation at the college that they entered into an all-night campus prayer meeting. The next morning the planned service of seminary chapel hymn singing was changed. One student stood to relate how the college revival had affected him, and spontaneously others began to move to the front and kneel at the altar in prayer. Students and faculty members formed a line at the pulpit, awaiting their turn to give testimony or to relate spiritual needs.

The seminary and college merged into united meetings, and smaller group prayer meetings spilled over everywhere. Classrooms were often filled with intercessors and seekers. Local churches and townspeople were drawn in and began to participate. The chapel meeting was continuous. Even at 3:00 a.m., more than two hundred people would still be meeting for testimony, prayer, Scripture reading, and singing. For an entire week, 185 continuous hours, the auditorium was wholly or partially filled with worshippers.

Numerous other colleges were touched as well. At least 130 colleges, seminaries, and Bible schools across the world were affected by what happened at Asbury, estimated Henry C. James, a spokesman at Asbury Theological Seminary. From Asbury in the east to Greenville College in the Midwest (Illinois) to Azusa Pacific College on the West Coast (California), awakenings were underway. Those who participated in the overflow of the Asbury revival will never forget that unusual visit of God's grace.

Accounts of recent revival awakenings are encouraging. The college revivals of spring 1995 affected more than a dozen schools nationwide. Some have hesitated to call the times of confession and prayer "revival," preferring to speak of personal "renewal" among students. But Tim Beougher, professor of evangelism at Wheaton College and an expert on revivals and awakenings, said, "This [movement] bears all the marks of being a deep and genuine work of God" (Lee, 50).

These awakenings at Christian colleges provided a taste that motivates God's people to desire more. Yet so much more is needed. Hunger for God's intervention must come to the Christian people of every community, town, and city. When that happens, a continentwide revival will be possible. But where do we start?

## PEOPLE INVOLVEMENT IN AWAKENINGS

First, we must ask the question: How does a broad base of people involvement in revival awakening happen? Here are some of the answers.

### A Sovereign God Prepares People

The Devil is using his broad base of "people power" to keep his revival of evil spreading at a phenomenal rate. His success is beyond human challenge. So what is our response?

"But God …" Those two words have sparked every revival that has ever happened. That's because it's God who initiates and authors His powerful intervention. In His sovereign grace He prepares and moves people to revival.

Nehemiah knew this truth before he left the Persian capital. "And because the gracious hand of my God was upon me, the king granted my requests" (2:8).

God had prepared Nehemiah's heart well. As he journeyed toward Jerusalem, Nehemiah knew he faced an awesome task. Obstacles too great for any human solution faced him. He knew the remaining Jews were a demoralized people. He also knew his foes would never permit walls to be rebuilt, gates rehung, or a Jewish government reintroduced to Jerusalem. As he viewed the enormity of his task, his dependence upon his God kept deepening. Prayer was constant in his life: "The king said to me, 'What is it you want?' Then I prayed to the God of heaven, and I answered the king" (vv. 4–5).

After Nehemiah arrived in Jerusalem, his dependence upon the Lord increased. For three days he simply waited, observed, and doubtlessly prayed. Only God could move the people to believe with him that the city would be restored.

In like manner, the core of students at Asbury dedicated themselves to prayer—God used them to bring His intervention to their campus and the surrounding community.

As I write, I wonder: Who will join me and those others who carry a burden concerning revival awakening for our communities, our nations, and our world?

The people are there. Evangelical Christians are everywhere. Yet we seem demoralized, passive, and almost indifferent. Some wish revival would happen, but the desire for personal involvement is missing. Disillusionment with Christian movements abounds. Contentment with the status quo characterizes the average evangelical church. How will the church, the sleeping giant of spiritual power, awaken to the challenge for revolutionary revival? Sovereign, merciful grace from the hand of God alone will make it happen.

### Testimony and Timing Bring People Involvement

The right timing is necessary to inspire people's involvement. Consider Nehemiah's approach to enlisting the support of the people upon his return to Jerusalem: "I set out during the night with a few men. I had not told anyone what my God had put in my heart to do for Jerusalem. There were no mounts with me except the one I was riding on" (v. 12).

Imagine the curiosity that was aroused when this Jewish dignitary with royal credentials rode into the city. The priests, nobles, and officials of the Jewish remnant were abuzz with speculation. Why had he come? What was he doing? For three days Nehemiah kept quiet. The seeds of curiosity were allowed to grow and permeate the culture while he waited upon God, observed quietly, and listened attentively. He was creating a readiness for people to hear what he had to say.

At the end of the three days, under the cover of darkness, Nehemiah quietly slipped out of Jerusalem through the Valley Gate. A few trusted men joined him as he surveyed the ruins. He was intent on allowing the magnitude of the broken walls to fully impress these men. The rubble was so extensive he was forced to dismount and walk over the ruins. Rebuilding could not be done without enlisting all the people. As Nehemiah retraced his steps, a burning awareness captured his heart. God must stir His people to action. God would do it.

In the meantime, curiosity had done its work. The officials didn't know where or why he'd gone, but they knew he'd left the city. As their curiosity reached a fever pitch, Nehemiah called together all of those "who would be doing the work" (v. 16). His testimony and God's timing made a perfect blend. The people were ready to listen to God's plan. Nehemiah told of the miracle of his coming and God's provisions. "I also told them about the gracious hand of my God upon me and what the king had said to me."

That must have been a powerful meeting. A quick, decisive response came from the people. "They replied, 'Let us start rebuilding.' So they began this good work" (v. 18).

Such a gigantic undertaking demanded that planning, organization, and administrative responsibility be worked out. It was a part of the beginning of "this good work." Nehemiah 3 unveils that the procedure was made possible because the people were behind it. Motivation through Nehemiah's testimony and God's timing had captured the people. They were ready for the challenge. As God graciously moves us toward a revival awakening, this same process of people involvement will emerge.

### Personal Interest Keeps People Involved

In Nehemiah's day, personal involvement was gained largely through personal interest. Some recurring phrases in Nehemiah 3 reveal the strategy. The chapter begins with, "Eliashib the high priest and his fellow priests went to work and rebuilt the Sheep Gate. They dedicated it and set its doors in place" (v. 1). The Sheep Gate was the gate through which the sacrificial sheep were brought to the rebuilt temple. Not only did the priests administer the sacrificial system, but most of them would live near the temple. Their personal interest gave them intensity of involvement.

Consider these phrases that reveal the personal nature of the repairs: "Jedaiah son of Harumaph made repairs opposite his house" (v. 10); "for his district" (v. 17); "in front of their house," "beside his house" (v. 23); and "opposite his living quarters" (v. 30). Similar statements occur at least ten times in the chapter. Clearly, a major consideration in the reconstruction was where a person would work. It was a winning strategy. Should fierce opposition rise up, weak-hearted dedication might quickly retreat. Yet when the threat was close to home, love and devotion would demand that they stay.

This principle has special application to revival effort. Before believers will be motivated, they must be touched personally with the crying need for revival. As we look around, the awareness of that need comes closer and closer. We even see it in our homes: Drug addiction or alcoholism are causing problems, we experience divorce or unwanted pregnancy, we are victims of rape or robbery, a child in our family has been abused, or a family member is drawn into pornography, or … you fill in the blank.

We can no longer say it's someone else's problem. The influence of the world, of Satan and other fallen angels, is my problem. It's your problem. Awareness is building. Everywhere I go, I find more and more people are alarmed. I hope it means we are ready to get involved.

### Encouragement Sustains Involvement

Saving a city, a nation, or a culture never comes easily. Revival requires time, hard work, patience, and an overflow of steady confidence. Nehemiah 4 tells us that some of the people grew fainthearted. The threats of the enemy got louder, the people were intimidated, and they spread alarm (v. 12). Nehemiah responded with tactful encouragement. He posted them "by families, with their swords, spears and bows" (v. 13). He then walked among them saying,

> Don't be afraid of them. Remember the Lord, who is great and awesome, and fight for your brothers, your sons and your daughters, your wives and your homes.… The work is extensive and spread out, and we are widely separated from each other along the wall. Wherever you hear the sound of the trumpet, join us there. Our God will fight for us! (vv. 14, 19–20)

We must have no misgivings about our need for constant encouragement. As God's people rise up with the repentance necessary to bring revolutionary revival, the opposition will be fierce. As believers exercise faith to clear away the rubble of sin and rebuild walls of spiritual integrity, all hell will be threatened by what we do. The kingdom of darkness will not take such a threat lying down.

We will have to be encouraged time and again to "remember the Lord, who is great and awesome," and to know that "our God will fight for us!"

We will need to remember that our brothers, sons, daughters, wives, and homes are worth defending from such assault.

## A Place to Begin

About now you may be asking, "How can I get involved to bring revolutionary revival?" A culturewide revival necessitates extremely broad involvement of God's people, but that starts one person at a time. As we noted in chapter 8, revival begins with personal renewal. In fact, renewal is a prerequisite for revival, for we must be cleansed of sin and selfish attitudes before we can help our community. After that, consider these six guidelines to begin to inspire our community first and eventually the country.

- **Start Close to Home.** Yes, involvement begins with you. Set aside at least a weekly time when, in the privacy of your own devotional life, you begin to pray for revolutionary revival to come to your heart, family, church, city, nation, and world. We will never believe God for revival on a large scale until we can believe Him in smaller dimensions. Ask God to bring forth more intercessors to pray for revival.

- **Be Open to Enlarging Your Circle.** Everyone interested in revival should desire and expect to find at least one other person with whom he can pray regularly. Schedule your prayer times with discipline. When your prayer group grows to three or four, start another. It's better to increase the number of groups than to grow too large. Distractions multiply as numbers grow.

- **Keep the Format Simple.** Read some Scripture and begin to pray. The seven suggested prayer patterns for revival presented in this book might help you. Those who can set aside a daily time can use a different one each day. Begin to pray them back to God with a planned dedication. Make them yours, or let them be a creative beginning for writing out your own prayer petitions.

  The suggested prayers in this book can be particularly helpful in group prayer. Each person could pray a different prayer when you meet, adding your own intercessions as you pray. Alternating paragraphs between those praying helps you concentrate on the subject at hand. Learning to pray doctrinally honors God and focuses His power against evil.

- **Read Good Books on Revival Awakenings.** Intercessors are motivated by keeping the testimonies of past revivals constantly in focus. A suggested bibliography on revivals has been supplied by Richard Owen Roberts in his excellent book *Revival.* His incisive comments on many of the books can help you determine your preference.

- **Seek a Communitywide Revival Prayer Focus.** Ask the Lord to enable you to be a part of an interdenominational revival prayer focus for your area. It's important that this gathering not become just another planning group for a program, crusade, or organized evangelistic effort. Revival requires God's people to humble themselves, seek God's face, and wait upon Him. God's timing and plan will always be made known to those who trust Him. A sample letter for beginning a city-wide prayer fellowship is included in appendix E.

- **Wait and Watch with Expectancy.** Patience, perseverance, and faithfulness are the most vital ingredients for those interceding for revival. As King David reminds us in Psalm 27:14, we are to "wait for the LORD; be strong and take heart and wait for the LORD."

Believing God for revival requires an expectant, anticipating heart. Ask God to give you such expectancy, and thank Him for the work He's about to do.

## REVIVAL PRAYER PATTERN: REVIVAL PRAYER GROUPS

*Loving heavenly Father, I worship You as the God who loves people. You have declared in Your Word that You are patient with people, not wanting anyone to perish, and You have provided opportunity for everyone to come to repentance. Thank You for Your patience that brought me to saving faith in Jesus Christ. I praise You, heavenly Father, for demonstrating Your love by having Jesus Christ die for ungodly people while we were still in our sins. It is wonderful to know that You have loved humanity with such outreaching sacrifice that provides forgiveness and eternal life for all who will believe. Thank You, Lord Jesus Christ, for praying for those who would believe in You. Thank You for the other sheep that You must bring to Yourself.*

*I pray with You, dear Savior, for those other sheep that You must bring. Multitudes are bound by sin and Satan, and I ask forgiveness for me and for other believers who have cared so little for those perishing people. I acknowledge that the same sinful culture that blinds and binds the lost has made my heart cold and apathetic. Please forgive me. Grant me a burden for the lost around me. I pray for (name persons you care for who are lost). In the name of the Lord Jesus Christ, I tear down the blindness Satan is putting upon _____. I pray You will bring these dear ones to saving faith in our Lord Jesus Christ.*

*Thank You, Father in heaven, for the revival awakenings of history. I praise You for giving revival blessings in various places even in recent years. Thank You for opening my eyes to see the need for a revolutionary revival from Your omnipotent hands that will glorify You, startle the world, and bring multitudes into saving faith. I ask You to grant me a burden for such a revival. Help me to believe that it can come to my city. I humbly offer myself as an intercessor for such an awakening. Lead me to at least one other person with whom I can pray regularly for its coming. I ask You to raise up revival prayer groups in every city, town, suburb, and rural area of our nation. I ask You to build a broad base of people nationwide who are expecting revival. Grant to each group a consuming burden for You to bring revival. Make the involvement of people broad enough so that, when You sovereignly know we are ready, You will visit us with Your holy presence. Your promise is that, as we seek to draw near to You, You will draw near to us. I pray this nearness will truly be revolutionary. Make it humble us, break us, revive us, and change the direction of our disintegrating culture.*

*We desperately need a movement of Your mighty grace that will transform the lives of multitudes of people. Move our culture back to the absolutes of a Judeo-Christian ethic. Grant to us a legal system with courts that fear God and establish justice. Invade our penal system with such regeneration and reform that our jails will gradually empty until we wonder what to do with the unoccupied buildings.*

*I ask for such a transformation of our educational system that the humanistic, atheistic trends of our day will be completely reversed. I pray this revival will touch every political leader, every business enterprise, and every person in the mass media and entertainment industry. May revival clean up the music industry. I ask that the poverty, drunkenness, drugs, immorality, and violence so common in our inner cities be overwhelmed by the transformed lives of regenerated people who live there. Bring the pornography industry to its knees through the repentance of the producers and consumers. Melt the divorce scandal away into nothingness because of the righteous, forgiving, encouraging lives of families made right with You.*

*The need for revolutionary revival in the churches, Lord Jesus Christ, is perhaps the greatest need of all. I invite You to walk among us who are believers and expose our sins as You see them. Grant to Your church a thoroughly repentant spirit where jealousies, suspicions, and competitiveness evaporate in the abundance of joy that revival brings. I ask that every denomination and church that honors You and proclaims Your Word will so overflow with people that petty differences will disappear and worship that honors You will be established in the land. Enable the people to enjoy their preference of worship style in the fullness of Your Spirit.*

*Loving heavenly Father, we are people with needs far greater than we understand. Come in the fullness and power of Your Holy Spirit and minister to them all. I open my life to You. Take every part of me and do with me whatever You know needs to be done. I hold back nothing from You. I believe there is sufficient grace supplied in the person and work of Christ to do far more than I have even begun to ask. I acknowledge that the Holy Spirit is mighty enough to humble a whole world with conviction of sin and the exalting of righteousness. I acknowledge, almighty God, that You can quickly bring a world to judgment or to revival. In the name of my Lord Jesus Christ, I plead for revolutionary revival to sweep over us like a fire that cannot be quenched. Amen.*

*Chapter 12*

# PROTECTING THE PARTICIPANTS

*Be self-controlled and alert. Your enemy the devil prowls around like a roaring lion looking for someone to devour. Resist him, standing firm in the faith, because you know that your brothers throughout the world are undergoing the same kind of sufferings.*

*1 Peter 5:8–9*

Pastor Bubeck, I just had to call you. I've been a pastor here for seven years. Your counsel helped me about three years ago when I called about my own spiritual warfare problem. Practicing the warfare principles you taught me has freed me from the problem with pornography and immoral thoughts. I have victory over that, but now I'm facing something else that baffles me. In fact, my wife and I are both frightened. It's our eight-year-old boy!"

He paused in an effort to hold back the tears. Then he said, "He hears voices. Whenever he's around little girls or women these voices tell him to do immoral things. He's so tormented it's about to destroy him—and us. Can you help?"

The words the voices were using were vile, and the pastor said, "Our boy has lived a sheltered life. He couldn't think those things up himself."

Since writing my books on the believer's warfare, I have received frequent calls like this, and an increasing number come from pastors. It's fresh evidence of the battle. They face family problems or church-related problems that point directly to Satan's work. My book *The Adversary at Home* provides some specific, helpful suggestions for dealing with such spiritual warfare issues.

## The Fierce Battle

Paul warns all believers that they will encounter spiritual opposition in their life of faith. "Our struggle is not against flesh and blood, but against the rulers, against the authorities, against the powers of this dark world and against the spiritual forces of evil in the heavenly realms," he wrote in Ephesians 6:12. And Peter added, "Your enemy the devil prowls around like a roaring lion looking for someone to devour." He called on believers to "resist him, standing firm in the faith" (1 Peter 5:8–9).

The fierce battle between light and darkness is heating up. The bolder the sin of our culture becomes, the more arrogant and daring is the Enemy's intrusion.

The battle started in the garden of Eden and has plagued humanity ever since. At certain times, though, it becomes more obvious and fierce. A sinful culture filled with immorality, occultism, violence, and drug addiction arouses problems for Christians that demand action, and the battle intensifies because any move toward a spiritual revival threatens Satan's kingdom.

## As the Battle Heats Up ...

Nehemiah found the battle heating up as he proceeded with God's plans for rebuilding the walls, rehanging the gates, and reestablishing a viable government in Jerusalem. We can be sure the kingdom of darkness was not pleased. The battle was brewing even before Nehemiah began to build.

The work of "the spiritual forces of evil in the heavenly realm" usually appears first through the lives and attitudes of people under Satan's control. That's his tactic. Those of us who work with demonized people have witnessed this innumerable times. Even as I began this writing effort, people who had been looking to me to help began to feel intensified oppression. Also, the number of distressed phone calls during my first month of writing increased phenomenally.

As we will see, the battle can be subtle. But often it will heat in intensity. The more threatened the opposition feels, the more determined they become to do something about it. The opposition threatens war, bloodshed, and even death.

Wheaton College experienced a revival in 1950 much like the Asbury revival mentioned in the last chapter. Jim Elliot and Ed McCully, two of the five missionaries who would be martyred by Auca Indians in Ecuador in 1956 (and subjects of the recently released movie *End of the Spear*) were student leaders in that revival awakening. Though Satan's effort to keep the gospel from the Aucas was violent, it was also futile. These men had a heart for God that even death could not stop.

The results of their sacrifice are well known. God in His sovereignty used the shock of these men's deaths to move many others to volunteer for missionary service. The Aucas were reached. Even some of those who committed murders became evangelists and leaders of the new church.[†]

Perhaps I should warn you that the Devil hates your nation's history of Christ-exalting churches. He hates your freedom and prosperity, which enable believers to support world evangelization and missionary outreach. He hates your technology that makes possible wide and diverse means of communicating the gospel. He hates the large numbers of Christians who pray, love, and support the proponents of God. His hatred is so great he'd rather destroy us than fight us.

Even if he gets your nation's majority totally coming his way, Satan is still terribly threatened by believers. He knows the awesome potential of even a remnant of Bible-believing Christians. If we unite behind God's will and plan for world revival, mighty advancement for Christ will result—even a desire for a revival awakening terrifies the kingdom of darkness. It's the one remedy that can intervene in a national downward plunge toward total destruction.

## ... Believers Can Stay Cool

Proper understanding and use of warfare principles and praying will provide secure protection. No believer need fear Satan's threats or intimidations. As discussed in earlier chapters, if a believer carefully uses his God-supplied protection, he's more than a match for Satan's schemes. Fearless courage in the face of Enemy threats belongs to prepared believers. "The God of heaven will give us success. We his servants will start rebuilding" (Neh. 2:20).

---

[†] For a description of the impact of the five missionaries' deaths, see Olive Liefeld, "The Auca Five" in John D. Woodbridge, ed., *Ambassadors for Christ* (Chicago: Moody, 1994), 127–33.

When Nehemiah's enemies tried to get him to visit them and enter into a dialogue, his reply was fearless and firm: "I am carrying on a great project and cannot go down. Why should the work stop while I leave it and go down to you?" (6:3). If he had not been sure of his higher authority of protection, it would have been foolish for him to face these murderous enemies with such courage. Many of the other Jews working with him, because they did not know the same surety that God had taught Nehemiah, nearly fell apart under such threat (4:11–12).

For Christians to face satanic warfare with confidence and without fear they must keep two truths in mind:

- It is utter folly to presumptuously walk into battle against evil super-naturalism. When believers arrogantly assume that Satan cannot cause harm, they are soon brought to disaster. The writer to the Hebrews speaks of the Devil as the one "who holds the power of death" (2:14). He would kill believers if he could. "He was a murderer from the beginning," Jesus tells us (John 8:44). In our own strength we are no match for Satan's destructive power.

- Believers can launch a fearless warfare against the Enemy. When believers are careful to put on their armor of God's protection and claim His sovereign presence between them and violent demons, Satan's murderous intent becomes an idle threat. Once we gain bibli-cal understanding of our position in Christ and use our God-given authority protectively, our abiding, moment-by-moment appropria-tion of Christ's victory provides complete protection (see, for instance, 1 John 4:4 and Eph. 6:13).

When you become serious about praying for revolutionary revival, you may be threatened by intimidations, taunts, even clouds of death, but you are invincible to do God's will in God's way.

## THE NATURE OF OUR STRUGGLE

It's important for revival intercessors to know their battle. As we engage in this ministry, we must wear our weapons and be ready to fight while at the same time remaining absolutely fearless. We must never shrink back in the face of this war. To do so would lead to disaster.

Let's look at the nature of our struggle, which covers four key areas.

### *The Battle Will Be Insidious and Subtle*

Satan's opposition is always subtle, sometimes so elusive we miss it completely. Paul warns of this in Ephesians 6:11 "Put on the full armor of God so that you can take your stand against the devil's schemes."

The Greek word translated "schemes" is *methodeias*; other translations render schemes as "wiles" and "craftiness." Paul is talking about an evil, clever trick designed to deceive. That's how Satan approached Eve in the garden temptation, and it's how he approaches us today. He lies, and he makes the deception so clever that we miss it.

That kind of opposition came to Nehemiah. In 2:10, he shows Sanballat and Tobiah disturbed and angry. It wasn't long before their nonviolent opposition became threatening: "They mocked and ridiculed us. 'What is this you are doing?' they asked. 'Are you rebelling against the king?'" (v. 19).

The subtle threats and innuendos of these powerful political leaders were lethal. People with less dedication than what God had built into Nehemiah might have succumbed quickly. Knowing the effect the threats might have on the less committed Jewish leaders, Nehemiah responded quickly and boldly: "The God of heaven will give us success. We his servants will start rebuilding, but as for you, you have no share in Jerusalem or any claim or historic right to it" (v. 20).

Years ago when our own citywide revival prayer focus first started, my friends and I sought a neutral meeting place. One of the leading hotels offered to rent us a room overlooking the city for a reasonable fee. We rented the room for several months. Although the charge was fair enough, over the months the cost still became difficult for our small number to meet.

Someone suggested we try to influence management to lower the amount in light of the noble purpose of our prayer for our city. The managers' response was almost sarcastic scorn. Obviously, revival prayer was not wanted there. God met our need by providing a free meeting room at a local hospital, but the hotel's rejection of our preferred place was one of those subtle attacks. It stung!

We need to be watchful for the sneak attacks Satan makes on our lives. We'd be wise to memorize Nehemiah's appropriate response: "The God of heaven will give us success." Then when the subtle attack comes, we are armed and ready.

### The Adversary Will Be Deceptive and Full of Lies

Even when Satan tells the truth, he uses it to promote deception. He knows no other tactic. "There is no truth in him," Jesus has told us. "When he lies, he speaks his native language, for he is a liar and the father of lies" (John 8:44).

As the progress on the walls of Jerusalem went forth and the gaps were filled in, a consortium led by Sanballat tried a new tactic; one probably devised by Satan himself. They sent a conciliatory letter to Nehemiah with the invitation "Come, let us meet together in one of the villages on the plain of Ono." The letter seemed to say, "We see that you're determined and progressing well, so let's try to live together. Let's talk it over in a friendly way." Nehemiah wisely read the description. He stated, "But they were scheming to harm me" (6:2). He responded to their conference to Ono with, "Oh, no!" His work was too important for him to leave for any such negotiations. Four times the invitation came and four times the response was the same.

The fifth letter was a clever, devilish lie that could have produced great trouble for Nehemiah. The entire project could have been put in jeopardy. Here's what it said:

> It is reported among the nations—and Geshem says it is true—that you and the Jews are plotting to revolt, and therefore you are building the wall. Moreover, according to these reports you are about to become their king and have even appointed prophets to make this proclamation about you in Jerusalem: "There is a king in Judah!" Now this report will get back to the king; so come, let us confer together. (vv. 6–7)

Several factors reveal the insidious nature of this lie. First, the letter expressed a possible unspoken longing of Nehemiah and probably every Jew in Jerusalem. They desired to be a viable nation again, and to have Nehemiah as their king could well have been a part of that longing. No doubt Satan already planted the thoughts of the letter in Nehemiah's mind many times. Satan's forces can and do project thoughts into our minds that tempt us to act independently of the will of God. But Nehemiah was a man of integrity. He would not yield to such a temptation. Artaxerxes had trusted him to keep his word and remain loyal, and Nehemiah would do so.

Second, this lie could have tempted the Jews to try for the very thing it suggested. Word would spread through the ranks, excitement could build on the rumors, and some of the people might well have become motivated to do what the letter inferred.

Third, this lie could have undermined Artaxerxes' confidence in Nehemiah. A written accusation of this nature from these leaders could have been due cause for the king to recall Nehemiah.

Nehemiah put his answer in writing: "Nothing like what you are saying is happening; you are just making it up out of your head" (v. 8). I'm sure he kept all the correspondence on file in case further documentation might be needed, and he probably sent copies of everything by courier with his regular reports to the king. Nehemiah had nothing to hide.

This incident reveals a strategic element of Satan's methods. Though he lies about our motives, he usually touches dangerously close to where our hearts are. For example, he might accuse those forming a prayer group for revival of wanting to have a place of prominence when revival comes. Or he might tempt them to desire praise for leading a revival prayer group. Who of us in leadership positions have not been tempted to reach for some glory?

A few years ago the Billy Graham Evangelistic Association celebrated the fortieth anniversary of the Los Angeles Crusade, the early effort that would draw major attention to Billy Graham and his ministry. During Graham's LA tent meetings, I was a young man beginning my own ministry, and one report from the crusade spoke deeply to me.

A college faculty member at Northwestern College (where Billy Graham once was president) attempted to visit him in his hotel room. As he reached the door of the room, he heard the evangelist praying. Not wanting to interrupt, he turned and left, but he did overhear Dr. Graham walking and praying in his room: "Oh God! Help me to see that it's not my doing. Help me to see that it's not I. Give me grace to let You have all the glory."

We understand a prayer like that. We understand the temptation to elevate ourselves, and we understand feelings of guilt when we do. The Accuser is always busy, and he tempts us where we're vulnerable. He projects the temptation into our minds—and then he haunts us with accusations about that very temptation. It's one of his most proficient tricks.

## *The Battle Can Produce Fear*

We have already mentioned that a believer can keep cool in the battle. Nevertheless, we must acknowledge that fear is a common response. Certainly Nehemiah's enemies played on the people's tendency to fear (4:11; 6:9). Next to the lie, fear is the Enemy's most effective tool. The most direct attack upon faith is that which makes us afraid.

In the African bush where lions roam freely, the stronger lions rarely roar. They prefer to stalk their target, relying upon a quick ambush to destroy them. The older lion, whose quickness and strength is failing, relies on his roar to paralyze his prey with fear. Then he continues his charge for the kill. When fear is present, even a weakened enemy can capture and destroy the one targeted.

The roar of the Devil, who "prowls around like a roaring lion looking for someone to devour," is meant to make us afraid, but Satan is not a lion. He may roar like one, but it is just another attempt to be like God, who is the "Lion ... [who] has triumphed" (Rev. 5:5; see also Hos. 11:10; 13:7–8; Jer. 49:19; 50:44).

Jesus Christ has weakened our foe. The best Satan can do is roar. His growls are not to be feared by the Christian. The Lord Jesus Christ has defeated him. Christ alone is worthy to be reverenced and feared by believers.

The Lord Jesus Christ instructs us not to be fearful of our enemies, including Satan himself:

> So do not be afraid of them. There is nothing concealed that will
> not be disclosed, or hidden that will not be made known.... Do not

be afraid of those who kill the body but cannot kill the soul. Rather,
be afraid of the One who can destroy both soul and body in hell.
(Matt. 10:26, 28)

Fear is the complete antithesis of faith. Fear must be recognized for what
it is—the Enemy's war club. The believer's greatest weapon against it is the
Word of God. Used in doctrinal praying, as illustrated in the written prayers
of this book, God's Word puts fear to flight.

## The Battle Will Induce Religious Leaders to Speak for the Enemy

Historically some of the Enemy's best spokesmen have been respected religious leaders. Eli's two priestly sons, Hophni and Phinehas, had to be judged
with death because of their sinful example and wicked deeds (1 Sam.
2:22–36). The religious leaders of Jerusalem under the high priest Caiaphas
were used to instigate our Lord's crucifixion. They later actively opposed the
spreading of the gospel (Matt. 26:57–67; Acts 5:17–42).

Religious leaders in our day are often a part of the Enemy's camp too.
They promise "instant heaven" and superior rewards for those willing to be
killed in their "holy wars." And one does not need to look outside the
Christian faith to see religious leaders being used for the Enemy's cause.
Extravagant lifestyles, immoral living, and financial dishonesty of recognized
Christian leaders repeatedly gain top billing in the media. Disgrace comes to
the cause of Christ through those leaders who allow sin to rule them.

Religious leaders with notable scholastic credentials likewise can become
cohorts of Satan's deceptions. Some of their "educated" pronouncements cast
doubt on the authority of Scripture, on the deity of Christ, and on other major
doctrines. This makes these leaders some of the Enemy's most effective allies.
They often oppose revival awakenings, especially in the early stages. They
brand these efforts as a move toward emotionalism or fanaticism. They refer to
those who speak of revivalism as "escapists," accusing them of wanting to evade
the real world and their responsibility to meet the urgent issues of the day.

I've had such words addressed to me. After I preached a message on the
need for revival, a fellow pastor confronted me about making revival a door

of escape from my duty to act. He was very sincere. He believed the way to meet the sin challenge of our day was to confront it with organized opposition. He saw my emphasis on revival as an excuse not to be involved.

I have no quarrel with those who organize and oppose sin's advance. That has its place. But so much more is needed. The confrontational approach by itself will never be enough to turn the tide. The satanic influence in America has gained too much ground. While the good effort is being put forth to confront sin, the revival of evil keeps accelerating. Only revolutionary revival can bring the changes in people's hearts that will make the stand against evil effective. Confrontational challenge will be much more successful when regenerated legislators, born-anew judges, and converted leaders of the executive branches of government have righteous interests.

The Enemy uses many approaches to oppose God's work done in God's will. Subtle opposition will always be present. The battle may become fierce, even murderous. Half-truths and outright lies will be employed. Fear will lurk in the shadows. We may even see religious leaders joining the Enemy's entourage to defeat revival effort. Satan and his kingdom will do all they can to turn us back from God's will and plan, but Nehemiah's example confirms that victory consists of faithfully using our weapons of warfare in fearless application.

## REVIVAL PRAYER PATTERN: PROTECTION FROM THE ENEMY

*Loving heavenly Father, I worship You as the provider of my protection from the hurtful, murderous intent of my enemies. I desire not to passively assume my safety but to step deliberately with faith and understanding into that victory You have provided. Teach me how to appropriate my victory. I am listening for wise insights from You even as I address You in prayer. Teach me deeper love and understanding of Yourself even as I open my whole person to You right now.*

*I plead that mighty name You have exalted above every name—Lord Jesus Christ—over my personal life and my walk with You; over my spouse, my children, and all for whom I am responsible in my family; and over the ministry You have given to me and all for whom I am responsible in ministry. I hold the name of my Lord Jesus Christ over Your church and all of Your will and plans for the bringing of revolutionary revival. I worship my Savior. I affirm that He is*

*Lord—He is Jehovah God—the more we know of Him the more we know of You. He is Jesus, Savior. He is my Savior—there is no Savior but Him. I worship Jesus as the one who took away my sins. He is the Christ—the Anointed of God. He is the anointed Prophet who proclaimed the way and who is the way. He is the anointed Priest who offers a better sacrifice and is Himself that sacrifice for sin. He is the anointed King who now rules in His sovereign power and who will one day rule as King of Kings and Lord of Lords.*

*I seek to abide in my Lord Jesus Christ and to hide in the protection of His almightiness and my oneness with Him. I abide in His incarnation, His human-ity. How wonderful that You planned that our Savior should be one of us. The mystery of that remains beyond my capacities for full understanding.*

*I abide in the surety that He experienced all of life's temptations and never failed to meet sin's fullest challenge. He fulfilled all righteousness. He obeyed every particle of Your expectancy for us as expressed in Your law. As one of us, He pleased You, His heavenly Father, as a child, as a youth, and as an adult in every aspect of His life.*

*Thank You that as one of us He completely overcame sin. In His humanity, He never yielded to sin's enticements, though He was made in "the likeness of sin-ful flesh." The world was never able to entice Him to accept its values or to press Him into its mold. Thank You that though Satan himself and all of his demons tried to cause Him to sin, in His humanity He willed not to sin. With joy I enter into His sinless, worthy human life and expect Your blessing because You have placed His worthiness upon me. There is safety and peace here and I abide in it.*

*By faith, I abide in the death and sufferings of my Lord Jesus Christ. I claim the shelter of His precious blood over myself and those for whom I am responsi-ble. It was in the work of His sufferings and the cross that You have removed the guilt of my sins. Cleanse me through His blood from all my sins of omission and commission that would hinder my fellowship with You.*

*I abide in the suffering and death of the Lord Jesus Christ who "destroyed him who had the power of death, that is the devil." I hold the victory of the cross against the Devil and his entire kingdom. In the power of the sufferings and shed blood of my Savior, I resist all of Satan's efforts to harm me or those for whom I am responsible.*

*I affirm the mighty triumph of the Lord Jesus Christ in His resurrection from the dead. In the practical outliving of my life today, I desire to be clothed with that same mighty power that raised Jesus Christ from the dead. In His resurrection power, enable me to walk in newness of life. I address resurrection power directly against Satan and his kingdom in all his efforts to rule me and to hold back revival awakenings from coming to Christ's church.*

*By faith, I enter into the ascension of my Lord Jesus Christ, where He is seated far above all principalities and powers. Thank You, heavenly Father, for raising me up with Christ and seating me with Him in the heavenly realms. Teach me more perfectly how to rest in the safety of that lofty position and how to use that authority to pull down all of Satan's ruling tactics.*

*I abide in my Savior's glorification. I submit to Your lordship over my life, my family, and Your church. I ask You to shepherd me in Your will and to hold me in the safety of your faithful protection. I ask You to shepherd Your church to revival awakening in this day of great darkness.*

*Heavenly Father, I reach out for Your Holy Spirit and the wonder of His work. I rejoice that He came in fulfillment of the promise of both the Father and the Son. I rejoice that He convicted me and brought me to Christ, opened my eyes to see, and caused me to be born of the Spirit. Thank You that He came to live within me the moment I was saved. I invite the Holy Spirit to enable me to walk in Him, so that love, joy, peace, patience, gentleness, goodness, meekness, faithfulness, and self-control may overflow from my life. May others see this, especially those close to me. May I see His fruit, but most of all may His control be evident to You, O Lord.*

*I abide in His sealing, protecting work. I abide in His having made me a member of Christ's body. Help me to minister to the body of Christ today. I depend upon Him to breathe His quickening life and power into me. May the Holy Spirit pray through me and may He endue me with His power to witness of You before others. I pray for the mighty work of the Holy Spirit as God's "holy finger" directly against Satan and his kingdom. May the mighty power of the Holy Spirit confront and defeat the Devil in all of his hurtful designs for this day. I ask the Holy Spirit to increase His powerful work of convincing our world of sin, of righteousness, and of judgment to come.*

*By faith, I reach out for the wholeness of Your armor, heavenly Father. I receive the girdle of truth, and by faith, I wear it. Help me not to deceive or be deceived in any way.*

*I wear the breastplate of righteousness. Having none of my own righteousness, I desire to walk in the adequate supply of Your righteousness.*

*Help me to walk in my shoes of peace. I claim my peace with God through justification and my peace of God through prayer, the Spirit's work, and the near presence of the God of peace who, when my ways please Him, makes even my enemies to be at peace with me.*

*Be my shield today, dear Lord. May Your presence hedge me in and quench all of Satan's flaming arrows.*

*Protect my head with Your salvation helmet. May the Savior cover my mind to protect me from Satan's intruding thoughts. May the Lord Jesus Christ think His thoughts in my mind today.*

*I receive the Word of God as the Spirit's sword. Teach me to use it proficiently in my protection and in my witness. Help me to memorize it and to know its power.*

*I thank You, heavenly Father, that my victory in Christ is not merely protective. You have provided me safety, so that I might be bold to address my Lord's victory against everything that opposes Your will. In the name of my Lord Jesus Christ, I tear down all that Satan has strategized to hinder revival. I invite my living Lord Jesus Christ to sovereignly shepherd and lead His church into all that is necessary to bring revival. I invite the Holy Spirit to sovereignly move to prepare the people whom You have chosen to be the leaders in each phase of revival preparations. I invite the Holy Spirit to prepare those special servants through whom the call for revival will come.*

*I give myself to You, loving God and Father of our Lord Jesus Christ. In the worthiness of my Lord and in the enablement of Your Holy Spirit, I offer myself to You for any purpose You may have. Through Jesus Christ my Lord, I pray. Amen.*

*Chapter 13*

# RESOURCES AND WEAPONS FOR THE BATTLE

*For though we live in the world, we do not wage war as the world does. The weapons we fight with are not the weapons of the world. On the contrary, they have divine power to demolish strongholds.*

*2 Corinthians 10:3–4*

The servant arose early one day and stepped out on the flat roof overlooking the town of Dothan. Both he and Elisha the prophet were guests in the home of Elisha's friend. Elisha had risen earlier and was quietly praying and reading the Holy Scriptures when his servant arrived. The war with the king of Aram (called Syria in the King James Version) was going well. Every action the king of Aram attempted was thwarted—the king of Israel seemed to have advance warning about all of Aram's plans, and Israel was winning all the battles.

Yet the war had made most people in Israel very tense, and Elisha's servant felt uneasy. Word had circulated that Elisha was funneling information to Israel's king, and that meant trouble. The Aramean king would be filled with rage against Elisha.

The servant felt relieved to see Elisha seated on the rooftop, so completely at ease. As the wings of the dawn spread their brightness over the city, Elisha's servant thought, *With Elisha so calm, all must be well.*

He stretched his arms and flexed his knees in his struggle to fully awaken. Suddenly, he saw them. During the night, a great army had surrounded the city. Chariots and horses were everywhere. Enemy soldiers were quietly waiting, poised for attack. The Israelite troops stationed at Dothan were hopelessly outnumbered. Elisha's servant panicked. It was his responsibility to protect the prophet, but what could he do? Instinctively, he knew those troops were after Elisha.

Frantic desperation overtook him. He turned to Elisha, who was still calmly reading the Scriptures. "Oh, my Lord, what shall we do?" he cried. Many thoughts raced through his mind. *Doesn't he see the danger? Doesn't he care that these troops are after him? Why isn't he hiding? Why doesn't he try to escape?*

The servant's response was typical of the way God's people react when they face spiritual battles. He saw only what his physical eyes beheld. Locked into the natural perspective, he didn't consider the spiritual realm of truth. On the other hand, Elisha had more than physical sight—he had spiritual vision. Though Elisha couldn't physically see into that unseen spiritual realm where angels dwell and God's armies reside, he knew they were there. To him it was more real than the world he saw.

When he was Elijah's servant, Elisha had seen the evidence many times. Since being anointed as Elijah's successor, Elisha had grown in his awareness of the unseen world of the heavenly realm.

Elisha responded to his distraught servant with quiet calmness. "Don't be afraid.... Those who are with us are more than those who are with them" (2 Kings 6:16).

## The "More" Principle

What an important truth to know. Elisha's statement conveys to God's obedient people what we need to know in our hour of confronting satanic opposition. The forces of righteousness surpass the opposition in both numbers and power. No matter how large and threatening the opposition becomes, "Those who are with us are more than those who are with them." That's an absolute for believers who prayerfully walk in the Lord's will.

This truth rests upon the foundation of God's omnipotent, omnipresent, omniscient, immutable, and eternal attributes. He's always "more." Knowing and applying such an important truth is a must of spiritual warfare. Our resources and weapons are far superior to what Satan and the other fallen angels possess. We need only to use those weapons.

Elisha's response to the danger baffled his servant. An incredulous look portrayed the servant's inner thoughts: *There aren't enough Israeli soldiers within miles to come to our rescue. How can Elisha say such a thing?*

Seeing his servant's befuddlement, "Elisha prayed, 'O LORD, open his eyes so he may see.'" In answer to that prayer "the LORD opened the servant's eyes, and he looked and saw the hills full of horses and chariots of fire all around Elisha" (v. 17).

The servant probably experienced not only a severe shock but also a life-transforming enlargement of his faith. A mortal doesn't see supernatural, angelic scenes and remain the same.

## GOD'S GOOD ANGELS

Which kind of vision characterizes us? That's the heart of this chapter. We need to recognize and use the supernatural resources we have.

As the army of the king of Aram advanced to take Elisha captive and bring him back to their king, God's servant prayed again, saying, "Strike these people with blindness" (v. 18).

It happened in an instant. The God who opened the eyes of Elisha's servant to the supernatural now closed the eyes of the Aramean army to the natural. Blind and in a stunned stupor, the soldiers were helpless. Elisha led the enemy troops into the very presence of the king of Israel at Samaria. At Elisha's suggestion the king did not harm them. Their sight then returned and Israel's king treated them to a royal banquet instead of violent death. Afterward he sent them home to their nation and families. The king of Aram was so amazed by this whole turn of events that he stopped his war raids into Israel's territory. Peace prevailed.

What a beautiful story to give God's people—a true vision of our victory. We need to know of our spiritual allies and their infinite superiority over all adversaries. Yes, the fallen angels remain our enemies, but God's good angels are our allies, mighty helpers who serve God and us in the battle against satanic forces.

## The Reality of Evil Supernaturalism

God seems to be bringing back to His church a renewed perspective of what Ed Murphy has termed "evil supernaturalism." Overseas, believers do recognize the spiritual nature of the battle. During the summer of 1989 in Manila, for instance, delegates to the Lausanne II Congress on evangelism approved twenty-one affirmations, including a focus on spiritual warfare. Affirmation No. 11 stated: "We affirm that spiritual warfare demands spiritual weapons, and that we must both preach the Word in the power of the Spirit, and pray constantly that we may enter into Christ's victory over the principalities and powers of evil" (*Manila Manifesto*).

In North America, however, the idea that believers are involved in close struggle with evil has been neglected as a biblical view. The concept of influencing nations and people has been generally dismissed as irrelevant. A believer's conflict with spirit beings has been relegated to the realm of superstition or ignorance. Evangelicals have preferred psychological answers for almost all problem areas.

Westernized, evangelical Christianity appears to have suffered from a "secularized brainwashing," because God's Word extensively recognizes this battle. Certainly Christ's apostles recognized that evil spirits existed; such spirits were a crucial part of the apostles' worldview. The believer's battle with evil spirits is a major theme in epistles like Ephesians, Colossians, and 1 and 2 Peter. God never intended that warfare with darkness be relegated to a mental nod of friendly assent. Evil supernaturalism must be faced directly and boldly by using the spiritual weapons of warfare.

Several of the epistles clearly set forth the believer's day-by-day battle with Satan's kingdom:

"Resist the devil, and he will flee from you" (James 4:7).

"Resist him [the Devil], standing firm in the faith" (1 Peter 5:9).

"Dear friends, do not believe every spirit, but test the spirits to see whether they are from God" (1 John 4:1).

"We know … that the whole world is under the control of the evil one" (1 John 5:19).

"Put on the full armor of God so that you can take your stand against the devil's schemes. For our struggle is not against flesh and blood, but against the rulers, against the authorities, against the powers of this dark world and against the spiritual forces of evil in the heavenly realms" (Eph. 6:11–12).

These samples of texts from the New Testament epistles speak plainly of the believer's authority and responsibility. One wonders how evangelicals could become so neglectful of resisting the Enemy in our daily battle with evil supernaturalism—the biblical worldview stresses it so strongly. Hope for world evangelization and revolutionary revival demands that believers recognize the truth: The world of darkness fiercely opposes the good. The fallen angels hate revival. If we ignore Satan's work, we will never overcome his schemes against a revival awakening. Our only hope is to aggressively apply Christ's victorious work over Satan. That's a truth we must not ignore.

## VICTORY THROUGH CHRIST'S AUTHORITY

Paul's epistle to the Colossians establishes firm ground for confidence in our battle with Satan. Let's examine some major points.

First, Paul declares the full authority of the Lord Jesus Christ over darkness. "[God] has rescued us from the dominion of darkness and brought us into the kingdom of the Son he loves" (1:13). Then, he declares our Savior's deity through His creation work and shows that this establishes His authority over Satan's kingdom: "He is the image of the invisible God [His deity], the firstborn over all creation. For by him all things were created … whether thrones or powers or rulers or authorities; all things were created by him and for him" (vv. 15–16).

Christ created Satan and all of those angelic beings that serve Satan. He created them perfect, but rebellion caused their fall. Still, by right of the creator being greater than His creation, He retains full authority over them. This argument is stated even more forcefully in the next verse: "He is before all things, and in him all things hold together" (v. 17).

We have a striking picture here: Jesus Christ alone holds together that which He has created, including the entire kingdom of darkness. It would immediately disintegrate into nothingness without Christ holding it together. If it were not within God's sovereign purpose to allow it to continue for a reason, satanic thrones, powers, rulers, and authorities would fly apart.

That's a dramatic revelation concerning our Lord Jesus Christ's total authority and total victory over Satan's kingdom.

Here's something even more dramatic: The Lord Jesus Christ chose to share this great victory and authority with His church (vv. 18–29).

In His bodily human form, Christ won our victory, and His full authority over darkness and over Satan's kingdom is transmitted to us who believe.

> For in Christ all the fullness of the Deity lives in bodily form, and you have been given fullness in Christ, who is the head over every power and authority ... having been buried with him in baptism and raised with him through your faith in the power of God, who raised him from the dead. (2:9–10, 12)

This victory came to us because Christ paid the penalty for our sins: His oneness with His church transfers His victory to believers. His resurrection bestows upon us newness of life (vv. 13–15). In His ascension He lifts us into the heavenly realm. "Having disarmed the power and authorities ... triumphing over them by the cross," Christ gives us authority over darkness in our oneness with Him (v. 15).

## THE DISARMED ENEMY

Through the redemptive work Christ did in His humanity, the power of Satan and his kingdom over the lost no longer applies to believers (Eph. 2:1–2). Christ has disarmed our Enemy.

When a believer knows and stands by faith in such promises, he has complete confidence of his authority and can apply his victory with courage.

In working with those suffering with demonization, I've never yet found (and I know I never will) any power of darkness manifesting itself that didn't have to admit that the believer has this full authority over all wicked spirits. Believers are "more than conquerors through him who loved us" (Rom. 8:37).

There may be even deeper ramifications to the believer's positional authority than most believers have been bold enough to practice. I refer to biblical statements such as these:

"In fact, no one can enter a strong man's house and carry off his possessions unless he first ties up the strong man. Then he can rob his house" (Mark 3:27).

"I tell you the truth, whatever you bind on earth will be bound in heaven, and whatever you loose on earth will be loosed in heaven" (Matt. 18:18).

"I am sending you to them to open their eyes and turn them from darkness to light, and from the power of Satan to God, so that they may receive forgiveness of sins and a place among those who are sanctified by faith in me" (Acts 26:17–18).

"Be self-controlled and alert. Your enemy the devil prowls around like a roaring lion looking for someone to devour. Resist him, standing firm in the faith, because you know that your brothers throughout the world are undergoing the same kind of sufferings" (1 Peter 5:8–9).

"Submit yourselves, then, to God. Resist the devil, and he will flee from you. Come near to God and he will come near to you" (James 4:7–8).

Each of these texts has to do with the believer exercising his authority over Satan, the kingdom of darkness, and the work that kingdom desires to do. The careful use of one's authority within the prescribed will of God is not only a privilege but also a responsibility.

The Bible teaches that Satan's demons carry forth his program through strongholds of darkness throughout the earth and that his rule is powerful enough to cause spiritual blindness to unbelievers everywhere. As Paul wrote, "The god of this age has blinded the minds of unbelievers, so that they cannot see the light of the gospel of the glory of Christ" (2 Cor. 4:4). Paul told the believers at Ephesus that Satan controlled unbelievers, calling Satan "the ruler of the kingdom of the air, the spirit who is now at work in those who are disobedient" (2:2).

Thus Satan's extensive work seems to include every nonbeliever, no matter where he or she is located.

## Satan's Organization

Since Satan is not omnipresent like God, how can he do such an extensive work, blinding unbelievers everywhere and cleverly working within them to keep them disobedient? He does it through the highly structured kingdom that he holds in his powerful rule.

Colossians and Ephesians give us limited insight into the organized structure of this evil kingdom. Satan is the commander-in-chief (Eph. 6:11), and under him there seem to be at least six levels of authority overseeing his worldwide program. Colossians 1:16 identifies thrones (*thronoi*) and dominions or lordships (*kouriotates*) as the first two levels of authority under Satan. Both Colossians and Ephesians list the next two levels as rulers (*arkai*) and authorities (*exousei*). Ephesians 6:12 carries the organized structure on to the two remaining levels of powers of this dark world (*kosmokratopas*) and spiritual forces of evil (*ponarias, pneumatika*). The structure appears like a human military chain of command with everything funneling to and from Satan. This means that, although Satan is not omnipresent, he does have a semblance of an omnipresent kingdom working to govern humanity and control their inner lives. That's a formidable network of darkness holding unbelievers in bondage.

This organized kingdom affects believers also. Passages like Ephesians 6:10–18 remind us that those in Satan's network are our formidable foes. They wrestle against us to hinder our walking in God's will and fulfilling God's plans.

### *Territorial Control*

The Old Testament seems to verify the concept of satanic forces being assigned to carry out Satan's program in various geographic areas. Daniel had a vision concerning a coming "great war." His understanding of the meaning of what he'd seen was limited, so he sought more enlightenment from God. Daniel 10 records his three-week fast and humbling before the Lord as he sought further insight. A heavenly messenger finally arrived with these words for Daniel:

> Do not be afraid, Daniel. Since the first day that you set your mind
> to gain understanding and to humble yourself before your God,

your words were heard, and I have come in response to them. But the prince of the Persian kingdom resisted me twenty-one days. Then Michael, one of the chief princes, came to help me because I was detained there with the king of Persia. (10:12–13)

After delivering God's message to Daniel, the messenger revealed more of this struggle between holy and evil angels:

Soon I will return to fight against the prince of Persia, and when I go, the prince of Greece will come.… (No one supports me against them except Michael, your prince. And in the first year of Darius the Mede, I took my stand to support and protect him.) (10:20—11:1)

This passage shows unseen forces of evil angels on the "prince" level who exercise some territorial control over Greece and Persia. These spirit beings battled against this unnamed holy angel and Michael, "one of the chief princes," who is also called "the archangel" (Jude v. 9). He seems to be the holy angel with special assignment to protect Daniel and, by implication, the nation of Israel.

Scriptures indicate that unseen demonic powers work behind the scenes in every visible government, seeking to influence their philosophies, policies, courses of direction, and political actions. This influence is particularly evident in those governments that hinder the gospel, persecute Christians, or terrorize people. Who could doubt the Nazi policy to destroy the Jews was of demonic origin?

### Activity Assignments

The Scriptures imply that this large-scale, highly organized system of evil powers carries on an extensive warfare against God's plan (Matt. 12:25–26; John 12:31; 14:30). The assignments given to these malevolent powers can affect virtually every facet of human life. The Word of God speaks about numerous areas where the Enemy is active:

- They promote idolatry, witchcraft, sorcery, and all manner of false religious teachings and systems (Deut. 32:17; Ps. 94:4–5; 1 Tim. 4:1–4; 1 John 4:1–4; Rev. 13:4, 15).

- They cause or intensify physical ailments or hurts. They can cause seizures (Mark 9:20; Luke 9:39); physical crippling (Luke 13:11, 16); blindness (Matt. 12:22); the inability to hear or speak (Matt. 9:33; Mark 9:17–29); and some physical injuries (Mark 5:5; 9:22).
- They promote sexual perversions and the vilest kind of human behavior (Rom. 1:18–32; 1 Cor. 5:1–5; Eph. 2:1–3; Rev. 18:2–3).
- They influence God's people and cause them to dishonor the Lord Jesus Christ (Acts 5:1–6; 1 Tim. 4:1–4; Rev. 2:12–17, 20–26).
- They can conceal the truth of the gospel from unbelievers (2 Cor. 4:3–4; 2 Thess. 3:1–3).
- They cause severe emotional disorders and try to bring individuals to self-destruction (Mark 9:22; Luke 8:27–35).

When people are involved in these problems, it cannot always be directly attributed to Satan's work, but in many cases it can.

How do we defeat this formidable force of evil that functions from the advantage of an unseen realm? The satanic enemy is highly structured, cooperative, organized, myriad in number, and all conspiring together to defeat and destroy God's people and God's work. How can we cope with that?

Nehemiah used holy weapons to gain his victory over the enemy. For us to defeat Satan and the other fallen angels, we need to use these weapons as well.

### An Understanding of Doctrinal Authority

Nehemiah rallied his followers back in Jerusalem, basing his bold authority on a revealed truth: God is powerful and good, and He will remain faithful to His people. Here are his words to the people and his rebuke to their opponents.

> I answered them by saying, "The God of heaven will give us success. We his servants will start rebuilding, but as for you, you have no share in Jerusalem or any claim or historic right to it." (2:20)

Understanding his God-given authority underlies every phase of Nehemiah's victory over his enemies. A solid doctrinal foundation is essential for the application of spiritual warfare victory. Nehemiah knew that his plan to rebuild the walls, rehang the gates, and reestablish a viable government in Jerusalem was founded on God's promises. He had the promise to Abraham and the writings of prophets like Isaiah and Jeremiah to claim.

In contrast, the detractors under Satan's control had no God-given right or historic biblical claim to Jerusalem. Any victory over darkness must rest on the sure promises of God expressed in His Word. This requires that we understand doctrinal truths about God's character and promises.

## A Total Dependence upon God—and Expressing It in Prayer

Nehemiah's prayer life was aggressive in resisting the enemy and causing trouble for him. He knew where the victory lay—in God alone. Hear both his urgency and forcefulness in calling upon God to assist the people:

> Hear us, O our God, for we are despised. Turn their insults back on
> their own heads. Give them over as plunder in a land of captivity.
> Do not cover up their guilt or blot out their sins from your sight,
> for they have thrown insults in the face of the builders. (4:4–5)

"Turn their insults back on their own heads" is the kind of praying that reverses the demonic curses of our enemies and creates pain of their own making among their ranks.

Whenever the enemy pressed in, Nehemiah resorted to prayer. "But we prayed to the God of heaven" was his constant refrain as the enemies' threats increased.

## Alertness to the Battle and a Willingness to Fight

Prayer was backed up with great emphasis on watchfulness and readiness to do battle. In Nehemiah 4, we can see this attitude on three different occasions:

"But we prayed to our God and posted a guard day and night to meet this threat" (v. 9).

"After I looked things over, I stood up and said to the nobles, the officials and the rest of the people, 'Don't be afraid of them. Remember the Lord, who is great and awesome, and fight for your brothers, your sons and your daughters, your wives and your homes'" (v. 14).

"Neither I nor my brothers nor my men nor the guards with me took off our clothes; each had his weapon, even when he went for water" (v. 23).

Nehemiah and the people practiced a constant state of alertness, just as Ephesians 6 instructs New Testament followers of Christ to put on their armor and be ready (vv. 13–18). Our Enemy is no pushover. The battle is real, and it requires a high degree of attention to weaponry and alert guard duty as we utilize the weapons of our warfare.

### Assurance of the Victory

When God's people apply their biblical authority with prayerful dependence upon God, the ultimate victory is sure. We may not see it in "fifty-two days" or even in the time frame we desire, but God's promised victory always comes. With the promise of victory comes a confidence, an assurance that allows us to continue strong in the battle. That's why the apostle John wrote to us, "This is the victory that has overcome the world, even our faith" (1 John 5:4).

Such assurance motivated the Jewish builders back to the wall, and they continued at the task until success was theirs:

> When our enemies heard that we were aware of their plot and that God had frustrated it, we all returned to the wall, each to his own work. (Neh. 4:15)

> So the wall was completed on the twenty-fifth of Elul, in fifty-two days. (6:15)

It's good to see how Nehemiah's enemies, who seemed such a strong threat to the whole project in the first six chapters, faded into insignificance. After the wall was completed, they were scarcely mentioned in the remaining seven chapters. A proper use of authority won the victory.

### A Heart of Courage

Someone said, "When you're in trouble and your knees knock, kneel on them." That's the secret of the believer's fearless courage. Courage is not the absence of fear; it is the mastery of it.

Again, it is based on knowing our resources in God. Nehemiah and his people mastered fear by recognizing their resources. Faced with a threat of death and told to hide in the temple from would-be assassins, Nehemiah refused. Instead he answered: "Should a man like me run away? Or should one like me go into the temple to save his life? I will not go!" (6:11).

When one enters into warfare against Satan's kingdom, the roar of threat will sometimes be exceedingly strong. Death may even be faced, but that is really no threat for a believer. We need only to remember Jesus' promise to Martha and all who believe in Him: "I am the resurrection and the life. He who believes in me will live, even though he dies; and whoever lives and believes in me will never die" (John 11:25–26).

For a believer in Jesus Christ, courage in the face of death is a birthright. Our Savior entered death and came back out, victorious over the grave. As the apostle John wrote, "They overcame him by the blood of the Lamb and by the word of their testimony; they did not love their lives so much as to shrink from death" (Rev. 12:11).

### An Expectation of God's Sovereign Provision

In spiritual warfare, it's always God's divine provision that defeats the Enemy and wins the victory. The apostle Paul tells us that the believers' warfare weapons are sufficient to "demolish strongholds" (2 Cor. 10:3–5). Satan has organized his supernatural, unseen, powerful strongholds into thrones, dominions, principalities, authorities, powers of this dark world, and spiritual forces of evil. Yet the psalmist reminds us, "The LORD is the stronghold of my life—of whom shall I be afraid?" (27:1) and "the LORD is ... a stronghold in times of trouble" (9:9).

Nehemiah knew and lived that truth. The mighty are not really mighty when confronted by the Almighty. All strongholds of Satan must yield to God, who is our stronghold.

"When all our enemies heard about this," wrote Nehemiah, "all the surrounding nations were afraid and lost their self-confidence, because they realized that this work had been done with the help of our God" (6:16).

I challenge each reader to become confrontational and address the victory of Christ against Satan's hindrances to revival. The following prayer pattern for revival focuses on coming against the Enemy by using these divinely appointed weapons.

## REVIVAL PRAYER PATTERN: COMING AGAINST THE ENEMY

*Loving heavenly Father, You are the stronghold of my life; of whom shall I be afraid? I worship You and love You for being omnipotent, almighty, and absolute in Your transcendent greatness and unequaled power. Thank You that, no matter how formidable and threatening the forces of darkness become, those who are with us are always "more" than those who are with them. I affirm that Your almightiness is unapproachable by any challenger and that Your power is full of glory.*

*I worship You, heavenly Father, in the worthy merit of the Lord Jesus Christ. I affirm that He is Lord to the glory of God the Father. I hold all of His person and work directly upon my life as my protection during this time of prayer. I choose to abide in His incarnation, His cross, His resurrection, His ascension, and His glorification.*

*I come in humble obedience to use the weapons of my warfare against the darkness that is seeking to rule the people of my city, country, and world. I affirm that the weapons You have given me to use are filled with divine power that is sufficient to demolish every stronghold Satan has built to hold back Your will and plan.*

*I confess the awful wickedness and sins that I, my family, my fellow believers, and my culture have committed. Wash me afresh in the blood of my Lord Jesus Christ that there may be no hindrance to Your fellowship and blessing upon me. I apologize to You for the offense against You represented in the wicked sins characterizing our culture. I recognize that when people abandon themselves in such sinful rebellion, much ground is being given to Satan to rule in our culture. My only hope is knowing that the finished work of my Lord Jesus Christ is sufficient payment for even these. I ask you to bring about all that is necessary to grant us the gift of repentance and a broken humility before You. I invite You to draw near to the people of our day until we are humbled and broken before You in a revival awakening greater than any that has ever been.*

*In the mighty name of my Lord Jesus Christ, I use the weapons of my warfare to demolish and weaken every throne, dominion, princely ruler, authority, power of darkness, and wicked spirit in the heavenly realm that is organized and* strategized to hinder revival. I ask the Holy Spirit to hold the mighty power of the shed blood and finished work of my Lord Jesus Christ constantly against these strongholds to cause their destruction and defeat.

In the name of the Lord Jesus Christ and by the power of His blood, I pull down all levels of the stronghold of _____. (Choose items from the following list of areas of Satan's strongholds that you desire to pull down and smash. You may think of other things—the list is suggestive, not exhaustive.)

Pornography
Perverted sexual practices
Adultery and prostitution
Drug use and promotion
Alcohol addiction
Abortion practices and promotion
Unbelief and humanism
Neo-pagan teaching
Occult promotion and activity
Satan worship
Television and media distortions
Religious cults and isms (name those you know)
Liberal theology and false doctrines
Divisive influences in the body of Christ
Violence and abuse
Child abuse in all its forms
Divorce and family disunity
Materialism and greed
Peer pressure
Spiritual deafness and spiritual blindness
Blocking of people from sharing their faith
Blocking of people from receiving Christ
Lack of care for the homeless and hurting
Disunity and distrust in Christ's body
Attacks on pastors, Christian workers, and their families

*Interest in spiritism and evil supernaturalism*

*Promotion of hate, rage, and violent anger*

*Hindrance of the recruitment and funding of missionaries*

*Pride, spiritual haughtiness, and indifference*

*Neglect of Bible study and prayer*

*I pull down these strongholds in the name of my Lord Jesus Christ, and I pray their wicked work back upon themselves. I ask my loving Father in heaven to assign His holy angels to engage in direct combative defeat of these strongholds of evil. I bind the work of evil powers in each of these strongholds, and I invite the Holy Spirit to unleash His mighty, convicting power upon the people who are in bondage to them.*

*I ask Him to exalt the ways of righteousness before the spiritual understanding of such people and to convict them deeply of their accountability to God in coming judgment. I ask the Holy Spirit to open their spiritual eyes to see their need for the saving grace of our Lord Jesus Christ. May this revival for which I pray bring multitudes into a saving relationship with Him.*

*I address my prayer against the strongholds assigned to keep God's people from believing You for revival awakening. Surely there must be many who are working to make Your people lukewarm and satisfied with our materialism and blind to our spiritual needs. I pull down all such strongholds, named and unnamed, and I pray for a great moving of the Holy Spirit to bring to us a hungering and a thirsting after righteousness. May the Holy Spirit arouse in Christ's body an insatiable appetite to memorize, study, and know God's Holy Word.*

*In the name of my Lord Jesus Christ I plead for a revolutionary revival to visit my heart, my family, my church, and the whole body of Christ until it spills over upon the world around us and brings many souls into glory. Amen.*

*Chapter 14*

# UNITED WE STAND

*Be completely humble and gentle; be patient, bearing with one another in love. Make every effort to keep the unity of the Spirit through the bond of peace. There is one body and one Spirit—just as you were called to one hope when you were called—one Lord, one faith, one baptism; one God and Father of all, who is over all and through all and in all.*

*Ephesians 4:2–6*

The following letter from a church member added to the frustration and hurt I was already feeling in my pastoral role. Sara (name has been changed) was blunt and yet sincere. I reread a portion of the letter.

Preacher Bubeck:

Why don't you just leave our church? You're causing so much trouble with your horrible, negative leadership. We always had a church of marvelous unity until you came as our pastor. Under our beloved Dr. Adams we all got along so well together.

I understand some of our leaders asked you to leave quietly, and you've refused. Why do you have to do this to us? Remember, God is listening and expecting your resignation to insure the ongoing of our great church according to His future plans for us. It is up to you to answer our request as soon as possible.

For the good of our church,

Sara Jones

In my twenty-four years of pastoral ministry, I never had faced anything like this. The churches I had been privileged to pastor had been wonderfully united with a positive outlook upon ministry. My preaching had been commended for its expository, doctrinal style. Any threatened troubles had quickly vanished when handled with humility and prayer. My pastoral leadership had enjoyed strong support from the people.

Now, though, the problem would not disappear. We held several "clear the air" forums where I answered any questions anyone had submitted in writing, but afterward a minority group still wasn't satisfied. They were determined to force my resignation.

## The Story of "Divide and Conquer"

It all began two and a half years earlier when I had accepted a nearly unanimous call to become the senior pastor of this large historic church in the heart of one of our great cities. Though the pastorate there was difficult in many ways, it had also been rewarding. I had never witnessed so many people growing spiritually in such a short time. The majority of members seemed hungry for God's Word.

The major battle was in the spiritual realm. Frequently, I would get to church before any other staff members arrived and walk and pray in the sanctuary. I will never forget the battles fought there. I also sensed great struggle when I preached; unseen forces seemed determined to resist me and the message. It was difficult not to be discouraged, even though I knew I was in the place of God's appointment.

### The Ad Hoc Committee

The crisis came during the summer while I was away on vacation. A long-tenured staff person cast some negative aspersions upon my pastoral leadership and resigned. When I returned, an ad-hoc committee of seven asked to have a private conference with me. I agreed, although I was not comfortable with such a meeting when our constituted church leadership was bypassed.

At the meeting, the committee suggested my pastoral leadership was not meeting the expectations of a "large number" of influential congregation members. They had no desire to "dirty my name" by bringing the matter to a church vote—but if they had to, they would. They reminded me of a peculiar bylaw of that church: In case a vote of confidence was requested, the pastor would need a 75 percent supportive vote to stay. They assured me I would never receive that percentage.

Their request was completely unexpected and very confrontational, yet I sensed within myself a quiet, deep inner peace. I responded with, "I sensed a strong call from my Lord to come to this church, and I will have to sense just as strong a release from Him before I can resign. Unless He gives me such a sense of release, I will have to stay, regardless of any dirtying of my name that might result."

Their determination and my response set in motion months of deep turmoil in the church. Petitions calling for a vote of confidence were circulated. Both major boards expressed strong majority support for my continued pastoral leadership, but clouds of disunity were everywhere. Some of the most painful experiences possible occur when believers quarrel with one another.

## The Vote

The day for the confidence vote was set. Much prayer ascended, and most of the leaders and congregation expected a supportive vote.

However, an unexpected development altered the situation. A key issue had been whether I intended to lead the church out of the denominational convention with which it was affiliated. I'd stated clearly in the forums that I would not do that, but a week before the vote, one of my detractors received a solicited letter from a man in my former pastorate. This man's letter stated that I had never been a strong supporter of the convention, and I probably would lead the church out.

The letter was copied and circulated widely just before the vote. Though the man who authored the letter wrote a retraction letter, it was too late. Some people assumed, "Where there's smoke, there's fire."

The vote was 69 percent supportive for me to stay on as pastor. My resignation became necessary. Some rejoiced, but the majority were crushed. Tears flowed freely. People were in a state of shock. Some were very angry, and they determined to reverse the decision.

They had private strategy meetings and later presented me with a number of alternatives. Many felt the provision requiring 75 percent approval violated state laws and wanted me to let them appeal it to the courts. But I could not allow that in good conscience. I had known the provision was in the bylaws when I accepted the call. Besides, God could have sovereignly given me a 75 percent majority vote as well as 69 percent.

Other suggestions came. I should lead in the formation of a new church. Or I should just not resign and continue in this ministry, forcing the minority to take it to court.

Any of these suggestions, though well intentioned, would have violated my personal integrity. I felt I could do nothing but resign and allow the church to come back together under a new pastor. This might not be the Lord's direction in every similar situation, but I knew it was His plan for me. I did sense His release, so I resigned. The majority gave my wife and me a royal farewell, presented us with a phenomenal love gift, and continued my full-time salary for four months. They also changed the bylaws immediately, so that a minority could never again dismiss a pastor. The majority chose the pastoral search committee and led in the call of a new pastor.

I had hoped the new leader would be able to unite the body, but it did not happen. The minority group took him and the church to court several times but without success. They ultimately left the church, and the church did eventually withdraw from the convention—the very thing I would not have allowed.

The sovereign workings of our Lord are indeed beyond finding out, and His disciplines are at times strangely ironic.

## THE PROBLEMS FROM WITHIN

That account from the journal of my life focuses on the greatest problem God's people ever face. The most threatening and painful area of attack upon any group of God's people is from within, not without. As we have seen, the external enemies of Nehemiah and his fellow builders were formidable. Yet the problems within the Jewish community were even more threatening to his call to rebuild the walls. It's the same in Christ's church.

A number of years ago Bruce Shelley, a gifted seminary professor and church historian, quoted a late medieval manuscript: "The church is something like Noah's Ark. If it weren't for the storm outside, you couldn't stand the smell inside" (Brown, 17).

Such is the case in the church today. Our internal problems have devastated the witness of the church. Arguments over choice of hymns, a pastor's preaching style, and even what is served at a church potluck[†] have led to divisions within local churches and even church splits. Local churches feel the impact of such dissension the most, but denominations also feel it in battles over troubling issues. Parachurch organizations are torn by internal dispute. Yet in spite of all these expressions of internal dissension, God's sovereign ability to work out His will has enabled Christ's work to move forward. That's to the praise of His glory.

An admonition from the apostle Peter has an important message for believers who are hoping for revival: "For it is time for judgment to begin with the family of God; and if it begins with us, what will the outcome be for those who do not obey the gospel of God?" (1 Peter 4:17).

We believers need to clean up our act before the eyes of a holy God and the eyes of a scorning world. Our internal problems are terribly destructive.

## How Nehemiah Handled Disunity

As Nehemiah exhorted the people to rebuild the city walls, he was able to rebuff the conspiracy of Sanballat, Tobiah, the Arabs, and others (4:7–9). But the internal dissenters threatened to undermine the project in a few short days. The problems were so threatening that Nehemiah declared, "When I heard their outcry and these charges, I was very angry" (5:6).

Although we are not given the detailed accounts of these internal problems, we can synthesize the situation from biblical evidence. A serious famine broke out within Jerusalem. Several factors contributed to this problem. With Sanballat, Tobiah, and the others opposing the people's efforts to rebuild, there was no flow of commerce between them and the builders.

---

[†] Robert Moeller in *Love in Action* (Multnomah, 1994) describes a major church battle that began as an argument about whether Cool Whip or real whip cream should be used as a topping to a gelatin salad. Eventually the church split; today it no longer exists, "due in part to [the] incident that took place in the church kitchen one Sunday afternoon." The story introduces an appropriately entitled article, "How to Split a Church," in *Moody*, February 1995, 22.

Also, at Nehemiah's request, most of the Jewish people were putting all their efforts toward rebuilding the walls, leaving them little time to grow food. Their large families created a constant demand for food, and, since they couldn't grow it, they had to buy it. When money ran out, they had to borrow, and they put up their fields, vineyards, and houses as surety. They also had to pay a real estate or "ground tax" to the king of Persia.

The common Jewish folk faced a dilemma. They had to borrow from their more wealthy Jewish brothers, and they were to pay the loans back with generous interest. Not earning any money, they could not repay their loans, so the creditors took advantage of the situation. They took the debtors' children into service to work off the debt (5:1–5). This debt slavery happened within the Jewish community and not with foreign lenders. These wealthy Jews were clustering around dire circumstances like vultures hovering over a wounded animal.

Nehemiah responded to this internal problem in several ways, including anger over the injustice of Jewish people profiteering at the expense of their countrymen, taking time to think things through carefully, and confronting the wrongdoers (vv. 6–7). Three other actions he took suggest how seriously Christians should regard disunity and work to maintain (or restore) harmony within the local church, the body of Christ.

### Nehemiah Assembled the Larger Body to Solve the Problem

There are times when our guilt renders us silent. That happened to those who had charged their brothers high interest rates and then enslaved their children to pay the debts. The law of Moses had forbidden the wealthier Israelites to charge high interest to poorer people (Ex. 22:25; Lev. 25:35–37; Deut. 23:19–20).

> So I called together a large meeting to deal with them and said: "As far as possible, we have bought back our Jewish brothers who were sold to the Gentiles. Now you are selling your brothers, only for them to be sold back to us!" They kept quiet, because they could find nothing to say. (Neh. 5:7–8)

Nehemiah let their silence hang for several moments, letting the time lapse do its work. One can sense a change of mood taking place. The combative confronter became the correcting teacher.

"What you are doing is not right," Nehemiah then said. He recognized how the action was undermining their influence in the pagan world. "Shouldn't you walk in the fear of our God to avoid the reproach of our Gentile enemies?" (v. 9). The appearance of disunity should not be ignored or denied; it must be addressed by the local body in a meeting of the membership.

### Nehemiah Identified with the Sins of His Nobles

When we want to help those who are sinning greatly, we'll do a better job if we can identify with them on a common ground. Nehemiah's investigations had revealed that his own family was doing some of the same types of things that made Nehemiah so angry. "I and my brothers and my men are also lending the people money and grain," he said. "But let the exacting of usury stop!" (v. 10).

The Hebrew text implies that Nehemiah not only acknowledged the sins of his own family members, but he also assumed the responsibility for what they were doing. It always adds weight to the correction process when the corrector admits his own guilt. Nehemiah was a master at that (Neh. 1:6–7).

### Nehemiah Stated the Correction Necessary, and He Built in Accountability Safeguards

When restitution is necessary, it's good to spell it out clearly, leaving no room for misunderstanding. Nehemiah's call for restitution was specific:

> Give back to them immediately their fields, vineyards, olive groves and houses, and also the usury you are charging them—the hundredth part of the money, grain, new wine and oil. (5:11)

These wealthy people were on the spot. Their sins had been exposed, and a pattern of correction was made clear. To their credit, they affirmed their willingness to correct the wrong.

> "We will give it back," they said. "And we will not demand anything more from them. We will do as you say." (v. 12)

Nehemiah was glad to hear their agreement, but knowing human nature, he also built accountability into their verbal agreement. He insisted that they formalize it with a solemn oath before the priests. This was not merely a verbal oath; it also carried a commitment. The priests in such instances were like a court of appeal. If a noble failed in his oath, the sufferer could appeal to the priests for help. Nehemiah then reminded the men that if they failed to fulfill their agreement, God would deal with them (vv. 12–13).

Accountability of this nature provides motivation for proper living within God's family. When we realize that God holds each of us accountable for righting our wrongs, we become strongly motivated. That's a notable ingredient in revival. It's also an absolute: No believer ever gets away with wronging his brother. If not made right, it either will be dealt with in discipline now (Heb. 12:1–15) or be fully rectified at the judgment seat of Christ (2 Cor. 5:1–10)

## KEEPING THE BODY HEALTHY

When believers' hearts are not right with one another or with God, He holds back His power. The very heart of revival, therefore, needs to be a focus of believers getting their internal problems remedied.

The church is known as the body of Christ, based on Paul's metaphor in 1 Corinthians 12. Keeping the body healthy is crucial to revival power. Let's examine seven important ingredients suggested by biblical passages for keeping the internal unity of the body functioning properly.

### Be Alert to the Threat

Paul expressed the constant attitude we should have concerning our relationships with other believers: "Be alert and always keep on praying for all the saints" (Eph. 6:18). Pastors, elders, deacons, and spiritually concerned believers need to be alert continually. We must maintain an attentive and prayerful watch for any internal threat to the body.

"We need to get back to the New Testament church!" I heard that expression a lot during my pastoral training years. It implied that the New Testament church always did things the way they should be done. When I heard that, I often would respond with, "Which New Testament church?"

Not every church was worthy of following as an example. The church at Corinth, for instance, was filled with tragic internal problems, including: a four-way split brought on by carnal pride (1 Cor. 1:11–17; 3:1–9); a believer living with his father's wife (5); use of godless, secular courts to resolve disputes with each other (6:1–11); sexual immorality and marital disharmony (6:12–20; 7); eating food offered to idols without considering that others could connect that to worship of evil spirits (8); drunken, self-centered love feasts in connection with the Lord's Supper (10 and 11); and confusion concerning spiritual gifts, a lack of love among the people, and a chaotic abuse of tongues (12—14).

That is not the kind of church most of us would want to join. It was a spiritual mess. Yet it was a correctable mess. That's why Paul wrote his letter. (A remarkable change occurred by the time he wrote his second epistle to the Corinthians.) In the beginning the internal problems threatened the church constantly, and Paul's prayers and admonitions dealt with those internal needs. As spiritually concerned Christians, we will remain attentive to any threat to the body. When we fail to do that, we open ourselves to internal disaster. Remember, the threat of disunity is always present.

### Be Doctrinal in Upholding the Unity Already Established

On several occasions, churches with internal problems have called me to help them come together in unity. That's never easy for a church. When anger, resentment, hatred, jealousy, and defensive self-righteousness have festered internally, healing comes slowly. Careless words, vindictive actions, and choosing sides allow little chance for internal harmony. That is what's behind most church splits—believers just agree to go their separate ways. Where do we begin to resolve such emotionally fired problems?

The essential starting place is for those involved to focus upon an important point of doctrinal truth that they may have neglected. Ephesians 4:3-4 states, "Make every effort to *keep* the unity of the Spirit through the bond of peace. *There is one body* and one Spirit."

Believers are never called upon to create oneness in the body. We are asked to maintain what has already been accomplished by the redemptive work of Christ and the baptizing work of the Holy Spirit. "For we were all baptized by one Spirit into one body" (1 Cor. 12:13). If we are true believers, we are already united with one another and with our Lord Jesus Christ, who is the head of His body. That's an indisputable fact. Grace has already accomplished it.

It's difficult to hate a part of your own physical body. We usually treat even the parts that hurt with great love and tenderness. Only when a member of our physical body is hopelessly diseased or injured do we consent to removal. When that does happen, we may feel great pain over the loss.

The church body works the same way. When we understand how essential each member is, we treasure every one. We put up with a lot. We are patient and loving when we know the other believer is a part of us. Instead of amputation, we think of medication and tender, loving care, and we seek to nurse the hurting part back to health. Focusing on the essential oneness of Christ's body not only helps to heal broken churches, but it also helps to keep healthy churches functioning in unity through maintaining supportive, understanding attitudes among the believers.

### Be Exemplary in Leadership

Bill Yeager, while serving as pastor of the First Baptist Church of Modesto, California, spoke at an institute on church leadership, stressing that three ingredients are essential to a healthy, thriving church. In order of importance they are: leadership, leadership, and leadership. An important biblical truth is that much responsibility for what happens in a local body of believers rests upon the leadership.

In Nehemiah 5:1–13, after relating the confrontation with the greedy moneylenders and the resulting corrective measures, Nehemiah declared his own personal philosophy of being an exemplary role model leader in financial matters. He humbly cataloged what his practice had been during his governing rule. He had forgone the customary salary, avoided land speculation, provided food for more than 150 officials, and entertained and fed visiting dignitaries.

The point he made is important to leadership: As a leader, he felt responsible both to the people and to God.

Nehemiah's leadership reached beyond financial integrity. He set the precedent for frequent and fervent prayer; his faith was magnificently displayed; his courage was undaunted; and his capacity for moral indignation boiled over with corrective action. He confronted even the most influential dignitaries willingly. Social justice and compassion for the oppressed were his trademarks, and his work focused upon the approval of God rather than man.

There is no substitute for exemplary spiritual leadership. We desperately need Nehemiah-style leaders who practice lifestyles that are beyond reproach and who challenge their people to strive for spiritual and moral excellence.

Similarly, followers are to obey their leaders "and submit to their authority. They keep watch over you as men who must give an account. Obey them so that their work will be a joy, not a burden, for that would be of no advantage to you" (Heb. 13:17–18).

No leader except Christ can ever be completely faultless, but he can be careful to measure his progress toward exemplary leadership. Leaders must also be exemplary in their willingness to say, "I'm sorry. I was wrong. Will you forgive me?"

## *Be Protecting*

Whenever strife arises in the body of believers or even between two individual believers, you can be sure Satan's kingdom is participating. We must protect one another from an active Enemy. One of his chief functions is to accuse and find fault. He is always trying to cause us to think accusing, negative thoughts about fellow believers. The solution is to think the best of our Christian brothers and sisters and to protect them from accusation. (Remember that Satan is called "the accuser of our brothers" in Revelation 12:10.)

Galatians 5:19–21 makes very clear that much trouble and strife between believers can flow out of our fleshly nature. However, no sin more quickly aligns us with Satan's work than allowing negative, accusing thoughts and words toward others to dominate us. They open the door to accusing spirits of darkness, and the power of evil supernaturalism can begin to rule that area of our life. Anyone who has been a part of a church quarrel knows the satanic ugliness of it all. Satan's kingdom is quick to move in and superintend the increasing disaster.

What can believers do to combat this problem? In addition to not listening to gossip and thinking the best of others, we can practice biblical spiritual warfare. Faithful use of the weapons of our warfare is vital.

Suppose you sense a hostile relationship building between you and another believer for no apparent reason. Here's a warfare prayer approach you can take, silently in your mind, even while you continue your conversation:

*In the name of my Lord Jesus Christ and by the power of His blood I pull down all hurtful relationships between _____ and me that Satan and his kingdom are seeking to build. I will only accept relationships between _____ and me that are authored by the Holy Spirit in the will of God.*

That little prayer of resistance is a powerful tool for regular use in all negative relationships. You can enlarge the scope of the prayer to apply to quarreling relationships between other individuals or groups, like this:

*In the name of my Lord Jesus Christ and by the power of His blood, I come against all powers of darkness trying to promote accusations and negative attitudes among the believers of our church. I take full authority over them, and in the name of the Lord Jesus Christ, I bind them until they are inactive, and I command them to leave our presence and to go where the Lord Jesus Christ sends them. I invite the Lord Jesus Christ and the Holy Spirit to sovereignly work to create relationships between us that are in God's loving will and plan.*

Persistent usage of such prayer is notably productive. I've witnessed many reversals of divisive problems by such prayer. This practice is in accordance with our authoritative responsibility to resist the Devil steadfast in the faith, thus forcing him to cease his wicked work and flee.

### Be Forgiving

We are forgiving because we know that often we must share in the guilt. We touched upon this earlier when noting that Nehemiah identified personally with the moneylenders he was rebuking. He included himself and accepted responsibility for those in his own household who'd been doing similar things (5:10). We are never in greater spiritual trouble than when we see only the sins of others and not our own.

The development of a forgiving heart necessitates close familiarity with our own sinful capacities.

The offenses of those who sin against us are always small when compared to the whole spectrum of sins God has forgiven and removed from us. The Lord Jesus taught us to pray: "Forgive us our debts as we forgive our debtors." The greatly forgiven are responsible to forgive greatly. Failure to do so always spells disaster.

In the parable of the unforgiving servant (Matt. 18:21–35), the master eventually gave his heartless servant "over to the jailers to be tortured, until he should pay back all he owed" (v. 34). In this parable, the jailers probably represent demonic tormentors unleashed to discipline the offending servant.

At the end of this story, our Lord Jesus remarked, "This is how my heavenly Father will treat each of you unless you forgive your brother from your heart" (v. 35). I personally am convinced that believers never open their lives more tragically to invite demonic affliction than when we allow accusing, negative, unforgiving attitudes and actions in our dealings with others.

## Be Patient

It's better to err on the side of patience and tolerance than to rush into judgment only to hurt others by fierce censure. That is the whole tenor of Scripture. God deals with His people in patience. He is long-suffering and willing to wait. It's part of the strength of His grace. Patience does not signal weakness.

Nehemiah dealt swiftly with the offenses of the moneylenders because it was urgent in that situation. Sometimes believers must be quick to act. The rebellious moral sin noted in 1 Corinthians 5 was also such a time.

The teaching of wrong doctrine is another practice that needs immediate correction. Yet, even in these cases, the spirit behind such action must be patient and understanding. Harsh, vindictive actions against other believers are always out of order. The focus must always be love, correction, and healing.

Nehemiah's correcting, loving approach brought far-reaching results among the people. Not only was the money-lending problem rectified, but the people also dealt with a host of other spiritual problems. In chapter 10, Nehemiah catalogs these measures: an end to intermarriage with heathen families (v. 30); respect for the Sabbath; restoration of the policy to cancel debts after seven years (v. 31); and proper tithing (vv. 32, 35–39); resumption of the sacrificial system (vv. 32–34); renewed honor for the priesthood (vv. 34, 38–39); and a whole new emphasis on worship and love for God's house (vv. 37–39).

Nehemiah's patient, correcting, loving approach played a great part in moving the people toward this revival. This is an Old Testament picture of grace in action: Grace is never a license to sin; grace is loving confrontation expressed in patience; grace is faith that allows God's sovereignty to bring about heart changes others may need.

## Be Loving

*Agape* love loves those who do not want or deserve love. That's the way God loved us as lost sinners: "God demonstrates his own love for us in this: While we were still sinners, Christ died for us" (Rom. 5:8).

God's love remains the most amazing of all theological concepts. The greatest philosophical minds reach for an understanding of its extremity and power. God's love reached out to a man who persecuted Christ and took part in the brutal murder of Stephen. That love redeemed Saul of Tarsus, transformed him, and used him as one of history's greatest defenders of the faith.

The capacity of God's love to save and change an undeserving sinner seems measureless. The only thing that can quench that power is persistent unbelief. Such love, which can save the vilest of sinners, leaves us breathless. It saved a man of power in the White House who broke the law—special counsel to the president, Charles Colson—and sent him into a ministry as leader of Prison Fellowship. It saved a mass murderer, Ted Bundy, whose "life was dramatically changed by his confession of faith" (Zettersten, 154).[†] This same love of God invades the believer's life: "God has poured out his love into our hearts by the

---

† Rolf Zettersten reports that John Tanner, who led Bundy to the Lord and discipled him over several years, said Bundy's conversion was real.

Holy Spirit, whom he has given us" (Rom. 5:5).

This love also can keep believers united, expressing the oneness God has created in them.

## REVIVAL PRAYER PATTERN: UNITY IN THE BODY

*Dear God and Father of our Lord Jesus Christ, I worship You in the wonder of Your triune oneness. I grope to understand the mystery of how three unique persons remain one God. I praise You for its truth, and I bow before You in the wonder of such revelation of Yourself. By faith, I ask You to increase my capacity to appreciate and understand Your triune oneness, that I might share new insights with others.*

*I also praise and worship You, Lord Jesus Christ, for the scope of Your finished work that unites me with You. I hold Your powerful name, Lord Jesus Christ, over my personal life, my family, my work, and the whole body of Christ for benefit, protection, and all that You have for us.*

*I rejoice that Your salvation has united me inseparably not only with Yourself but also with every other believer. Thank You, blessed Holy Spirit, for Your great work of baptizing me into this body of Christ. I rejoice to be a part of such perfect fellowship. Thank You, Lord Jesus Christ, for continuing Your mighty work of readying Your body to present her to Yourself as a radiant church without stain, wrinkle, or blemish of any kind. Thank You that this body will be holy and blameless in the mystery of Your finished work. I glory in the wonder of such truth.*

*I enter into repentance and confession before You to acknowledge how often I personally have violated the essential oneness of the body. Cleanse me of my wickedness of not honoring each part of the body as You do. I also confess the sins of my family and fellow church members in not living out the unity of the body that You have created. I confess the divisiveness existing in Your visible church as a violation of Your holy plan. I worship and praise You, dear heavenly Father, for Your sovereign ability to use even our divisiveness to glorify Your name and finish Your work.*

*Yet I long and pray for the bringing together of Your born-again ones in a united movement for revival awakening. We have been so terribly wounded by those things that have divided us. Our capacity to bring about change in our world has been reduced to a feeble squeak. In humble embarrassment I repent over this fact and ask Your Holy Spirit to move over Your body to cause change.*

*Help us to come together under the oneness of the Holy Spirit's control. May His oneness of intercession wait before heaven's throne of grace in the hearts of millions of believers who ask God for revolutionary revival.*

*Thank You, Lord Jesus Christ, for planning for unity rather than uniformity. The diversity of Your body is part of its beauty and functional appeal to the lost. It adds to Your glory. Bless Your church in its wide diversity of expression in patterns of worship and songs of praise. Help us to love one another in our diversity.*

*Help me not to condemn my fellow member for what he is not. Grant me the wisdom to understand and the capacity to appreciate him for what he is. Above all, help me to love each part of the body. May that love express itself in patience and in the capacity to hold my thoughts in check when I see the failures of another member of Your body. Forgive me for my quick practice to take comfort about my own failures when I see the sins of others.*

*Blessed heavenly Father, I recognize that Satan and his kingdom are relentless in their efforts to keep believers divisive toward one another. As the accuser of the believers, he continually plants suspicions in believers' hearts. In the name of my Lord Jesus Christ, I pull down that work of darkness and bind our Enemy that he might not succeed. I ask the Holy Spirit to supplant all divisive works with the unity of the Spirit actively working in believers.*

*O Holy God, only Your sovereignty can move Your body into united action. May Your Holy Spirit brood over Your church and cause it to breathe out a united cry for revival awakening. I wait before You for this. Only You can work it out in a way that will startle the world and glorify Your name. Raise up the human leaders You can trust to touch not the glory that belongs only to You. I affirm again that what You have accomplished through the finished work of my Lord Jesus Christ is sufficient to do more than I ask. In Jesus' precious name I pray. Amen.*

# Chapter 15

# THE WORK OF THE WORD

*For the word of God is living and active. Sharper than any double-edged sword, it penetrates even to dividing soul and spirit, joints and marrow; it judges the thoughts and attitudes of the heart. Nothing in all creation is hidden from God's sight. Everything is uncovered and laid bare before the eyes of him to whom we must give account.*

*Hebrews 4:12–13*

As my wife and sister-in-law returned from lunch, they saw a strange truck leaving the driveway. The driver had attached the trailer holding my brother's two snowmobiles and was pulling the trailer away. He was stealing them.

The scene unnerved the two, yet they followed the thief to get his license number. There was no license plate on the rear of his vehicle, so they pulled ahead to see the tag on the front. The driver had it tucked in the windshield of his cab. When he realized their intent to see it, he quickly hid the plate. Turning down a side street, he managed to lose them.

One of the investigating policemen said, "Snowmobiles are pretty valuable. What were they doing in your driveway?"

"I moved them there from summer storage so we could take them to the mountains," my brother explained.

The policeman replied, "Well, we'll do all we can, but you'll probably never see your snowmobiles again. These guys are pretty smooth operators, and they usually cover their tracks well enough that they avoid getting caught. It's pretty hopeless in a city the size of Denver."

My brother and his wife accepted the loss with Christian grace, but I felt tremendously resentful. In my study for the writing of this book, I had spent much time documenting the accelerating decay of morality in our culture. This firsthand evidence of arrogant, lawless conduct angered me deeply. I prayed with righteous indignation: "Loving heavenly Father, put Your holy finger on that thief. In the name of the Lord Jesus I ask You to bring him quickly to account for such bold sin against You. Bring confusion to him and cause him to make foolish mistakes that will expose him and reverse his apparent escape." I found myself frequently praying this way, and the other family members prayed too.

Returning from the Denver Seminary Library the following Saturday afternoon, I was astonished to see the snowmobiles back in the driveway. I could scarcely wait to hear the story. The man had tried to dispose of them at a ridiculously low price at the local flea market. Suspicions arose, police computers were checked, the snowmobiles were impounded and retuned to my brother, and the thief—now in great trouble—was made accountable. We all praised our Lord for such quick justice.

## ACCOUNTABILITY TO GOD

That incident reminds me of how every person is responsible for their actions before a holy God, and He could just as quickly bring any of us to face that accountability through His Word. He can bring us to swift, sure justice. Yet His mercy and great love delay our answering to that justice: "Because of the LORD's great love we are not consumed, for his compassions never fail" (Lam. 3:22).

The desire for profound revival springs up in people who understand their accountability to God. Such awareness breaks hearts concerning personal sin, and repentance quickly follows. Intimate fellowship with God is restored; the joy of that new relationship overflows and the revival process starts to move. Witnessing to the lost through the power of God occurs. When people are won to Christ, a whole culture begins to change. Sinful people are transformed, and they become God's people who desire holy living.

## THE EFFECT OF GOD'S WORD

The real presence of revival begins when God's Word, the Bible, penetrates hearts and becomes intensely personal to every believer (Heb. 4:12–13). When that happens, revival is on its way.

### Excuses to Sin

Good people, even Christian people, can easily become sinful in their lifestyles. Sin enters in so subtly that we fail to sense its presence. People conceal it from their own sight and from the sight of others. God's dealings with their sins are unrecognized, or they are excused with self-serving thoughts such as, "He'll forgive me"; or "He understands my weaknesses"; or "He knows what I have to live with." Only by knowing and focusing on the Scriptures can we be alert to the temptations to disobey God.

King David is a reminder that good people can become wicked and sinful in their actions without any apparent awareness. David excused himself from a whole catalog of sins as he was drawn into adultery and eventually murder. He knew God's Word, but he ignored God's plan for man to be morally clean and to have only one wife. Kings had the "right" to have multiple wives and concubines. Self-will spread through his inner soul and clouded his spiritual perceptions.

The fact that Bathsheba was the daughter of one of David's "mighty men" and the wife of another didn't deter him in his lust. As he gave his sexual desire unbridled expression, he gave up his integrity, his loyalty to his fighting troops, and his sacred trust in God. David's downfall was a series of excuses, and he was too blind to comprehend his condition.

David's experience illustrates how subtly Satan works. It also demonstrates how we believers show our need for spiritual revival. When we become oblivious to our sinful ways, we lack motivation for corrective actions. Questionable spiritual conduct becomes so accepted that God's holy ways are overlooked. When such conditions prevail in a culture, pastors and Christian leaders fail to speak convincingly to the sin issues of the day. People's spiritual sensitivity becomes so dull they cannot recognize the obvious. If it happened to David, "a man after [God's] own heart" (Acts 13:22), it can happen to us.

### The Scriptures' Power to Expose

God eventually brought David to account in a significant way. God sent Nathan, a humble, lowly prophet, to speak to David. Through Nathan, David heard God say, "You're the man."

Revival begins when believers hear God's Word speaking to their own hearts: "You're the one. This is what the Lord God says. It's your prayerlessness, your carnality, your indifference, your bitterness, your hardness, your unfaithfulness!" When revival awakening comes near, the Scriptures begin to speak personally to each individual. "You're the one!" begins to echo in the heart of each believer.

## GOD'S WORD AND REVIVAL IN JERUSALEM

### Instruction

After the walls were rebuilt under Nehemiah's direction, a beautiful thing happened in Jerusalem. As a direct result of the reading of God's Word, revival came to the people. Nehemiah's inspiring leadership and Ezra's teaching ministry created a hunger for God's Word in the people's hearts (Ezra 7:10). They wanted to hear what God expected of them.

Since they did not have personal copies of God's Word, they came by the thousands and gathered in the court area before the Water Gate. "Men and women and all who were able to understand" depicts the inclusiveness of the crowd—everyone came except the youngest children (Neh. 8:2).

It must have been a dramatic moment. To facilitate sight and hearing, Ezra and other officials stood on an elevated platform. With the scrolls of the Torah in his hands, Ezra began to praise and worship God. The people joined by raising their hands heavenward as they bowed down in worship. "Amen! Amen!" they cried.

We are not told what Ezra read, only that the reading went on from daybreak until noon (v. 3). Long readings from Genesis, Exodus, and Deuteronomy must have sounded forth. As the Levites, Nehemiah, and others explained the Word of God, feedback from the people became a vital part of what was happening.

### Repentance

Quietly and intensely, a repentant brokenness for sin settled upon all those gathered. "For all the people had been weeping as they listened to the words of the Law" (v. 9). The effects went deeper than mere feelings. The people's tears expressed a repentance that brought life changes, and revolutionary revival began to move through the culture. The Word of God remained the focus of all that was happening—at least six hours each day were devoted to its reading. The remorsefulness, tears, and repentance moved the people to such emotional levels that Nehemiah and the Levites felt constrained to calm them and encourage them to rejoice (vv. 9–11). Tears of repentance ultimately produced fountains of inner joy. It was in this revival setting that Nehemiah uttered these immortal words: "The joy of the LORD is your strength" (v. 10).

The first stage lasted for seven days. The Israelites camped together, living in booths and tents, and they observed their spiritual festivals. As the revival matured, the people's rejoicing developed a stable consistency. "Their joy was very great" (v. 17). That's what revolutionary spiritual revival brings to all who are touched by it.

The revival didn't end after this first week. On the twenty-fourth day of the month, another gathering took place. The revival spread. Hearing about this spiritual renewal, more people wanted to experience what God was doing. Awareness of sin once again motivated life changes:

> The Israelites gathered together, fasting and wearing sackcloth and having dust on their heads. Those of Israelite descent had separated themselves from all foreigners. They stood in their places and confessed their sins and the wickedness of their fathers. They stood where they were and read from the Book of the Law of the LORD their God for a quarter of the day, and spent another quarter in confession and in worshiping the LORD their God. (9:1–3)

### Balancing Instruction and Response

The revival format in Nehemiah illustrates balance between instruction and expression. Six hours devoted to reading and exhortation from the Word of

God were followed by six hours of testimony, confession, and praise. The people vented their joy through music, psalm singing, and other worship expressions. The rest of the day was for sleeping and family time. These are the ingredients common to most revival awakenings.

We are not told how long this revival expression ultimately lasted, but the resulting cultural changes were dramatic. The remaining five chapters of Nehemiah record these changes. Nehemiah's project of rebuilding Jerusalem would probably have failed without the revival—too much suspicion, scheming, and greed had controlled the people—but the impact of the revival allowed completion of the project and led to lasting cultural reforms.

## The Role of God's Word in Revival

Believers frequently suffer from spiritual hearing impairment—we don't hear what God is saying to us. As the glorified Christ addressed each of the seven churches in Revelation 2 and 3, He kept repeating, "He who has an ear, let him hear what the Spirit says to the churches" (2:7, 11, 17, 29; 3:6, 13, 22).

Hearing God's Word brings hope and spiritual healing. Paul wrote, "Faith comes from hearing the message, and the message is heard through the word of Christ" (Rom. 10:17). Revival necessitates each believer hearing "the word of Christ" in his inner heart.

We've seen that the Holy Scriptures were a vital element in renewing the hearts of the Jewish people in Nehemiah's time. How can the Word of God bring revival to your nation in this new day and age? Here are six ways.

### Exalt the Scriptures in Public Reading (Neh. 8:1—9:3)

In Nehemiah's revival, the Word of God was exalted to where the people gave it a deep, personal hearing.

To neglect the reading of the Word of God in our public or private worship is a calamitous error. Paul urged Timothy, "Until I come, devote yourself to *the public reading of Scripture,* to preaching and to teaching" (1 Tim. 4:13). We sense a lofty touch of infinite majesty when we read the Word of our eternal God. Significantly, when Ezra opened the book of the law, "the people all stood up" (Neh. 8:5).

Catch the dignity and respect that the people assigned to the reading of God's Word: They "stood up."

These people did not have our ready access to the sacred Scriptures. Reproductions had to be handwritten, and no one had his own copy. They were so starved for the Word that God's Spirit energized them to stand and listen to it being read for six hours at a time. Today we need God's people to get involved in reading and hearing the Word as enthusiastically as they did in Nehemiah's day.

Innovative ways must be discovered to promote the reading of the Word. Here are a few ideas:

> Have believers commit to a one-on-one Bible-reading plan with another believer. Accountability for Bible study and memorization would be the focus. Large sections of Scripture can be committed to memory with such steady liability. Enhance motivation by meeting regularly and maintaining a disciplined procedure.
>
> Church leaders can hand out schedules that take people through the entire Bible in a set time period. This would promote Bible reading among their members.
>
> Have a pastor preach from a biblical text after the congregation reads it earlier at home. One church has developed a three-year schedule that takes its people through the New Testament twice and the Old Testament once. The people read the weekly section at home; on Sunday a portion of that week's assignment is read in the church service, and the pastor then preaches from the text.

The plan for reading is not the important issue. God's people will be blessed if meaningful and increased reading of God's Word emerges as the most important aspect. Absorbing God's Word to the largest dimension possible is crucial to our hope for revolutionary revival.

### Exalt the Scriptures through Repentance (Neh. 8:9, 11–12; 9:1–2)

Repentance is a beautiful grace from God. As Ezra read the Word and the people listened, their sins came into perspective. They expressed their intense sorrow for those sins through repentance. At first it was just tears, but as the Word continued to be read, the repentance deepened. They expressed it by "fasting and wearing sackcloth and having dust on their heads" (9:1). They also stood up and openly confessed their wicked practices (v. 2). This repentance resulted from the reading of God's Word.

Repentance is not some kind of emotional frenzy. Emotions are involved, but biblical repentance involves the whole person—conduct and thoughts. It requires acknowledgment that we have violated the revealed will of God. It calls us to deliberately cease sinful thoughts and actions and to supplant them with righteous thoughts and deeds. Only the constant ingesting of God's Word can keep that spiritual process in balance.

As revival moves toward the transformation of a culture, hearing the Word of God must lead to repentance.

### Exalt the Scriptures through Prayer (Neh. 9:5–37)

Nehemiah 9:5–37 records a long prayer that the people expressed as a body. We are left to conjecture as to how this was done, but from the textual evidence it appears the Levites led by an antiphony pattern. One group "called with loud voices to the LORD their God" (v. 4). This group kept their prayer phrases short, enabling another group of Levites to lead the people in repeating each phrase. The second group of Levites instructed the people, "Stand up and praise the LORD your God, who is from everlasting to everlasting" (v. 5).

This got each person involved in the prayer. The participation was wonderful. The people spoke the prayer to God with their own lips. As this antiphonal pattern progressed, each person's involvement deepened.

This type of prayer greatly honors God because it focuses upon praying His Word back to Him. What they'd heard, as the sacred Scriptures were read, was now verbalized in worshipful praying. It illustrates the use of God's Word in doctrinal praying. It appropriates His Word in the application of His promises.

The seven prayer patterns for revival included in this book are designed to develop this style of praying. We must recite such prayers with sincerity and conviction, not in routine or ritual. The prayer in Nehemiah 9 deserves emulation by every believer. In addition, biblical passages, such as the Lord's

Prayer in Matthew 6:9–13 or David's prayers in Psalm 27 and 139, can be recited in your church or home.

### Exalt the Scriptures through Corrected Living (Neh. 10:29–39)

Nehemiah's cultural reforms rose from a solid basis. The people, with their leaders, pledged themselves "to follow the Law of God given through Moses the servant of God and to obey carefully all the commands, regulations and decrees of the LORD our Lord" (v. 29). They followed the absolute standard of God's revealed will.

Nehemiah 10 shows the living patterns instituted by the people. As they proceeded in their efforts, they frequently referenced what was written in the law. Their changes were necessary for carrying out the commands of God.

Earlier this century God's moral law formed a base of absolutes in American culture that affected even our own government. Though God's law was not lived out in total perfection, it was there. Today, it is remembered only as a part of our history. In fact, today the Supreme Court and our legislators seem to studiously avoid making decisions based on biblical revelation. Separation of church and state is interpreted to mean separation from any reference to God or the Bible. Humanism, which exalts man over God, and pluralism, which gives equal honor to all religions and even nonreligions, have led our culture to the near annihilation of biblical absolutes.

Any society moves into chaos when human reason becomes the measure for moral living. When people choose that route, values become relative and society's standards of conduct lose stability.

Vested interests and warped prejudices of those with influence soon become the accepted standards. In America, the humanistic die has been cast as the standard for the future function of our nation. Only revolutionary revival could make a difference now.

Encouragement comes to us from Nehemiah's experience. How quickly the chaotic disaster of that ruined culture was changed by revival. The change came because the people changed. They began to say, "We promise"; "We assume the responsibility"; and "We will not neglect the house of our God" (Neh. 10:30, 32, 39).

Any government "of the people, by the people, and for the people" will function with biblical absolutes when its people become personally related with God. As Christians, we must set the example with lives that exalt the Scriptures.

### Exalt the Scriptures through Worship, Praise, and Celebration (Neh. 12:27—13:1)

After such transformation, the people worshipped, praised, and celebrated before the God of Israel. The dedication of the rebuilt walls of Jerusalem was a colossal event. Two large choirs sang from the joining walls of the city. Cymbals, harps, lyres, trumpets, and other musical instruments added to the crescendo of music and praise. The priests and Levites functioned again in the biblical pattern. Nehemiah summarizes this majestic event in chapter 12:

> The choirs sang under the direction of Jezrahiah. And on that day they offered great sacrifices, rejoicing because God had given them great joy. The women and children also rejoiced. The sound of rejoicing in Jerusalem could be heard far away. (vv. 42–43)

When worship and praise flow from hearts made right with God through the understanding of His Word, the joy knows no bounds. It affects even the little children. The young people, the women, and the men let their hearts overflow with gladness. Everyone got in on the joy of the Lord. One of the great delights of revival is its joy.

In our churches and in our homes, we Christians can know such joy when, through the Word of God, we focus on God's love, power, and care for us. This can bring renewal to our hearts. Such joy also can draw the attention of a despairing society. It can be a catalyst for spiritual revival in our land.

### Exalt the Scripture by Continuing Reform, Repentance, and Correction (Neh. 13)

A mighty revival like the one that came to Jerusalem under Nehemiah's leadership doesn't really have a conclusion. Chapter 13 reveals the deepening insights that enabled the people to continue to bring their cultural practices more perfectly in line with God's will. As new comprehension came to the people, more of their sinful ways of living were corrected.

Nehemiah expressed continuing concern that his own leadership would remain worthy of the Lord's favor and blessing. He pleaded, "Remember me … O my God" (v. 14). This leader's relationship with his Lord was a growing process.

Many revivals last for years, and the resulting blessings pour out indefinitely. Such was the case of the revival that began at Pentecost. The blessings of that revolutionary revival movement lasted for at least thirty years and overflowed into most of the Roman Empire. Fresh outbreaks happened in many cities.

However, people are not fashioned to live constantly at such a high emotional pitch. The prayer time and the celebration at the dedication of the walls of Jerusalem required an abnormal elevation of emotion. As reviving and meaningful as these things were, their duration was limited. No revival movement can ever remain at such a high level of intensity.

## LASTING RESULTS

The emotional aspects of revivals fade quickly, and if that's all there is, the results will do little to change a culture. Emotionally charged revivals are like light from a shooting star, rapidly dissipating as the darkness settles back in. Brief revivals are important to the spiritual life of any church, area, or nation, but something much deeper is needed to change the course of an entire culture. The base must be extremely broad and deep, and, for revolutionary revival to defeat the satanic uprising, it must have a long-range, staying application. The revival under Nehemiah continued to impact the people of Jerusalem because it was rooted deeply in God's Word.

Our prayer is that God, in His mercy and grace, will bring a revival awakening to our day that will bear such a long-range benefit. We cannot settle for anything less.

## REVIVAL PRAYER PATTERN: THE WORD OF GOD

*Loving heavenly Father, I come to worship You in the wonder of what You have chosen to reveal in Your Word about Yourself. The majesty of Your creation displays*

*Your awesome greatness. I see Your omnipotence when I look upon the vastness of the universe. I praise You that You are everywhere present in the extremities of the universe and that You are greater than Your creation.*

*I look upon the immensity of man's accumulated knowledge and remember Your omniscient possession of all knowledge. The steady march of time causes me to reflect upon the fact that You are eternal, without beginning or end. The lying, sinful ways of humanity evident everywhere cause me to long for the one who is truth and who reigns in absolute justice.*

*I praise You, loving God and Father of our Lord Jesus Christ, for what You have revealed about Yourself in the written Word of God. I affirm that Your Holy Word is an inerrant revelation of Your holy truth. I ask forgiveness for my neglect in reading, memorizing, and meditating upon Your Word. What an ugly, sinful wrong it is for me, my family, and my fellow believers to treat Your Holy Word so lightly when it has been made so available to us. Wash away our guilt, and create within believers' hearts a longing to know and read Your Word.*

*Through Your Word, heavenly Father, I came to know the Lord Jesus Christ as my Savior from sin. In Your Word, He is revealed as the one who became God in human flesh and was victorious in Himself over the world, the flesh, and the Devil. In Your Word I learn that, though He was tempted in every way I am tempted, He never sinned. Your Word declares that, as one of us, He fulfilled all righteousness. Your Word declares that He was wounded for my transgressions and bruised for my iniquities. It declares that He became sin for me and that my sins and offenses against You were laid upon Him when He died in my place upon the cross.*

*It is in Your Word that the mighty truth of His triumph over death and the grave in resurrection power is established. Your Word declares with assuring detail the Lord Jesus Christ's ascension into heaven and His present, glorified overseeing of His church. Because of the declarations of Your Word, I look for my Savior to come again with power and great glory. I love You, heavenly Father, for having given me Your Word.*

*I praise You, loving God, that You have graced us with the coming of the Holy Spirit at Pentecost. Thank You for revealing Your Word to me in the wonder of His mighty work in this world and in believers. Thank You for declaring in Your Word that the Holy Spirit came to convict the world of its sinful guilt. I ask for the Holy Spirit to greatly intensify His work of convincing people of their sin against a holy God. May the Holy Spirit so open people to the spiritual seeing and hearing of Your Word that they again will cry out in repentance. Thank You, also, that the Holy Spirit exalts righteousness by revealing the righteous things of Your Word. I ask Him to do that with powerful persuasion.*

*I pray that the Holy Spirit will, by Your Word, reveal to human hearts the certainty of an approaching accountability to God. May that sobering fact settle upon people until they can find no rest apart from coming to our Lord Jesus Christ.*

*Blessed Holy Spirit, You are the one who breathed out God's Word in divine revelation through human instruments. I ask You now to use that Word to speak personally to believers. Grant new insights to God's appointed leaders to promote interest, reading, memorization, and meditation upon God's Word among God's people. I ask You, Holy Spirit, to raise up anointed revivalists, evangelists, and preachers who will be able to make the Bible known with compelling power to a lost world.*

*I pray the mighty power of God's Holy Word against Satan and his kingdom. Confront and defeat Satan's lies with the truth of Your Word. May the comfort of Your Word relieve people from Satan's accusations, torments, and terror. I ask that the warnings of Your Word will alert people to Satan's tactics to bring them into bondage. Invade Satan's kingdom with salvation's message in Your Word and bring multitudes from the darkness of hell into the kingdom of light and eternal life.*

*I recognize, heavenly Father, that revival will never come unless a deep, personalized hearing of God's Word comes to human hearts. In the name of my Lord Jesus Christ and by the power of His blood, I pull down Satan's power to dishonor and discredit God's Holy Word. I bring in prayer the power of the Holy Spirit against all satanic strongholds assigned to hinder the Word of God from being heard and understood by the hearts of people. I invite the blessed Holy Spirit to exalt the Word of God and to reveal its mighty power in ways that will confound the enemies of truth. Cause people to hear Your Word with a new, profound depth, and move pastors and churches to proclaim and teach Your Word with a contagious freshness.*

*I affirm, heavenly Father, that Your Word is alive and powerful. I rejoice that, though heaven and earth will pass away, not one tiny word of Your holy truth will ever fail. Grant to Your Word great success in our day. Use Your Holy Word to move our nation to revolutionary revival. I love Your Word, O Lord, and I give myself to know it better and to live it more. I offer this prayer in the name of Him who is the Living Word, my Lord Jesus Christ. Amen.*

## Chapter 16

# THE TIME IS NOW

*You are going to have the light just a little while longer.*
*Walk while you have the light, before darkness overtakes*
*you. The man who walks in the dark does not know*
*where he is going. Put your trust in the light while you*
*have it, so that you truly become sons of light.*

*John 12:35–36*

Has the dawn of revival vision broken over the horizon of your life? When the sun's rays lift above the horizon, they spread a pervasive light. It's quiet, but it's deliberate, relentless, and inclusive. It warms the entire landscape. Only the most tightly closed places can shut out the light and the warmth. Revival is like that when it has the revolutionary dimension.

There is an urgency to get involved. God has placed that which will bring revival awakening into the hands of believers who are ready, who have God's burden and have experienced renewal in their own lives.

Revival will put holy living back into the deep, inner desires of the heart. God's people don't do the sinful or even questionable things they once did, because His holy fire has once more ignited their passion for Him.

### SIGNS OF REVIVAL AWAKENING

Are there signs that revival is near?

Unfortunately, we do not see much evidence yet of a true revival awakening. Little outbursts happen here and there in the world, but in today's culture where it is needed so much, things appear static. Perhaps the renewal that swept more than a dozen American campuses in the spring of 1995 (see chapter 11) will return in modern-day colleges to provide a more pervasive movement of the Spirit.

Certainly the very desperation of our times can give us hope of a revival in our day. In *The Awakening That Must Come*, Lewis A. Drummond lists three awakening signs that precede revival. They are (1) social, political, and economic crises; (2) feelings of hopelessness within the church; and (3) a concern for world evangelization and missions (109). These signs are evident in our day.

### *The Sign of Social, Political, and Economic Crises*

Times of crisis have a way of shocking us out of our temporal, physical world. Trials bring us face-to-face with the eternal and spiritual dimensions of life. Part of our crises flows from the natural chaos that sinful living injects into everything it touches. However, the possibility of sovereign, divine intervention also must be recognized. After bringing revival awakening to Solomon and the people at the dedication of the temple, God spoke to Solomon about what He would do when the need for revival arose: "When I shut up the heavens so that there is no rain, or command locusts to devour the land or send a plague among my people" (2 Chron. 7:13).

Drought, pestilence, and plagues. For any culture, these things spell crises with a capital C. God does sovereignly use various types of crises to get people's attention and to awaken them to the urgency of the need.

Volumes could be (and have been) written about the many aspects of the social crisis of our times:

- The breakdown of family and home life displayed in high levels of divorce and child abuse, including incest
- Alcohol and drug addiction
- The ever-increasing presence of AIDS and other largely sexually transmitted diseases
- Increased paganism and satanic imagery

The educational needs of our children stand out. Despite our efforts, increasing numbers pass through the educational system but are still illiterate.

Some statistics say up to 14 percent of adults in the United States cannot read, write, or do simple math.

Good medical care is moving beyond the cost limits of many. Jails and prisons can't be built large enough or fast enough.

Social crisis is everywhere, and it's mounting. We see little hope of relief through human wisdom.

The political crises loom. People in the highest elected offices are paraded before the world for ethical violations, immoral conduct, and even illegal activities and criminal fraud. We can be thankful when our systems can root out some of the political corruption, but that offers little comfort. Those who know tell us that we see only a small part of the corruption present in the political realm and world of business.

The economic crisis appears destined to come home to every citizen's pocket. Efforts by governments to balance their budgets are noteworthy, yet the requirements for an austere life make many citizens unwilling to sacrifice, and politicians hesitate to act.

The social, political, and economic crises should get our attention. Hopefully, they are signs that will turn people toward a spiritual revival. If we respond to the crises by revival praying, it will come.

### The Sign of the Feelings of Hopelessness within the Church

As we look at the church today, these words of the psalmist seem most appropriate:

> They mounted up to the heavens and went down to the depths; in peril their courage melted away.
>
> They reeled and staggered like drunken men; they were at their wits' end. (107:26–27)

The image here is a ship on a tossing sea with little hope for survival. The church has indeed been staggered by the events of our day. The moral scandals surrounding religious leaders touch every denomination and every believer. How far it will go no one knows. Guilt by association is widespread. To the wary, watching public, a cloud of suspicion lurks near most religious groups. Unfortunately, sound Christian organizations suffer with the unworthy ones.

Our youth are skeptical of organized religion. In increasing numbers, fifth- and sixth-grade children are following in the path of teenagers; they want nothing to do with organized religion. Satanism seems to have increasing appeal. Meanwhile, cults and non-Christian religions capture youth from traditional Christianity by the multitudes. Secularism, humanism, and New Age philosophy pick up many more. Our youth are in crisis. The church is in crisis.

But it's not hopeless. The psalmist continued the passage quoted above with these rescuing words of promise:

> Then they cried out to the LORD in their trouble, and he brought them out of their distress.
>
> He stilled the storm to a whisper; the waves of the sea were hushed.
>
> They were glad when it grew calm, and he guided them to their desired haven. (vv. 28–30)

The church always has a resource of hope; rescue is available. Revival is a viable option—it does offer hope. When we are overcome with feelings of helplessness, when we are unable to cope with staggering demands, when we are overwhelmed: that's a good situation to be in. It's time then to believe God for revival. The answer begins with crying out to the Lord, who can "bring them out of their distress." There is no problem beyond the solution of our Lord. He's waiting to respond to our cry with reviving intervention. Psalm 107 closes with great hope:

> He lifted the needy out of their affliction and increased their families like flocks.
>
> The upright see and rejoice, but all the wicked shut their mouths.
>
> Whoever is wise, let him heed these things and consider the great love of the LORD. (vv. 41–43)

That's a promise of revival blessings flowing out so strongly that "the wicked shut their mouths." Revival does that. It sends wickedness into retreat. It can reverse the influence of Satan and other fallen angels.

## The Sign of Concern for World Evangelization and Mission

Not all signs of an impending revival awakening are dark. Through his evangelistic association, Billy Graham broadcast the gospel to 180 countries in spring 1995 through the Global Mission. Based in San Juan, Puerto Rico, Global Mission allowed Graham to issue "the first worldwide invitation for individuals to make a profession of Christian faith." Mission officials estimated that the gospel was spread to one billion people through delayed transmissions that were broadcast across all twenty-nine time zones (Morgan, 36–37).

The Billy Graham Evangelistic Association has provided wonderful leadership in promoting world evangelization, which has included many other organizations and individuals. Both nationally and internationally, evangelists Luis Palau and John Guest have led large evangelistic crusades. Organizations such as Campus Crusade for Christ, Operation Mobilization, World Vision and other world relief agencies, and denominational and missionary organizations are doing great work. More movements than we could ever name keep promoting world evangelization and missionary outreach.

More than a thousand Asian missionaries from seven Asian countries are now a part of this expanding vision to evangelize the world, and more seem destined to follow soon. The vision for world evangelization appears to burn brighter than it ever has.

Rapid travel, technological advances, communications networking, and satellites like those used in Graham's Global Mission are among the new tools and methods being used to spread the gospel. These are exciting days for Christians. Never has the church had more concern or more capacity for the task of world evangelization.

The one ingredient desperately needed is spiritual revival, hopefully beginning in the United States, but spreading quickly into a worldwide move of God's mercy and grace. A legitimate, heartfelt revival here would have many outcomes:

- Revival would enlarge the needed manpower reserve in a short time. Revived people become eager missionary volunteers.
- Revival would enlarge God's people with spiritual power for prayer. United prayer pushes the Enemy into hasty retreat.
- Revival leads to repentance and cleaned-up lives. God's power flows freely through a clean people.
- Revival would secure the needed funds to finance the evangelism projects. Revived people become joyful stewards.
- Revival would help create a political climate favorable to world evangelization. Changed people translate into changed political leaders who open doors for the gospel.

There is great encouragement for us. I personally believe that revival is not just a possibility, but a probability. My prayer is that an ever-increasing number of believers will envision that probability and enter into those activities that will help bring it to pass.

## ACTIVITIES AND ATTITUDES THAT PROMOTE REVIVAL

Now it's time to give you some practical suggestions. Revival knowledge would have little significance if it stimulated only a surface interest in the subject. More must take place. Attitudes must become expectant. Actions must head toward goals. Motivation must produce fortitude.

Revival material and tools need to be simple in format, applicable to every believer, and adaptable to each situation. In appendix E, we have included some samples of printed materials that we hope will be helpful to you. These may be photocopied for your personal use.

Revival is not complicated. God gave the formula for it to Solomon in less than fifty words:

> If my people, who are called by my name, will humble themselves and pray and seek my face and turn from their wicked ways, then will I hear from heaven and will forgive their sin and will heal their land. (2 Chron. 7:14)

As we have noted earlier, revival begins personally, with each of us. Spiritual renewal is a personal response and the foundation for any cultural revival. Here are four things you and I can do personally to promote revival in our land.

### Walk in Personal Victory over the World, the Flesh, and the Devil

God is pleased when people who are concerned for revival commit themselves to godliness. Those He chooses to use in a revival movement must know they are called to holiness. As we've seen, one of the first marks of revival awakening is when sin is recognized as exceedingly sinful. Those burdened for revival need to be on the cutting edge of a desire to live above sin.

"Offer your bodies as living sacrifices, holy and pleasing to God," urges Paul, who adds that Christ's followers should no longer be conformed "to the pattern of this world, but be transformed by the renewing of your mind" (Rom. 12:1–2).

Ask the Lord daily to reveal areas of compromise or sinful indulgence that need to be removed from your life. Be quick to confess such sins and appropriate God's cleansing.

An important factor in God's formula for bringing revival is that the people who desire it would "turn from their wicked ways." Through Christ's finished work, God has given believers the power and grace to win the victory over the world, the flesh, and the Devil. My books *The Adversary, Overcoming the Adversary,* and *The Adversary at Home* give biblical insight into this spiritual victory. Spiritual victory must be a factor in a believer's life. There is so much at stake.

### Commit to Personal Prayer for Revival

People who influence others are themselves deeply committed to their cause, so personal prayer for revival must come first. Put private prayer at the top of your priority list and develop it.

Accept no substitute for private, personal prayer. You benefit greatly, and you also honor God when you develop your shut-away time with Him. Jesus' instruction on the matter is clear: "When you pray, go into your room, close the door and pray to your Father, who is unseen. Then your Father, who sees what is done in secret, will reward you" (Matt. 6:6).

For effective private prayer, be sure to determine a set time and place. Most people cannot work protracted prayer times into a daily schedule, but nearly everyone can do it several times a week. Some of those regular times should be devoted exclusively to a revival focus. If our very survival demands revival, then prayer for revival is not an option. It's a necessity.

You may develop your own style of intercessory prayer for revival, or you may wish to use the prayer patterns suggested in this book. They emphasize key doctrinal truths. You will find the seven prayers at the ends of chapters 8, 10–15. In addition, you may want to consult the several topics listed in appendix D under "Prelude Praying" in the table "Features and Prayers Before Revival."

Momentum in developing habitual prayer is vital. Revival prayer should be sharply focused. Like Nehemiah's prayer, it needs to express worship, burden, and repentance (1:5–11). It should include biblical doctrine, and it should focus on God's revealed will. It should confront and resist Satan in all that he is doing to hinder revival. Remember that the basic ingredient of the broad-base revival is the personal prayer life of believers. Pray that God will give us a base of millions of Christians who are privately and personally praying for revival. "Then your Father, who sees what is done in secret, will reward you."

### Become Part of a Revival Prayer Group

Though revival is always intensely personal, it is also group centered.

In the Old Testament, the spiritual leaders often were loners who heard from God as individuals. Abraham, Moses, Elijah, and Isaiah gave out their messages to the people as singular heralds of God's truth. In the New Testament, however, the emphasis is upon the body, the group, and the composite church that heard from God and moved with God. To be sure, individual New Testament leaders like James, Paul, and Peter were necessary, but they always functioned in harmony with the body.

The forward movement of the church was group centered from its inception—the Lord Jesus Christ had a group of twelve apostles. He also instructed the group of 120 faithful disciples to wait in Jerusalem for their enduing of power from heaven through the Holy Spirit (Luke 24:49; Acts 1:12–13). As the disciples waited in a room for the promised Holy Spirit, "They all joined together constantly in prayer, along with the women and Mary the mother of Jesus, and with his brothers" (Acts 1:14).

Notice that men and women (and probably children) prayed together. Revival began with this group.

The place to begin a group prayer gathering for revival should be in one's local church, God's chosen entity to evangelize the world and to edify the body. God assigns the local church great importance. Sadly, in this day in most local churches, the number of prayer meetings seems to be at an all-time low, and some churches have even ceased having them. This is just one more indication of the desperate need for revival in our time.

Innovative plans promoting church prayer are needed. Most of these meetings have a scattered focus: physical illnesses, family problems, job changes, employment needs, the programs of the church, and the missionaries. These all deserve prayer support, but it's difficult to include much revival prayer in addition to those needs. Some groups should meet just to pray for revival. Revival praying requires more attention than it's currently getting.

Believers who sense God's burden for revival need to confer with their pastor for his blessing and support. The revival-focused prayer sessions should be listed in the weekly church announcements. The time and place should be chosen in the best interests of the participants. Early mornings serve many people well; noon hours sometimes work; some groups schedule meetings from 9:00 to 10:00 p.m. after the children are in bed. It is advisable to have a time limit, and people should be free to come and go as their schedules permit. Revival prayer groups in local churches are a must.

Interdenominational group prayer times for revival are also needed. These may flow out of existing interdenominational fellowships, such as Christian businessmen's committees, womens' ministry groups, and interchurch Bible studies. It is vital that interdenominational groups see the urgent need for revival to visit all churches. When revival comes, all churches will be filled, and praying together for revival is an important foundation of preparation.

## Wait upon the Lord with Persistence for Revival

God can move quickly to bring revival awakening. The 120 people gathered in the upper room at Jerusalem had to wait only ten days. The sound of a blowing wind and the sight of a burning fire announced its beginning. Once that happened, thousands responded almost immediately. Yes, God can move quickly, but ...

Remember, the groundwork for that revival had taken much longer. Its foundations reached back into the three years the Lord Jesus Christ spent fulfilling His earthly ministry. Without those years, there would not have been a revival. Even the revival of Pentecost required a protracted time of preparation. God's great and "sudden" movings have deep roots.

God is responsible for the times—believers are responsible for persistent intercession. Those who "stay by the stuff" will surely see the refreshing come. As Ronald Dunn notes,

> In the recorded history of the church there has never been a mighty outpouring of the Spirit in revival that did not begin in the persistent, prevailing prayers of desperate people. Revival has never come because men placed it on the calendar. It has come because God placed it in their hearts. (227)

## Protect the Results of Revival

The duration of revivals has varied widely. Martin Luther felt the outer limits to be about thirty years, and he thought the church needed a new awakening at least that often.

Some revivals have had a much shorter duration. The Welsh revival of 1904 ended rather quickly. The chief leader in that revival, Evan Roberts, and author Jessie Penn-Lewis, both felt it ended prematurely. Their book, *War on the Saints*, first published in 1912 after the results of the 1904 revival had largely abated, deals with the subtle ways Satan can hinder what God desires to do through believers. The authors presented Satan's deceptions and the believers' passive attitudes about spiritual warfare as the chief causes for spiritual defeats. They felt that aggressive spiritual warfare could have greatly extended that revival's influence.

Prayer for revival awakening needs to include petitions for its protection. The heavenly Father alone is able to protect revival awakening from the devious ways Satan will use to try to stop it.

The awakening changes hearts, reverses downward trends, establishes a new direction, and greatly strengthens the Christian faith in the culture where it happens. Once this new direction has been installed, the church continues to function at a much higher level of spiritual intensity. Everyone enjoys the blessings of renewed spiritual life even though the emotional intensity and elevated activity of revolutionary revival begin to tone down. The revived people settle into an enjoyment of long-term worship, evangelism, steady teaching, and missionary outreach.

We should pray for the revival duration just as fervently as we pray for it to come. What a complex, religious world a revival would encounter today. How quickly it could be weakened by a person's capacities to "quench the Spirit," to say nothing of Satan's work. Tangents of extremism could quickly divert its influence. Balance between sound doctrinal teaching and evangelistic outreach to the lost must remain the focus and the ongoing message of true revival.

World evangelization is the major outflow from revival awakening. God doesn't bring revolutionary revival just to bring us joy and make things better for His people. God loves the lost world, and He longs to reach every person in it. Watchful, protective prayer to that end is an indispensable part of revival praying. Pray that our heavenly Father will sovereignly superintend both the doctrinal soundness and the duration of revolutionary revival.

## How to Keep a Revival Fresh and Vital

Even before revival comes, your community can design programs to promote, protect, and continue its long-term freshness. We could argue for many programs to provide balance to revival awakening, including: (1) Bible-study nurture groups for new believers; (2) action brigades carrying Christ's love to the homeless and needy; (3) alert support teams assisting new converts exiting from paganism and satanism; (4) evangelism training that promotes varied outreaches to the lost; (5) seminars providing biblical balance in spiritual-warfare training; (6) prayer ministries to reinforce and protect the revival movement; and (7) individual and small group discipling strategies.

Like a long-distance walker who methodically organizes and trains to develop strong legs, revolutionary revival needs organized structure and skillful leadership to keep it going. The above seven programs (and several others) seem like sound strategies, and I could address the how-tos in greater detail. But I feel constrained not to do so, for two major reasons: (1) an abundance of evangelical Christian programs and organizational structures are already in place; and (2) revolutionary revival fuels its own continuance.

## Programs in Place

Consider the following programs and institutions already available to help during a revival:

Congregations of various sizes and denominations in communities across the world

Fast-moving parachurch organizations with defined ministries

The best in media communication already promoting worldwide evangelism

Widely available discipleship programs of proved performance

· Outstanding seminaries, Christian colleges, and Bible institutes, which are ready for more students

Denominational and faith missionary boards equipped to funnel new volunteers to the fields

World-hunger organizations and inner-city ministries, which are presently doing much great work

These structures would need Holy Spirit–led fine tuning to handle the rush created by revolutionary revival, but they are there, ready and waiting. More program-centered plans are not needed. God's sovereignty has already provided the direction.

## The Self-Propelling Power of Revival

In the world of nature, the mixture of wind and fire unleashes the most powerful elements of creation. The 1988 fires that roared through Yellowstone National Park and those that have visited Southern California in 2006 have displayed the unstoppable power of wind and fire. In any combustible environment, wind and fire created their own explosive fuel, defying massive control efforts. In any more-urban environment, people have had to return to smoking heaps where their homes once stood when wind and fire spread their engulfing fury. Even the best-trained firemen cannot stop such raging fires.

A revival unleashes similar overwhelming forces. That may explain why, in the Acts 2 account of the coming of the Holy Spirit and a subsequent spiritual revival, the revival during Pentecost began as "a sound like the blowing of a violent wind came from heaven." This sound of wind filled the whole house, and the people gathered there "saw what seemed to be tongues of fire that separated and came to rest on each of them" (vv. 1–3).

God planned only one Pentecost event, and it demonstrated important lessons we need to learn. The Holy Spirit's coming in the symbols of wind and fire illustrate far more than any of us fully understand. In part, I believe these volatile symbols communicate the unstoppable strength of Christ's Spirit-controlled church. When heaven-sent wind and holy fire combine in multiplied numbers of yielded believers, the results are explosively powerful.

When the Holy Spirit was poured out, the resulting revolutionary revival fueled its own continuance. The life, death, resurrection, and ascension of God's Son set in place all that was needed for the Holy Spirit's work. The long-term results were phenomenal:

- Program-centered disciples became power-filled apostles (Acts 2).
- Stephen, a church-elected table server, shone as a star of faith and laid down his life, following the forgiving example of his Lord (6—7).
- Hate-filled persecutors were transformed into giant defenders of the faith (9).
- Scattered, persecuted believers became missionary church planters (8).

- Racial, religious, and ethnic barriers melted away (8:26–40; 10—11).
- Religious traditions and deep disagreements were resolved (15).
- Worldwide evangelism moved through the known world (13—28).
- Satan's opposition was neutralized and rebuked (13:6–12; 16:16–18).
- Cruel, evil people became ardent believers (16:19–34).
- Entire cities and cultures were dramatically changed (19).

Though Satan and other fallen angels have alarming power and determined goals, a God-authored revival can meet Satan's challenge. God's people are called to see it happen. The tools are in our hands.

Such revival begins with each of us, as individuals, pursuing spiritual renewal. And it will continue as we wait patiently on the Lord to move through His Holy Spirit. In this hour, we do well to remember the words of King David:

> Wait for the LORD; be strong and take heart and wait for the LORD. (Ps. 27:14)

# A REVIVAL CRY

*G*racious, merciful heavenly Father, hear the cry of my heart. I sometimes feel such a need for personal revival. At times my heart seems cold as ice and hard as stone. Have mercy upon me.

I affirm that the work of our Lord Jesus Christ was sufficient to enable You in mercy and grace to draw near to us. I affirm that the mighty person and power of the Holy Spirit are sufficient to convict the lost of sin, of righteousness, and of the judgment to come, and can bring those lost to You. Our day, our lives, our world, and Your church desperately need revolutionary revival. I invite Your Holy Spirit to begin His work in me. I invite Him to work in Your church. I invite Him to work in all of Your created people in this awful day of engulfing evil.

Open the eyes of the lost to see their need of Christ. The overwhelming sense of Your power and presence through the Holy spirit can bring us all to revolutionary revival.

May it be so in Jesus' name. Amen.

# WORKS CITED

"Ann Landers," *Sioux City Journal*, August 10, 1989.

Arthur, Kay. *Lord, I Want to Know You.* Colorado Springs: WaterBrook Press, 2000.

Bridges, Jerry. *The Pursuit of Holiness.* Colorado Springs: NavPress, 1978.

Brown, Robert McAffee. *The Significance of the Church.* Westminster: Philadelphia, n.d.

Coleman, Robert E., ed. *One Divine Moment.* Old Tappan, NJ: Revell, 1970.

DeMoss, Nancy Leigh. "Proud People vs. Broken People List." FamilyLife.com: http://www.familylife.com/articles/article_detail.asp?id=222.

Drummond, Lewis A. *The Awakening That Must Come.* Nashville: Broadman, 1978. (Drummond cites the seven laws of revival found in James Drummond's excellent book on revivals, *Revivals: Their Laws and Leaders* [n.p.: 1960].)

Dunn, Ronald. *Don't Just Stand There, Pray Something.* San Bernardino, CA: Here's Life, 1991.

Kittel, Gerhard, ed. *Theological Dictionary of the New Testament,* vol. 3. Grand Rapids: Eerdmans, 1966.

Lee, Hellen. "Campus Revivals Spread Across Country." *Christianity Today*, May 15, 1995.

Lloyd-Jones, D. Martyn. *Revival.* Wheaton, IL: Crossway Books, 1987.

Luther, Martin. *What Luther Says: An Anthology*, vol. 2. Compiled by Ewald M. Plass. St. Louis: Concordia Publishing House, 1959.

Lutzer, Erwin W. *The Serpent of Paradise.* Chicago: Moody Press, 1996.

Malenke, Jake. Alongside Ministries, 4650 N. 35th Ave., Phoenix, AZ, 85017. Written report on revival at jail, 2005.

*The Manila Manifesto*, Manila International Congress on World Evangelisation, Manila, Philippines, July 1989.

Morgan, Timothy C. "From One City to the World." *Christianity Today*, April 24, 1995.

Murphy, Ed. Spiritual Warfare Series, 16 audiotapes, syllabus, Colorado Springs: Overseas Crusades, 1988.

Olford, Stephen F. *Heart-Cry for Revival.* Old Tappan, NJ: Revell, 1982.

Orr, Edwin, *The Fervent Prayer.* Chicago: Moody Press, n.d.

Ortlund, Anne. *Up with Worship.* Ventura, CA: Regal, 1975.

Roberts, Richard Owen. *Revival.* Wheaton, IL: Tyndale, 1982.

Rosenberg, Joel C. *The Ezekiel Option.* Wheaton, IL: Tyndale, 2005.

Shelley, Bruce L. *Church History in Plain Language.* Waco, TX: Word, 1982.

Ton, Josef. *Suffering, Martyrdom, and Rewards in Heaven.* Wheaton, IL: Romanian Missionary Society, 2000.

Walvoord, John F. *Israel in Prophecy.* Grand Rapids: Zondervan, 1962.

Watson, Russell. "The Last Days of a Dictator." *Newsweek*, January 8, 1990.

Zettersten, Rolf. "Part II of the Ted Bundy Interview." *Focus on the Family*, April 1989.

Additional copies of this and other
Victor Books products are available
wherever good books are sold.

If you have enjoyed this book,
or if it has impacted your life,
we would like to hear from you.
Please contact us at:

Victor Books
Cook Communication Ministries, Dept. 240
4050 Lee Vance View
Colorado Springs, CO 80918

Or visit our Web site:
www.cookministries.com

*Victor*®
The Bible Teacher's Teacher